A RAINBOW ORIGINAL

HOW TO DEAL WITH A PARENTAL KIDNAPPING

compiled by
Margaret Strickland

PLUS BOOK BONUS - *CHILD-SNATCHED*
by Margaret Strickland

HOW TO DEAL WITH A PARENTAL KIDNAPPING
COMPILED BY MARGARET STRICKLAND

Copyright 1983/All rights reserved
3rd Printing 1984

CHILD-SNATCHED
BY MARGARET STRICKLAND

Produced by Ratzlaff & Associates
Cover Design by Ronin Studio
Creative Advisor Jeffrey C. Black

Published by Rainbow Books/Betty Wright
2299 Riverside Drive/P.O. Box 1069
Moore Haven, Florida 33471

Library of Congress:
Card Catalogue No. 83-61766

Quality Hardback Edition
ISBN: 0-935834-20-6
Retail Price $15.50

Trade Softback Edition
ISBN: 0-935834-17-8
Retail Price $12.50

Printed in the United State of America

*Portions of this book have been excerpted or condensed, and reprinted by permission
from INTERSTATE AND INTERNATIONAL CHILD CUSTODY DISPUTES; A COLLEC-
TION OF MATERIALS, 2nd Edition, A Monograph by the Child Custody Project,
Patricia M. Hoff, Esq., Director, American Bar Association, Fund for Public
Education, Washington, D.C.

1987 SUPPLEMENT
HOW TO DEAL WITH A PARENTAL KIDNAPPING
ISBN: 0-935834-20-6

STEPS TO TAKE IF YOUR CHILD IS MISSING

1. File a Missing Person's Report with your local law enforcement agency.

2. Ask that the Missing Person's Report be filed with the National Crime Information Center (NCIC). If in Florida, ask that the Missing Person's Report be filed with the FCIC and the Florida Missing Children Information Clearinghouse (See page 27). To verify that the Missing Person's Report has been filed, contact the FBI. If not, ask the FBI to file the Missing Person's Report for you.

3. File criminal charges at the local level, if the abductor is known. Obtain a pick up order through your attorney.

4. Call a Help Group such as Children's Rights of America (813-593-0090) or the Adam Walsh Resouce Center (305-423-ADAM). For a more complete listing of such organizations, refer to page 17.

5. Call the National Center for Missing and Exploited Children (1835 K Street N.W., Suite 700, Washington, DC 20006) for advice and technical assistance at telephone numbers 1-800-843-5678 or 202-634-9821.

Since many parentally kidnapped children have been/are emotionally traumatized, a searching parent should use all available resources.

***

A. All states, except the District of Columbia, have laws against parental kidnapping.

B. All states comply with the Federal Acts: Parental Kidnapping Prevention Act (See page 81); Missing Children's Act (See page 77); and the Uniform Child Custody Jurisdiction Act (See page 47).

C. As state legislation continues to change, check with your State Attorney or Prosecutor to learn the current state statute on parental kidnapping, then file charges under a felony statute, if possible, so that the assistance of the FBI may be obtained. Otherwise, file a civil charge with the State Attorney or Prosecutor.

D. Make use of state laws and federal acts: Federal Parent Locator Service (See page 123), telephone number 301-443-4950; Military Locator Service, if applicable (See page 26).

Officials of Schools must inform the searching parent (if asked) where school records are sent through the Family Education Rights and Privacy Act.

NOTE

Greyhound Bus, Inc. and Quality Inn, Inc., in conjunction with the National Center for Missing and Exploited Children, will furnish free transportation and motel room for a parent or legal guardian and the missing child. Make requests for assistance at the National Center for Missing and Exploited Children, telephone number 1-800-843-5678.

***

Many states now have missing children agencies which can assist victim parents and law enforcement agencies. They are listed below with telephone numbers:

Alabama — (202) 261-4207
Alaska — (907) 264-6141
Arkansas — (501) 371-2007
California — (714) 834-3610 or (918) 739-5114
Canada — (403) 422-4698
Connecticut — (203) 566-4240
Delaware — (302) 736-5888
Florida — 1-800-342-0821 (in state) or (904) 488-5224
Georgia — (404) 244-2554
Illinois — (217) 782-6429
Iowa — (515) 281-6278
Kansas — (913) 232-6000
Kentucky — (502) 227-8708
Maryland — (301) 653-4433
Massachusetts — 1-800-447-5289 or
    (in state) 1-800-622-5999
Michigan — (517) 373-3700 ext. 680
Mississippi — (601) 987-1598
Missouri — (816) 524-1407
Montana — (406) 444-3817
Nevada — (702) 885-4170
New Jersey — (609) 984-5830
New Mexico — (505) 827-9181
New York — (518) 457-6326
North Carolina — (919) 733-7974
Ohio — (614) 466-6837
Oklahoma — (405) 682-6724
Rhode Island — (401) 647-3311
South Carolina — (803) 758-6048 (after 5:00 call 758-6000)
South Dakota — (605) 773-4614
Tennessee — (901) 528-2005
Texas — (512) 465-2810
Virginia — (804) 323-2023
Washington D.D. — National Center for Missing and
    Exploited Children — (202) 634-9821 or 1-800-843-5678
    T.D.D. for the hearing impaired — 1-800-826-7653
Washington — (206) 753-3960

If a victim parent believes a parentally kidnapped child has been taken to a foreign country, contact the Department of State (See page 155).

On October 9, 1986 the United States Senate voted to ratify the Hague Convention (See page 163).

For further information on the issue of parentally kidnapped children who had been taken to a foreign country, refer to . . .

PARENTAL KIDNAPPING: AN INTERNATIONAL RESOURCE DIRECTORY, Compiled by Margaret Strickland and Edited by Joe Teague Caruso.* (This book defines the laws of foreign countries in regard to parental kidnapping, addresses the European Convention and the Hague Convention, and provides Help Lists and other assistance to the victim parent.)

*This book may be ordered direct from the publisher, Rainbow Books, P. O. Box 1069, Moore Haven, FL 33471 for $20.00 postpaid.

Table of Contents

Organizations by states are listed, including the **Missing Childrens Information Clearing House;** toll-free number for Missing Children Clearing House. **Child Find** is a point of registration for a searching parent and a missing child; a toll-free number is reserved for use by children. Servicemen and Servicewomen are not immune to divorce or child-snatching. The various branches of the armed services operate **World Wide Locator.** Telephone numbers are listed; a valuable aid where children of military personnel are abducted.

All 50 states are listed with their statutes which are in effect in their jurisdiction. A state must have felony abduction and/or restraint laws to acquire the assistance of the Federal Bureau of Investigation.

The Uniform Child Custody Jurisdiction Act was designed to bring some sort of order to the existing chaos of parental kidnapping. It remedies the seize and run, self-help game and replaces it with an orderly process of law. Its application determines home states, discourages re-litigation and encourages enforcement, not modification. Policies of this Act extend into the international area.

The Missing Children Act applies to the collection of data, not to an active search, which requires a felony warrant. Thus, the Federal Bureau of Investigation's National Crime Information Center's computers can be used more extensively in the area of Missing Persons. Report and Request for National Crime Information Center entry included.

The Parental Kidnapping Prevention Act of 1980 does the following: (1) promotes full faith and credit between sister states honoring sister state custody decrees; (2) allows use of the Federal Parent Locator Services. (3) allows the Federal Bureau of Investigation to become involved under applicable state felony statutes. In 1983 a temporary change was made in obtaining an Unlawful Flight to Avoid Prosecution (UFAP) Warrant; **a parent no longer has to prove a child is in danger to secure a UFAP Warrant.**

Police - The most important function of the police is proper entry and official communications with other police departments and public agencies.

Prosecutor - An arrest warrant obtained through the prosecutor will usually mean official involvement. Your district or state attorney is **not** your private attorney. The role of the prosecutor is absolute and central to the issue, since the issuance of legal process necessary in the investigation, together with request for investigative assistance from other agencies, including the Federal Bureau of Investigation, **are** the responsibility of the prosecutor.

Parent - A parent should correlate collected information and develop leads, and pursue them to the extent that the parent is legally able, seeking assistance from the prosecutor, so that the laws in force may be applied effectively.

Formal Intervention - An arrest warrant, properly entered in the National Crime Information Center (NCIC) computer and the beginning of investigation activities are imperative. Fast legal actions relate directly to the length of time the child is missing.

Federal Bureau of Investigation - A prosecutor wishing to obtain an Unlawful Flight to Avoid Prosecution (UFAP) Warrant in a parental kidnapping case should follow those steps listed.

Federal Parent Locator Service - A search done exclusively with computers in addition to any field investigation undertaken by the Federal Bureau of Investigation pursuant to the Fugitive Felon Act.

State and Local Parental Resources and Responsibilities - Parents, assuming there has been a warrant issued, should alert airports, train and bus stations. Phone records, bank records, post office, credit cards, school records, state tax and welfare rolls should be examined.

Arrest and Recovery - Once the parentally kidnapped child is located, it is imperative that the police establish contact with the local prosecutor's office. To lessen the child's trauma, the custodial parent should arrive quickly with certified papers of custody.

Trial - Guilty verdicts are rare; jurors have a natural tendency to see the relationship of the defendant and victim, failing to focus on the adverse impact such conduct has on a child.

Conclusion - Parental kidnapping **is not** a domestic dispute. Here is a serious crime against children with long lasting harmful effects.

Other remedies: Tort Actions and Ethical Considerations - Abducting parents, and any person, including relatives, known or believed to have aided in the removal or retention of a child, may be held liable for damages. **Attorneys and judges have been disciplined for unacceptable conduct in counseling clients in parental kidnapping cases.**

ally from the harmful effects of their wrongful removal or retention and to establish procedures to ensure their prompt return to the State of their habitual residence as well as to secure protection for rights of access. The correct form for a **Request for Return** is included.

TO STEAL A CHILD IS NOT AN ACT OF LOVE;
IT IS AN ACT OF SELFISHNESS.

PREFACE

Having been personally involved in the Strickland "child snatching," I can recommend this publication as an excellent guide and tool to any person involved in the multi-faceted aspects of a "child snatching" case. What has been learned by Margaret Strickland, through several years of frustration, is now readily available to the reader in this publication. Once you have read this book, I encourage you to encourage your friends to join Margaret in her crusade to educate the public at large, as well as all practicing professionals, as to the enormity of the problem which "child snatching" and all of its ramifications present. Every attorney, law enforcement officer, family counselor, parent and concerned citizen should include this volume along with their library as a source of ready reference in case of unexpected need.

Joe Teague Caruso
Attorney-At-Law

SECTION I

AN OPEN LETTER FROM THE AUTHOR

AN OPEN LETTER FROM THE AUTHOR

In the middle of the night I awoke to a ringing telephone. When I answered, I heard the uncertain voice of a woman, saying, "My moccasins are following in the same path your moccasins walked, Mrs. Strickland."

What followed were the jumbled words of desperation, describing once again, the horror and terror of a parental kidnapping. I understood this woman perfectly. My own grandson, Danny, had been kidnapped by my son's ex-wife, presumed dead and miraculously found alive, after twenty-two months of intense searching.

Now -- since I have been listed by the American Bar Association to assist those in need of information and direction on how to deal with a parental kidnapping -- I receive approximately 1,000 telephone calls and letters a year from people who turn to me for help and hope. Though I am accustomed to such middle of the night awakenings, I shall never become accustomed to the cruelty and lack of concern for the child involved. Here was another typical case.

The woman's son had custody of the child. His ex-wife took the child and fled the state. Now her son was in prison for murdering his ex-wife. Presumably the second husband of the ex-wife had the child. He had returned to the state in which the woman lived. Then, he waited outside a store in which the woman was shopping. When she emerged from the store, he ran her down with his car, breaking her leg.

"I've been in the hospital," she told me in anguish, "and no one looks for my grandson. Please help me."

Although the father had legal custody of the child, I doubted his ability to help, since he was in prison. So I began to ask her a series of questions so that I might research her problem. Of primary importance was to investigate the laws of the States involved as they applied to her case. In this manner, I am able to assist others in dealing effectively with a parental kidnapping.

Meanwhile, since my grandson, Danny, was kidnapped, I have worked to see new laws passed on the Federal level. I have made speeches. I wrote articles. I appeared on a Gannett Newspaper television special, TODAY. I talked to knowledgeable and authoritative people across the country, not the least of which was the late Brigitte M. Bodenheimer, a professor of law from the University of California and an international authority on parental kidnapping.

13

With this effort and with that of many other concerned people, we have seen Federal legislation come to pass. Representative Charles E. Bennett (D-Fl.) and Senator Malcolm Wallop (R-Wyo.) were sponsors of the Parental Kidnapping Prevention Act of 1980, Public Law 96-611. However, no one was more supportive in this effort than Pat Hoff, an attorney in Senator Wallop's office, and a lady in the truest sense of the word.

I am pleased and proud to have been a part of this concern for children. I will continue to assist anyone and everyone whenever possible. Each letter or telephone call describing a parental kidnapping is different, but each of the letters and telephone calls carries the same theme: *HELP ME FIND MY CHILD!*

In every instance, I try to help. But much remains to be done to enhance the laws of our land. Each State should sign an agreement with the Director of Child Support Enforcement to fully utilize the Federal Parent Locator Service. All States do not consider child stealing a felony. Unless those State laws are changed to felony status, the assistance of the Federal Bureau of Investigation cannot be obtained.

If no criminal warrant is available in a State, the next step is to check the Uniform Child Custody Jurisdiction Act and the Parental Kidnapping Prevention Act for remedies. That done, do contact State senators and representatives, and urge State 'felony' statutes be passed.

The Federal law helps locate missing children. When a child is located, the custodial parent must take immediate and lawful action for the return of the child. But it doesn't end here -- not for the child.

The trauma the child has suffered lives on, often manifesting itself in the need for professional psychiatric help. The child pays a terrible price for the parent's thoughtless actions.

In September, 1982, the Child Custody Project and Family Law Section of the American Bar Association sponsored the First National Conference on Interstate Child Custody and Parental Kidnapping in Washington, D.C. Shortly thereafter, Florida's U.S. Senator Paula Hawkins, sponsored and acquired the passage of the Missing Children Act. Jay Howell, Chief Counsel in Senator Hawkins' Washington office, is helpful and knowledgeable on missing children.

Further, the 'Prints of Love' program, which is the fingerprinting of students, has begun to take hold across the country. Quite often, this is the only manner in which a missing child can be identified, since all too often many years pass before a child is found, and small faces grow and change.

All the while, I wear two bracelets as a constant reminder of what needs to be done to make people aware of the need for more definitive laws in the area of parental kidnapping and missing children. One of those bracelets is for a missing child, and the other bracelet is for a parentally abducted child.

Despite the giant strides made acquiring new laws on the subject of parental kidnapping and missing children, obviously much remains to be done. Education is the key. Thus, this book, *HOW TO DEAL WITH A PARENTAL KIDNAPPING*, has been compiled to give those victims of a parental kidnapping and those in a position of authority to assist the victims, the tools they need to take advantage of the laws currently in effect. This resource book is intended to outline the rights and avenues available under our present legal system.

Margaret Strickland
Merritt Island, Florida

SECTION II

ORGANIZATIONS THAT PROVIDE ADVICE AND ASSISTANCE TO PARENTS IN CASES OF CHILD ABDUCTION

PREFACE

The organizations contained in this directory provide advice and other assistance to parents whose children have been wrongfully abducted or retained in connection with child custody disputes. The Child Custody Project of the American Bar Association compiled this list as a reference tool for parents, social workers, law enforcement officers, lawyers and other interested people.

This list does not include organizations that may advocate or engage in snatchings to recover children, conduct which is strongly discouraged by the Child Custody Project. Also missing from the list are groups the Child Custody Project has yet to learn about, and organizations which are not primarily composed of parents. Members of the various groups may be good sources for referrals to other helping organizations and professionals. Organizations denoted by an asterisk (*) are derived from a list compiled by Child Find, Inc. of New York.

DIRECTORY

ALASKA

A National Network to Locate
Missing Children
P.O. Box 10-1938
Anchorage, AK 99510
Phone - (907) 243-8484 or
(toll free) 1-800-544-2212

Missing Children
of America, Inc.
P.O. Box 1938
Anchorage, AK 99510
Phone - (907) 243-0318
(toll free) 1-800-544-2212

ARIZONA

United Parents Against Child
Stealing, Inc.
P.O. Box 35428
Tucson, AZ 85740
Phone - (602) 791-3417

CALIFORNIA

Bay Area Center for Victims
1165 Meridian Ave., Ste. #112
San Jose, CA 95148
Phone - (408) 274-0869

Child Stealing Resource Center
431 South Commonwealth Ave.
Los Angeles, CA 90020
Phone - (805) 492-2411 or
(213) 738-7402

Child Stealing Project
Center for the Family
in Transition
5725 Paradise Dr., Bld. A,
Suite 100
Corte Madera, CA 94925
Phone - (415) 752-3431

Stolen Children
Information Exchange
210½ Main Street
Huntington Beach, CA 92648
Phone - (714) 960-8426 or
(714) 847-2676

Top Priority - Children
P.O. Box 2161
Palm Springs, CA 92263
    Contact person: Teddy Kieley
Phone - (619) 323-1559

CANADA

Abducted Children's Rights
of Canada
P.O. Box 262, Station M
Toronto, Ontario M65 4T3
Phone -(416) 487-7543

Abducted Children's Rights
of Canada
15 Trillium Village
Ste. #212
Chatham, Ontario N7L 4A2
Phone - (519) 354-7462

The Tania Murrell Missing
Children Society
9913-151 St.
Edmonton, Alberta
Canada T5P 1T2
    Contact person: Vivian Murrell
Phone - 486-7777

FLORIDA†

Adam Walsh Child Resource
Center, Inc.
Mercede Executive Park
Park View Bldg., Suite #306
1876 N. University Drive
Fort Lauderdale, FL 33322
Phone - (305) 475-4847

Children's Rights of Florida
P.O. Box 173
Pinellas Park, FL 33565
Phone - (813) 546-1593

Locators International, Inc.
1470 Gene St.
Winter Park, FL 32789
    Contact person: Harney Morse
Phone - (305) 831-2000

M.E.N.
2054 Loma Linda Way S.
Clearwater, FL 33513
Phone - (813) 461-3806

Missing Children...Help Center
410 Ware Blvd, Suite 1102
Tampa, TL 33619
    Contact person: Ivana DiNova
Phone - (813) 681-HELP or
(813) 623-KIDS

Missing Persons Nationwide
P.O. Box 5331
Hudson, FL 33562
    Contact person: Alfie Brideen
Phone - (813) 856-5144

National Association for
Missing Children, Inc.
300 South University Dr.
Plantation, FL 33324
    Contact person: Martin Fierro
Phone - (305) 473-6126

Dee Scofield Awareness
Program, Inc.
4418 Bay Court Ave.
Tampa, FL 33611
Phone - (813) 839-5025

Margaret Strickland
420 Milford Pl.
Merritt Island, FL 32952
Phone - (305) 452-8707
*(Author CHILD-SNATCHED,
Rainbow Books, 1979)*

§SEE: *Missing Children Information
Clearinghouse, page 27.*

GEORGIA

Find Me, Inc.
P.O. Box 1612
LaGrange, GA 30241
Phone - (404) 884-7419 or
(404) 883-5442

KANSAS

Parents Alone
Mary Anne Harvey
Dept. of Psychology
Wichita State University
Wichita, KS
Phone - (316) 684-7654

MAINE

COPE - Southern Maine Center
68 Deering St.
Portland, ME 04101
    Contact person: Peter Cyr
Phone - (207) 775-0258

MASSACHUSETTS

Child Search
6 Beacon Street, Suite #600
Boston, MA 02108
Phone - (617) 720-2760

People Against Parental
Kidnapping
298 Hurley Street
Cambridge, MA 02141
Phone - (No Listing)

MICHIGAN

HEART (Help every
abduction return today)
10937 Red Arrow Hwy., Rt. #1
Mattawan, Michigan 49071
    Contact person:
Leslie Campbell
Phone - (616) 668-3733

Fathers for Equal Rights
861 Honey Creek Drive
Ann Arbor, MI 48103
    Contact person:
Leigh Travis, Ph.D.
Phone - (313) 761-3427
(24 hour Hot Line)

Searching Parents Association†
P.O. Box 582
E. Tawas, MI 48730
Phone - (517) 362-7148
§*Updating through computer pictures of children long missing*

MINNESOTA

Missing Kids Action Agency
320-A, 310 East 38th St.
Minneapolis, MN 55407
  Contact person:
Patricia Crosby

NEW JERSEY

The American Society for the
Prevention of Cruelty to Children
1101 N. State Road
Princeton, NJ 08540
Phone - (609) 921-0500

Sgt. Dick Ruffino, Director
Missing Persons Bureau
Bergen County Sheriff's Office
1 Court Street
Hackensack, NJ 07601
Phone - (201) 646-2192

Search
560 Sylvan Avenue
Englewood Cliffs, NJ 07632
Phone - (201) 567-4040

Children's Rights of New York,
Inc.
19 Maple Avenue
Stony Brook, NY 11790
Phone - (516) 751-7840

OAR - Chemung County
Neighborhood Justice Project
Victim Assistance/
Dispute Mediation
300 Lake Street
Elmira, NY 14901
Phone - (607) 734-3338

OHIO

NEW YORK

Child Find, Inc.
P.O. Box 277
New Paltz, NY 12561-0277
Phone - (914) 255-1848
Phone - 1-800-431-5005*

Cobra International
P.O. Box 7016
Station A
Canton, Ohio 44705

OKLAHOMA

Friends of Child Find
of Oklahoma
P.O. Box 1063
Choctaw, OK 73020
Phone - (405) 842-7293 or
(405) 942-5086

Oklahoma Parents Against
Child Stealing
P.O. Box 2112
Bartlesville, OK 74005
Phone - (918) 336-1921

OREGON

Friends of Child Find of Oregon
P.O. Box 756
Springfield, OR 97477-0131
Phone - (No Listing)

National Missing Children
Locate Center, Inc.
#201 Yamhill Law Center
1123 S.W. Yamhill Center
Portland, OR 97205
Phone - (503) 224-5596

PENNSYLVANIA

Children's Rights of Pa., Inc.
"In Search of Missing Children"
P.O. Box 2764
Lehigh, Valley, PA 18001
   Contact person: Joan Bingham
Phone - (215) 437-2971

National Coalition for
Children's Justice
1214 Evergreen Road
Yardley, PA 19067
Phone - (215) 295-4236

Parents Against Child Snatching
P.O. Box 581
Coraopolis PA 15108
Phone - (412) 264-9025
Phone - (412) 526-5537

Phyllis Wonderling
Rt. #1
East Brady, PA 16028

RHODE ISLAND

Society for Young Victims
29 Thurston Avenue
Newport, RI 02840
Phone - (401) 847-5083

TEXAS

For Kids Sake
% Christine Scudder
12837½ Greens Bayou
Houston, TX 77015
   Contact person:
Christine Scudder
Phone - (713) 451-9349

Parents Against Legal
Kidnapping
1887 Wright Road
Buda, TX 78610
Phone - (512) 243-0649 or
(512) 472-3775

Parents Against Parental
Kidnapping
P.O. Box 14384
Austin, TX 78761
Phone - (512) 243-0649

UTAH

Child Industries
(formerly Identi-child)
P.O. Box 26814
Salt Lake City, UT 84126
   Contact person:
Michael J. Meredith
Phone - (801) 298-2900

VIRGINIA

Fathers United for Equal Rights
and Women's Coalition
Washington, D.C. and
Virginia Chapters
P.O. Box 1323
Arlington, VA 22210
Phone - (703) 892-1777
(For Recorded Information)
(703) - 451-9321 or
(703) 734-0202

WASHINGTON

Family and Friends of
Missing Persons
P.O. Box 2144
Seattle, WN 98111
Phone - (206) 782-8306

WASHINGTON, D.C.

Child Custody Clearing House
and Information Exchange
Patricia M. Hoff, Esq. Director
American Bar Association
1800 M Street, N.W., S-200
Washington, D.C. 20036
Phone - (202) 331-2256

Rae Gummel
Children's Rights, Inc.
P.O. Box 11458
Washington, D.C. 20008
Phone - (202) 363-9587

Parents Without Partners
7910 Woodmont Avenue
Suite #1000
Bethesda, MD 20814
Phone - (301) 654-8850

WISCONSIN

Children's Rights, Inc., Wisconsin Chapter
Edith St. John, President
121 Elliott Street
Janesville, WI 53545
Phone - (608) 752-8789

MILITARY

Military families are immune to neither divorce nor child snatching. This is true of families stationed in the United States or abroad. Where a serviceman or servicewoman stationed abroad marries a foreign national, the children of the marriage become likely candidates for international child snatching in the event of a break up of the marriage. The branches of the armed services operate "World Wide Locator" services which may prove valuable in such cases. To obtain information from the World Wide Locator Services, contact:

(1) **Air Force** World Wide Locator, (512) 652-5774.

(2) **Army** World Wide Personnel Information, (512) 221-2948 or (512) 221-3315. For information about officers on active duty and retired general officers, write to Personnel Records, Division (TAGO), Department of the Army, Washington, D.C. 20310. To locate active duty enlisted personnel, write to U.S. Army Personnel Service Support Center, Fort Benjamin Harrison, Indiana 46249.

(3) **Marines** To locate active duty personnel, write to Commandant of the Marine Corps, (CODE MSRP-22) Headquarters, Marine Corps, Washington, D.C. 20380. Information about retired marine personnel may be obtained by writing to Marine Corps Retired Branch, (CODE MMSR-2) Headquarters, Marine Corps, Washington, D.C. 20380.

(4) **Navy** To locate active duty personnel, address inquiries to Chief, Navy Personnel, Department of the Navy, Washington, D.C. 20370, (202) 694-2768. For information about Naval reserve personnel, write to Commanding Officer, Naval Reserve Personnel Center, New Orleans, Lousiana 70149.

(5) **Coast Guard** Requests for information about active duty personnel should be directed to Commandant, U.S. Coast Guards

26

(PE), 2100 2nd Street, S.W., Washington, D.C. 20593, (202) 426-8898. For reserved personnel, address inquiries to the Commandant, U.S. Coast Guards (G-RA-2) at the above address.

All letters should include the following information about the person being sought: full name, social security number, rank, and last known duty assignment, with the approximate date.

MISSING CHILDREN
INFORMATION CLEARINGHOUSE

The 1982 Florida Legislature appropriated funds for the Florida Department of Law Enforcement (FDLE) for the establishment of a Missing Children Information Clearinghouse (MCIC). The program is designed to collect, store, and disseminate information in an effort to locate Florida's missing children. Although the Clearinghouse will not conduct any investigations regarding missing children, it will provide a centralized file for the exchange of information.

LOCATION OF MCIC

The Clearinghouse is located in the Division of Criminal Justice Information Systems, which houses the state's central crime information computers, provides the connecting link to each law enforcement agency in the state and also provides state telecommunications to the National Crime Information Center in Washington. Storing information regarding missing children in this Division makes it readily and easily available to those who need it.

MISSING CHILD DEFINITION

For the purpose of this program, a missing child is:

*Any person, **under the age of 18, believed to be in Florida,** whose location has not been determined, and has been reported missing.*

The Clearinghouse will accept information on any child whose whereabouts is unknown, regardless of the circumstances (i.e., suspected foul play, parental kidnapping or runaway).

FUNCTIONS OF MCIC

The MCIC will monitor the various informational systems to insure that all available information involving juveniles is utilized to the fullest extent. The most important system monitored by MCIC is the existing Florida Crime Information Center (FCIC) Missing Persons File. This file provides a computerized focal point for all Florida law enforcement agencies to enter and inquire on missing persons. All entries regarding juveniles are a part of the Clearinghouse data base.

Concern has been voiced about those juveniles not immediately entered into the FCIC file by local law enforcement agencies. Therefore, a new file was created as a support to FCIC. This file will allow parents to enter a missing child into a statewide data base. Parents can enter information through the submission of a Missing Child Report, which may be obtained from Florida law enforcement agencies.

SERVICES PROVIDED BY MCIC

A 24-hour toll-free, in-state, WATS line (1-800-342-0821) is available to immediately report a child as missing.

Florida Department of Law Enforcement
P.O. Box 1489
Tallahassee, FL 32302
(904) 488-5221

Florida Department of Law Enforcement issues bulletins listing children reported missing by their parent(s).

STATE AND FEDERAL CHILD ABDUCTION AND RESTRAINT LAWS

A SURVEY OF STATE AND FEDERAL CHILD ABDUCTION AND RESTRAINT LAWS

Laws have been enacted by the states and by Congress to protect children from the harmful effects of "child snatching," the wrongful removal or retention of a child by a parent in violation of a court order, or in violation of the rights of the other parent where no custody decree has yet been made. What follows is a comprehensive survey of the child abduction and restraint statutes in effect throughout the country which apply to parents and/or their agents. (The statutes referred to herein as child abduction and restraint laws go by a variety of names, including "custodial interference," "child restraint," "child abduction," and "parental kidnapping.") In addition, the survey provides citations to kidnapping, unlawful imprisonment, and criminal restraint statutes which may cover child abduction and restraint by a parent or agent of a parent. Statutes expressly exempting parents from prosecution are also noted. Where available, explanatory comments are reprinted.

Of the 53 jurisdictions surveyed, 42 states have felony child abduction and restraint statutes; 35 have misdemeanors; 28 have felonies and misdemeanors; and only 2 do not criminalize this kind of conduct at all. Many of these laws are new. For instance, Congress passed a law at the end of the 96th Congress which expressly declares the intent of Congress that the Federal Fugitive Felon Act (18 U.S.C. 1073) shall be applied in state felony child abduction and restraint cases. This portion of Pub. L. No. 96-611 took effect on December 28, 1980 and is designed to provide F.B.I. assistance to state and local law enforcement officials in investigating state felony child abduction and restraint cases which involve interstate flight. Other laws have been on the books for years but have often gone unenforced for a variety of reasons.

In order for child abduction and restraint laws to be effective as deterrents to this conduct and as vehicles for the eventual return and prosecution of perpetrators, federal and state law enforcement officers, prosecutors, and extradition officials should familiarize themselves with, and vigorously enforce, the statutes in effect in their jurisdiction.

31

CRIMINAL CUSTODIAL INTERFERENCE LAWS

The following list provides citations to the custodial interference statutes in effect in each of the fifty states. In addition, the survey identifies kidnapping, unlawful imprisonment and criminal restraint statutes which may also cover the unlawful taking or retention of a child by a parent or agent of a parent. Statutes expressly exempting parents from prosecution are noted. Applicable federal statutes are cited at the end of the compilation. This survey is current through July, 1982.

ALABAMA

§ 13A-6-41   Unlawful imprisonment in the first degree; misdemeanor.
§ 13A-6-42   Kidnapping in the first degree; felony.
§ 13A-6-45   Interference with custody; class A misdemeanor.
                   (Eff. May 17, 1978)

ALASKA

§ 11.41.300(a)   Kidnapping; unclassified felony (affirmative defense to prosecution under §11.41.300(a)(2)(A) if defendant is relative of child under 18 and restrains the victim by secreting and holding him in a place where not likely to be found in order to assume his custody).
§ 11.41.320   Custodial interference in the first degree; class C felony.
§ 11.41.330   Custodial interference in the second degree; class A misdemeanor. (Eff. January 1, 1980)

ARIZONA

§ 13-1302   Custodial interference; class 6 felony unless child is returned unharmed prior to arrest, in which case it is a class 1 misdemeanor.

| § 13-1303 | Unlawful imprisonment; felony; may be reduced to misdemeanor as in §13-1302; defense that defendant was relative of person restrained and sole intent was to assume lawful custody and restraint was accomplished without physical force. |
| § 13-1304 | Kidnapping; felony; may be reduced to lesser felony. (Eff. October 1, 1978) |

ARKANSAS

§ 41-1702	Kidnapping; felony; may be reduced to lesser felony.
§ 41-1703	False imprisonment in the first degree; felony.
§ 41-1704	False imprisonment in the second degree; misdemeanor.
§ 41-2411	Interference with custody; class D felony if child removed from state; otherwise class A misdemeanor. (Eff. January 1, 1976)

CALIFORNIA

§ 207	Kidnapping; felony.
§ 236, 237	False imprisonment; misdemeanor; if effected by violence, menace, fraud, or deceit it is a felony.
§ 278	Child abduction; by a person having no right of custody; felony.
§ 278.5	Wrongful removal, retention or concealment of a child in violation of custody or visitation rights; misdemeanor. (Eff. July 1, 1977)

COLORADO

§ 18-3-301	First degree kidnapping; felony.
§ 18-3-302	Second degree kidnapping; felony; not applicable to person who takes, entices or decoys his own child with intent to keep or conceal child from his guardian; exclusion may **not** apply to parent's agent.
§ 18-3-303	False imprisonment; misdemeanor.

§ 18-3-304   Violation of custody; class 5 felony; affirmative defense that offender believed conduct was necessary to preserve safety or child over 14 was taken away at his own instigation or without enticement.

CONNECTICUT

§ 53a-92   Kidnapping first degree; felony.
§ 53a-94   Kidnapping second degree; felony.
§ 53a-95   Unlawful restraint first degree; felony.
§ 53a-96   Unlawful restraint second degree; misdemeanor.
§ 53a-97   Custodial interference first degree; class D felony.
§ 53a-98   Custodial interference second degree, class A misdemeanor. (Eff. October 1, 1971)

DELAWARE

§ 784   Affirmative defense to unlawful imprisonment and kidnapping if accused was relative of victim and sole purpose was to assume custody. Liability, if any, governed by §785.
§ 785   Interference with custody class E Felony; class A Misdemeanor; Family Court jurisdiction over such violation. (1979 Replacement Volume, Del. Ann. Code)

DISTRICT OF COLUMBIA

§ 22-2101   Kidnapping; felony; parents expressly excluded. (No specific custodial interference law.)
(D.C. Code Encyclopedia, Annotated, 1978)

FLORIDA

§ 787.01   Kidnapping; felony; includes confinement of child under 13 if without consent of his parents or legal guardian and if other elements of offense are present.

34

§ 787.02	False imprisonment; felony; comment, above, also applies.
§ 787.03	Interference with custody; first degree misdemeanor; applies to children 17 and under; defense that defendant reasonably believed action was necessary to protect child from danger or child was taken away at his own instigation without enticement; (Eff. August 2, 1977).
§ 787.04	Felony in third degree to remove children from state or to conceal child contrary to court order, to remove child during pending custody proceeding of which he has notice, or to fail to produce child in the court pursuant to court order. (Eff. October 1, 1980)

GEORGIA

§ 26-1308	False imprisonment; felony.
§ 26-1311	Kidnapping; felony; applies to a person over 17 when he forcibly, maliciously, or fraudulently leads, takes, or carries away, or decoys or entices away, any child under 16 against the will of the child's parents or other person having lawful custody.
§ 26-1312	Interference with custody; felony to remove from state; otherwise misdemeanor. Crime includes bringing child into state without consent of lawful custodian. (Eff. July 1, 1978)

HAWAII

§ 707-721	Unlawful imprisonment in first degree; felony.
§ 707-722	Unlawful imprisonment in second degree; misdemeanor; affirmative defense that (a) the person restrained was less than eighteen years old, (b) the defendant was a relative of the victim, and (c) his sole purpose was to assume custody over the victim.
§ 707-723	Custodial interference; misdemeanor; (Eff. 1972, repealed, 1981)
§ 707-726	Custodial interference in the first degree; class C felony; (Eff. June 17, 1981)
§ 707-727	Custodial interference in the second degree; misdemeanor. (Eff. June 17, 1981)

IDAHO

§ 18-4501   Kidnapping; felony; applies to every person who willfully... --2. Leads, takes, entices away or detains a child
under the age of sixteen years, with intent to keep or
conceal it from its parent, guardian or other person
having lawful care or control thereof, or with intent to
steal any article upon the person of the child...

§ 18-4502   Kidnapping first degree; for ransom; felony.

§ 18-4503   Kidnapping second degree; not for ransom; felony.
(No specific custodial interference law.)

ILLINOIS

§ 10-1   Kidnapping; felony; confinement of child under 13
considered against his will if without consent of his
parent or legal guardian.

§ 10-2   Aggravated kidnapping; felony; if violates §10-1 and ...
(2) takes as his victim a child under 13.

§ 10-3   Unlawful restraint; felony.

§ 10-5   Child abduction; class 4 felony; removal of child from
state, or concealing child within state with intent to
violate court order. Three affirmative defenses set forth.
(Eff. August 22, 1978)

INDIANA

§ 35-42-3-2   Kidnapping; felony.

§ 35-42-3-3   Criminal confinement; felony; includes knowing or
intentional removal of a person under 18 to a place
outside Indiana when the removal violates a child
custody order of a court. However, return of child to
custodial parent within 7 days of removal may be
considered as mitigating circumstances. (Eff. 1979)

IOWA

§ 710-2   Kidnapping in first degree; felony.

§ 710-3	Kidnapping in second degree; felony.
§ 710-4	Kidnapping in third degree; felony.
§ 710-5	Child stealing; class C felony.
§ 710-6	Violating custodial order; class D felony when removed from state; serious misdemeanor in described cases.
§ 710-7	False imprisonment; serious misdemeanor. (Eff. January 1, 1978)

KANSAS

§ 21-3420	Kidnapping; felony
§ 21-3421	Aggravated kidnapping; felony.
§ 21-3422	Interference with parental custody; class A misdemeanor. (Eff. July 1, 1970)
§ 21-3422(a)	Aggravated interference with parental custody; class E felony. (Eff. July 1, 1978)
§ 21-3424	Unlawful restraint.

KENTUCKY

| § 509.060 | Defense to any unlawful imprisonment or kidnapping charge that defendant was a relative of victim and his sole purpose was to assume custody of victim. |
| § 509.070 | Custodial interference; class D felony or class A misdemeanor if defendant is relative of victim. (Eff. 1980) |

LOUISIANA

§ 14.45	Simple kidnapping; felony; includes parent taking child in violation of custody order without consent and with intent to defeat the jurisdiction of court that issued decree. Amended by Acts 1962, No. 344, §1; Acts 1966, No. 253, §1.
§ 14.5.1	Interference with the custody of a child, misdemeanor. (Eff. September 11, 1981)
§ 14.46	False imprisonment; misdemeanor.

MAINE

17-A § 301	Kidnapping; class A crime. Defense that person restrained is the child of the actor.
17-A § 302	Criminal restraint; class D crime. Defense that the actor is the parent of the person taken, retained, enticed or restrained.
17-A § 303	Criminal restraint by parent; class E crime (apparently equivalent to misdemeanor). (Eff. 1979)

MARYLAND

Art. 27 § 337	Kidnapping; felony; specifically exempts parents.
Art. 27 § 2A	Child abduction; misdemeanor/felony. (Eff. July 1, 1982)

MASSACHUSETTS

265 § 26	Kidnapping; felony. The provisions shall not apply to the parent of a child under eighteen years of age who takes custody of such child unless such parent acts in violation of any court order or decree relating to the adoption or custody of such child. (Eff. 1971)
265 § 26A	Custodial interference by relatives; misdemeanor unless child exposed to danger, in which case it is a felony. (Eff. November 1979)

MICHIGAN

§ 750-349 (§ 28-581)	Kidnapping; felony.
§ 750-350 (§ 28-582)	Enticing away, etc., child under 14; felony.

MINNESOTA

§ 609.25	Kidnapping; felony. Commentary indicates the legislative intent is to distinguish parental from other kid-

napping; seems this statute would not be applied to parents.

§ 609.26 Obtaining or retaining a child; misdemeanor. (Eff. 1979)

MISSISSIPPI

§ 97-3-53 Kidnapping; felony; includes forcibly seizing, inveigling, or kidnapping of child under 10 without lawful authority and secretly confining child against the will of the parents or guardian or person having lawful custody. (Eff. 1974)

§ 97-5-5 Enticing child under 14 for concealment, prostitution or marriage; misdemeanor or felony.

MISSOURI

§ 565.110 Kidnapping; felony.
§ 565.120 Felonious restraint.
§ 565.130 False imprisonment; in state, misdemeanor; out-of-state, felony.
§ 565.140 Defense to false imprisonment for parents and relatives.
§ 565.150 Interference with custody; in-state, class A misdemeanor; if child removed from state, it is a class D felony. (Eff. January 1, 1979)

MONTANA

§ 45-5-301 Unlawful restraint; misdemeanor.
§ 45-5-302 Kidnapping; felony.
§ 45-5-303 Aggravated kidnapping; felony.
§ 45-5-304 Custodial interference; felony. Person who returns child within specified periods does not commit offense. (Eff. 1979)

NEBRASKA

§ 28-313 Kidnapping; felony.
§ 28-314 False imprisonment, first degree; felony.
§ 28-315 False imprisonment, second degree; misdemeanor.

§ 28-316   Violation of custody; class II misdemeanor unless violation contravenes court award of custody, in which case it is a class IV felony. (Eff. January 1, 1979)

NEVADA

§ 200.310
.320, .330   Kidnapping; felony; includes every person who leads, takes, entices, or carries away or detains any minor with the intent to keep, imprison, or confine it from its parents, guardians, or any other person having lawful custody of such minor.

§ 200.340   Penalty for aiding and abetting.

§ 200.350   Consent of person under 18 not a defense.

§ 200.359   Detention, concealment, removal of child from person having lawful custody or visitation in violation of court order; felony; can be reduced to misdemeanor (signed May 22, 1981).

NEW HAMPSHIRE

§ 633.1   Kidnapping; felony; includes knowingly confining another with purpose to avoid apprehension by law enforcement officials.

§ 633.2   Criminal restraint; felony; covers confinement of child under 16 if accomplished without consent of his parent or guardian.

§ 633.3   False imprisonment; misdemeanor applies to children in same manner as §633.2. (Eff. November 1, 1973)

NEW JERSEY

§ 2C:13-1   Kidnapping; crime of first or second degree includes kidnapping of child under 14 if accomplished without consent of a parent, guardian, or other person responsible for general supervision or welfare.

§ 2C:13-2   Criminal restraint; crime of third degree; affirmative defense to prosecution under subsection (b) if the person held was a child under 18 years old and the actor was a relative or legal guardian of such child whose sole purpose was to assume control of such child.

§ 2C:13-3   False imprisonment; disorderly persons offense; same affirmative defense as in criminal restraint.

§ 2C:13-4   Interference with custody; disorderly persons offense. (Eff. September 1, 1979)

NEW MEXICO

§ 30-4-1	Kidnapping; felony.
§ 30-4-3	False imprisonment; felony.
§ 30-4-4	Custodial interference; fourth degree felony; requires removal of child from state.(N.M.S.A. 1978)

NEW YORK

§ 135.15	Unlawful imprisonment; affirmative defense that (a) the person restrained was a child less than sixteen years old, and (b) the defendant was a relative of such child, and (c) his sole purpose was to assume control of such child. L. 1965, c. 1030.
§ 135.45	Custodial interference in second degree; class A misdemeanor.
§ 135.50	Custodial interference in first degree; class E felony. (Eff. July 27, 1981)

NORTH CAROLINA

§ 14-39	Kidnapping; felony.
§ 14-41	Abduction of children under 14; felony.
§ 14-42	Conspiring to abduct children; felony.
§ 14-320.1	Transporting or keeping child outside the state with intent to violate custody order; class J felony. (Eff. July 1, 1980)

NORTH DAKOTA

§ 12.1-18-01	Kidnapping; felony.
§ 12.1-18-02	Felonious restraint; includes secreting or holding person in place not likely to be found.
§ 12.1-18-03	Parents have defense to prosecution for unlawful imprisonment.
§ 14-14-22.1	Removal of child from state in violation of custody decree; class C felony. (Eff. 1979)

OHIO

§ 2905.01	Kidnapping; felony; includes removing another from the

place where found or restraining another of his liberty by any person by any means in the case of a victim under 13.

§ 2905.02	Abduction; felony.
§ 2905.03	Unlawful restraint; misdemeanor.
§ 2905.04	Child stealing; felony if committed by person other than relative or if relative removes child under 14 from state; misdemeanor in other cases. Affirmative defense that conduct was necessary to preserve child's health or welfare. (Eff. January 1, 1974)
§ 2919.23	Interference with custody; misdemeanor of third degree. (Eff. November 28, 1975)

OKLAHOMA

21 § 741	Kidnapping; felony; consent of victim no defense if victim 12 or younger.
21 § 891	Child stealing; felony or misdemeanor.

OREGON

§ 163.225	Kidnapping in second degree; felony; defense that person taken or confined is under 16 and the defendant is a relative whose sole purpose is to assume control of that person.
§ 163.235	Kidnapping in the first degree; felony.
§ 163.245	Custodial interference in the second degree; class C felony; (approved August 21, 1981).
§ 163.257	Custodial interference in the first degree; class B felony; covers removal of child from state or exposure of child to substantial risk of illness or injury; (approved August 21, 1981).

PENNSYLVANIA

§ 2901	Kidnapping; felony; covers unlawful removal or confinement of person under 14 if accomplished without the consent of a parent, guardian, or other person responsible for general supervision of his welfare.
§ 2902	Felonious restraint; misdemeanor of first degree.
§ 2903	False imprisonment; misdemeanor of second degree.

§ 2904 .   Interference with custody of children; misdemeanor in
                  second degree unless actor (other than parent) knew that
                  conduct would put child in danger, in which case it is a
                  misdemeanor in first degree. Three defenses provided.
                  (Eff. June 6, 1973)

PUERTO RICO

§ 4171   Restraint of liberty; misdemeanor.
§ 4178   Kidnapping; felony.
§ 4179   Kidnapping outside Puerto Rico and bringing or sending
                 victim into Puerto Rico; felony. (No specific custodial
                 interference law.) (Eff. 1974)

RHODE ISLAND

§ 11-26-1   Kidnapping; felony.
§ 11-26-1.1   Childsnatching; felony; removal or detention of child
                 under 18 outside the state with intent to violate R.I.
                 custody decree; (enacted by P.L. 1980, ch. 217, §1).

SOUTH CAROLINA

§ 16-3-910   Parents expressly exempted from kidnapping statute.
§ 16-17-495   Transporting or keeping child under 16 outside state with
                 intent to violate custody order; felony; if child returned to
                 jurisdiction of court within 7 days of his removal from
                 state, punishable as misdemeanor. (Eff. 1976)

SOUTH DAKOTA

§ 22-19-1   Kidnapping; felony; parents of unmarried minors
                 excepted.
§ 22-19-7   Taking away or concealing child under 12; felony or
                 misdemeanor.
§ 22-19-9   Taking away or keeping of unmarried minor in violation
                 of custody or visitation rights specified in custody
                 determination; class 1 misdemeanor.

§ 22-19-10   Removal of child from state in violation of §22-19-9; class 6 felony.

§ 22-19-11   Failure to report offense within 90 days as complete defense to prosecution under §22-19-9 and §22-19-10.

TENNESSEE

§ 39-2601   Kidnapping; felony.

§ 39-2602   Kidnapping children under 16; felony.

§ 39-2603   Aggravated kidnapping; class X felony; includes kidnapping of child under 13, but any seizure or kidnapping of a child by a parent shall not be considered a class X felony. (Eff. 1979)

TEXAS

§ 20.02   False imprisonment; misdemeanor unless victim recklessly exposed to substantial risk of bodily injury, in which case it is a felony; affirmative defense that actor was relative of child under 14 and sole intent was to assume lawful control of child.

§ 20.03   Kidnapping; felony; affirmative defense that abduction not coupled with intent to use or threaten use of force, actor was relative, and sole intent was to assume lawful control of the victim.

§ 20.04   Aggravated kidnapping; felony. No affirmative defense.

§ 25.03   Interference with child custody; felony of third degree; covers taking or retaining child out of state. Defense specified. (Eff. 1979)

§ 25.04   Enticing a child; class B misdemeanor. (Eff. 1979)

UTAH

§ 76-5-301   Kidnapping; felony.

§ 76-5-302   Aggravated kidnapping; felony; a detention or moving is deemed to be by force, threat or deceit if victim is under 16 and is accomplished without the effective consent of the victim's custodial parent, guardian, or person acting as parent.

§ 76-5-303   Custodial interference; class A misdemeanor unless child is removed from state, in which case it is a felony. (Eff. 1979)

VERMONT

§ 2401   Kidnapping; felony.
§ 2402   Kidnapping child under 16; felony offense committed regardless of child's consent.
§ 2451   Custodial interference; felony; defense specified. (Eff. April 24, 1980)

VIRGINIA

§ 18.2-47   Abduction and kidnapping; if committed by parent and punishable as contempt in the pending proceeding; class 1 misdemeanor unless child removed from state, in which case it is a class 6 felony. (Eff. 1980)
§ 18.2-49   Threatening, attempting, or assisting in such abduction; class 5 felony.
§ 18.2-50   Disclosure of information and assistance to law enforcement officers required by members of immediate family; class 2 misdemeanor.

VIRGIN ISLANDS

T.14 § 1051   False imprisonment and kidnapping; not applicable in any case when a parent abducts his own child. (Eff. 1974) (No specific custodial interference law.)

WASHINGTON

§ 9A.40.020   Kidnapping in the first degree; felony.
§ 9A.40.030   Kidnapping in the second degree; felony; defense that abduction did not include the use of, intent to use, or threat to use deadly force and actor is relative of person abducted and sole intent is to assume custody of that person. Provides that nothing in this defense constitutes a defense to, nor precludes conviction of, any other crime.
§ 9A.40.040   Unlawful imprisonment; felony.
§ 9A.40.050   Custodial interference; gross misdemeanor. (1975)

WEST VIRGINIA

§ 61-2-14   Kidnapping or concealing child; felony; mothers and fathers expressly excluded.

§ 61-2-14a Kidnapping for extortion, etc.; felony.
(No specific custodial interference law.)

WISCONSIN

§ 940.31   Kidnapping; felony.

§ 940.32   Abduction of child under 18 from his home or custody of his parent or guardian for unlawful purpose; felony.

§ 946.71   Interference with custody of child; class E felony. (Eff. August 1, 1980)

§ 946.715 Interference by parent with parental rights of other parent; class E felony; under specified circumstances, no violation committed. (Eff. August 1, 1980)

WYOMING

§ 6-4-201   Kidnapping; felony.

§ 6-4-203   Involuntary transfer of physical custody of child under 14; felony. (Eff. May 20, 1981)

§ 6-4-204   Concealment and harboring; felony. (Eff. May 28, 1977)

§ 6-4-205   Abduction for profit; felony. (Eff. May 28, 1977)

FEDERAL LAW

18 U.S.C. 1073   Unlawful flight to avoid prosecution.

18 U.S.C. 1073 note   Pub. L. No. 96-611, §10; 94 Stat. 3573

18 U.S.C. 1201   Kidnapping; felony; exempts parents from prosecution.

This survey was compiled by Patricia M. Hoff with the assistance of Janice Platner, law clerk to the Child Custody Project: INTERSTATE AND INTERNATIONAL CHILD CUSTODY DISPUTE: A COLLECTION OF MATERIALS, a Monograph by the Child Custody Project, 2nd Edition, Patricia M. Hoff, Esq. Director, American Bar Association, Fund for Public Education, Washington, D.C.

SECTION IV

UNIFORM CHILD CUSTODY JURISDICTION ACT AND THE MISSING CHILDREN ACT

UNIFORM CHILD CUSTODY JURISDICTION ACT
Table of Jurisdictions Wherein Act Has Been Adopted

Jurisdiction	Laws	Effective Date	Statutory Citation
ALABAMA	1980, No. 80-92	3-20-1980	Code 1975, §§ 30-3-20 to 30-3-44.
ALASKA	1977, c. 61	7-1-1977	AS 25.30.010 to 25.30.910
ARIZONA	1978, c. 16	4-21-1978*	A.R.S. §§ 8-401 to 8-424.
ARKANSAS	1979, No.91	7-20-1979	Ark.Stats.§§ 34-2701 to 34-2725.
CALIFORNIA	1973, c. 693	1-1-1974	West's Ann. Cal. Civ. Code §§ 5150 to 5174.
COLORADO	1973, c. 163	7-1-1973	C.R.S. 1973, 14-13-101 to 14-13-126.
CONNECTICUT	1978, P.A. 78-113	10-1-1978	C.G.S.A. §§ 46b-90 to 46b-114.
DELAWARE	60 Del. Laws, c.368	4-19-1976	13 Del.C. §§ 1901 to 1925.
FLORIDA	1977, c. 77-433	10-1-1977	West's F.S.A. §§ 61.1302 to 61.1348.
GEORGIA	1978, p. 258	1-1-1979	O.C.G.A. §§ 19-9-40 to 19-9-64.
HAWAII	1973, c.88		HRS §§ 583-1 to 583-26.
IDAHO	1977, c.214	7-1-1977	I.C. §§ 32-1101 to 32-1126
ILLINOIS	1979, P.A. 81-541	9-11-1979	S.H.A. ch. 40 §§ 2101 to 2126.
INDIANA	1977, H. 1040	8-1-1977	West's A.I.C. 31-1-11.6-1 to 31-1-11.6-24.
IOWA	1977, c.139	7-1-1977	I.C.A. §§ 598A.1 to 598A.25.
KANSAS	1978, c. 231	1-1-1979	K.S.A. 38-1301 to 38-1326.
KENTUCKY	1980, c. 69	7-15-1980	K.R.S. 403.400 to 403.630.
LOUISIANA	1978, No. 513	10-1-1978	L.S.A.-R.S. 13:1700 to 13:1724.
MAINE	1979, c. 481	9-14-1979	19 M.R.S.A. §§ 801 to 825.
MARYLAND	1975, c. 265	7-1-1975	Code 1957, art. 16, §§ 184 to 207.
MICHIGAN	1975, P.A. 297	12-14-1975*	M.C.L.A. §§ 600.651 to 600.673.
MINNESOTA	1977, c. 8	4-1-1977	M.S.A. §§ 518A.01 to 518A.25
MISSOURI	1978, H.B. No. 914	8-13-1978	V.A.M.S. §§ 452.440 to 452.550.
MONTANA	1977, c. 537	7-1-1977	M.C.A. 40-7-101 to 40-7-125.
NEBRASKA	1979, LB 18	8-24-1979	R.R.S. 1943, §§ 43-1201 to 43-1255.
NEVADA	1979, c. 85	3-23-1979*	N.R.S. 125A.020 to 125A.250
NEW HAMPSHIRE	1979, 345:1	9-1-1979	R.S.A. 458-A:1 to 458-A:25.
NEW JERSEY	1979, c. 124	7-3-1979	N.J.S.A. 2A:34-28 to 2A:34-52.
NEW MEXICO	1981, c. 119	7-1-1981	N.M.S.A. 1978, §§ 40-10-1 to 40-10-24.
NEW YORK	1977, c. 493.	9-1-1979	McKinney's Domestic Relations Law, §§ 75-a to 75-z.
NORTH CAROLINA	1979, c. 110	7-1-1979	G.S. §§ 50A-1 to 50A-25.
NORTH DAKOTA	1969, c. 154	7-1-1969	N.D.C.C. 14-14-01 to 14-14-26.
OHIO	1977, SB 135	10-25-1977	R.C. §§ 3109.21 to 3109.37.
OKLAHOMA	1980, c. 285	10-1-1980	10 Okl. St. Ann. §§ 1601 to 1627.
OREGON	1973, c. 375	10-5-1973	O.R.S. 109.700 to 109.930.
PENNSYLVANIA	1977, No. 20	7-1-1977	42 Pa.C.S.A. §§5341 to 5366.
RHODE ISLAND	1978, c. 185	7-1-1978	Gen. Laws 1956, §§ 15-14-1 to 15-14-26.
SOUTH CAROLINA	1981, Act. No. 102	7-1-1981	Code 1976, §§ 20-7-782 to 20-7-830.
SOUTH DAKOTA	1978, c. 190		S.D.C.L. 26-5-5 to 26-5-52.
UTAH	1980, c. 41		U.C.A. 1953, §§ 78-45c-1 to 45c-26.
VIRGINIA	1979, c. 229	1-1-1980	Code 1950, §§ 20-125 to 20-146.
WASHINGTON	1979, c. 98	6-7-1979	West's R.C.W.A. 26.27.010 to 26.27.910.
WEST VIRGINIA	1981, c. 207		Code, §§ 48-10-1 to 48-10-26.
WISCONSIN	1975, c. 283	5-28-1976	W.S.A. 822.01 to 822.25.
WYOMING	1973, c. 240	3-7-1973	W.S. 1977, §§ 20-5-101 to 20-5-125.

*Date of approval.

THE UNIFORM CHILD CUSTODY JURISDICTION ACT

The Uniform Child Custody Jurisdiction Act (UCCJA) was promulgated in 1968 by the National Conference of Commissioners on Uniform State Laws and approved by the American Bar Association in the same year.

The two jurisdictions which have not enacted the UCCJA are Massachusetts and Puerto Rico. The legislation is, however, presently pending in the legislatures of these two jurisdictions.

The Prefatory Note accompanying the UCCJA is reprinted on the next page. It describes the legal and social context which gave rise to the UCCJA, and serves as a concise summary of the law. The complete text of the UCCJA with Commissioners' comments follows.

The Committee which acted for the National Conference of Commissioners on Uniform State Laws in preparing the Uniform Child Custody Jurisdiction Act was as follows:

John W. Wade, Vanderbilt University School of Law,
    Nashville, Tennessee 37203
Chairman
William R. Burkett, Box 588, Woodward, Oklahoma 73801
Martin J. Dinkelspiel, 111 Pine Street, 10th Floor,
    San Francisco, California 94111
Frederick P. O'Connell, 341 Water Street, Augusta, Maine 04330
Willis E. Sullivan, Box 1466, Boise, Idaho 83701
Harry M. Weakley, Room 324, Capitol Building,
    Phoenix, Arizona 85007
Richard O. White, Legislative Building, Olympia, Washington 98501
Eugene A. Burdick, P.O. Box 757, Williston, North Dakota 58801
Chairman of Section F, Ex-Officio
Brigitte M. Bodenheimer, University of California School of Law,
    Davis, California 95616

Copies of all Uniform Acts and other printed matter issued by the Conference may be obtained from

National Conference of Commissioners
on Uniform State Laws
1155 East Sixtieth Street
Chicago, Illinois 60637

UNIFORM CHILD CUSTODY JURISDICTION ACT

PREFATORY NOTE

There is growing public concern over the fact that thousands of children are shifted from state to state and from one family to another every year while their parents or other persons battle over their custody in the courts of several states. Children of separated parents may live with their mother, for example, but one day the father snatches them and brings them to another state where he petitions a court to award him custody while the mother starts custody proceedings in her state; or in the case of illness of the mother the children may be cared for by grandparents in a third state, and all three parties may fight over the right to keep the children in several states. These and many similiar situations constantly arise in our mobil society where family members often are scattered all over the United States and at times over other countries. A young child may have been moved to another state repeatedly before the case goes to court. When a decree has been rendered awarding custody to one of the parties, this is by no means the end of the child's migrations. It is well known that those who lose a court battle over custody are often unwilling to accept the judgment of the court. They will remove the child in an unguarded moment or fail to return him after a visit and will seek their luck in the court of a distant state where they hope to find -- and often do find -- a more sympathetic ear for their plea of custody. The party deprived of the child may then resort to similar tactics to recover the child and this "game" may continue for years, with the child thrown back and forth from state to state, never coming to rest in one single home and in one community.

The harm done to children by these experiences can hardly be over-estimated. It does not require an expert in the behavorial sciences to know that a child, especially during his early years and the years of growth, needs security and stability of environment and a continuity of affection. A child who has never been given the chance

50

to develop a sense of belonging and whose personal attachments when beginning to form are cruelly disrupted, may well be crippled for life, to his own lasting detriment and the detriment of society.

This unfortunate state of affairs has been aided and facilitated rather than discouraged by the law. There is no statutory law in this area and the judicial law is so unsettled that it seems to offer nothing but a "quicksand foundation" to stand on. See Leflar, American Conflicts Law 585 (1968). See also Clark, Domestic Relations 320(1968). There is no certainty as to which state has jurisdiction when persons seeking custody of a child approach the courts of several states simultaneously or successively. There is no certainty as to whether a custody decree rendered in one state is entitled to recognition and enforcement in another state; nor as to when one state may alter a custody decree of a sister state.

The judicial trend has been toward permitting custody claimants to sue in the courts of almost any state, no matter how fleeting the contact of the child and family was with the particular state, with little regard to any conflict of law rules. See Leflar, American Conflicts Law 585-6 (1968) and Leflar, 1967 Annual Survey of American Law, Conflict of Laws 26 (1968). Also, since the United States Supreme Court has never settled the question whether the full faith and credit clause of the Constitution applies to custody decrees, many states have felt free to modify custody decrees of sister states almost at random although the theory usually is that there has been a change of circumstances requiring a custody award to a different person. Compare, *People ex rel. Halvey v. Halvey,* 330 U.S. 610, 67S. Ct. 903, 91 L. Ed. 1133 (1947); and see Comment, Ford v. Ford: Full Faith and Credit To Child Custody Decrees? 73 Yale L.J. 134 (1963). Generally speaking, there has been a tendency to over-emphasize the need for fluidity and modifiability of custody decrees at the expense of the equal (if not greater) need, from the standpoint of the child, for stability of custody decisions once made. Compare Clark, Domestic Relations 326 (1968).

Under this state of the law the courts of the various states have acted in isolation and at times in competition with each other; often with disastrous consequences. A court of one state may have awarded custody to the mother while another state decreed simultaneously that the child must go to the father. See *Stout v. Pate,* 209, Ga. 786, 75 S.E. 2d 748 (1953) and *Stout v. Pate,* 120 Cal. App. 2d 699, 261 P. 2d 788 (1953), cert. denied in both cases 347 U.S. 968, 74 S. Ct. 744, 776, 98 L. Ed. 1109, 1110 (1954); *Moniz v. Moniz,* 142 Cal. App. 2d 527, 298 P. 2d 710 (1956); and *Sharpe v. Sharpe,* 77 Ill. App. 2d 295, 222 N.E. 2d 340 (1966). In situations like this the litigants do not know which court to obey. They may face punishment for contempt of court and perhaps criminal charges for child stealing in one state when complying with the decree of the other. Also, a custody decree made in one state one year is often overturned in another jurisdiction the next year or some years later and the child is handed over to another family, to be repeated as long as the feud continues. See. *Com. ex rel. Thomas v. Gillard*, 203 Pa. Super. 95, 198 A 2d 377 (1964); *In Re Guardianship of Rodgers*, 100 Ariz. 269, 413 P. 2d 774 (1966); *Berlin v. Berlin*, 239 Md. 52, 210 A. 2d 380 (1965); *Berlin v. Berlin*, 21 N.Y. 2d 371, 235 N.E. 2d 109 (1967), cert. denied 37 L.W. 3123 (1968); and *Batchelor v. Fulcher*, 415 S.W. 2d 828 (Ky. 1967).

In this confused legal situation the person who has possession of the child has an enormous tactical advantage. Physical presence of the child opens the doors of many courts to the petitions and often assures him of a decision in his favor. It is not surprising then that custody claimants tend to take the law into their own hands, that they resort to self-help in the form of child stealing, kidnapping, or various other schemes to gain possession of the child. The irony is that persons who are good, law-abiding citizens are often driven into these tactics against their inclinations; and that lawyers who are reluctant to advise the use of maneuver of doubtful legality may place their clients at a decided disadvantage.

To remedy this intolerable state of affairs where self-help and the rule of "seize-and-run" prevail rather than the orderly process of the law, uniform legislation has been urged in recent years to bring about a fair measure of interstate stability in custody awards. See Ratner, Child Custody in a Federal System, 62 Mich. L. Rev. 795 (1964); Ratner, Legislative Resolution of the Interstate Child Custody Problem: A Reply to Professor Currie and a Proposed Uniform Act, 38S. Cal. L. Rev. 183 (1965); and Ehrenzweig, The Interstate Child and Uniform Legislation: A Plea for Extra-Litigious Proceedings, 64 Mich. L. Rev. 1 (1965). In drafting this Act, the National Conference of Commissioners has drawn heavily on the work of these authors and has consulted with other leading authorities in the field. The American Bar Association has taken an active part in furthering the project.

The Act is designed to bring some semblance of order into the existing chaos. It limits custody jurisdiction to the state where the child has his home or where there are other strong contacts with the child and his family. See Section 3. It provides for the recognition and enforcement of out-of-state custody decrees in many instances. See Sections 13 and 15. Jurisdiction to modify decrees of other states is limited by giving a jurisdictional preference to the prior court under certain conditions. See Section 14. Access to a court may be denied to petitioners who have engaged in child snatching or similar practices. See Section 8. Also, the Act opens up direct lines of communication between courts of different states to prevent jurisdictional conflict and bring about interstate judicial assistance in custody cases.

The Act stresses the importance of the personal appearance before the court of non-residents who claim custody, and of the child himself, and provides for the payment of travel expenses for this purpose. See Section 11. Further provisions insure that the judge receives necessary out-of-state information with the assistance of courts in other states. See Sections 17 through 22.

Underlying the entire Act is the idea that to avoid the jurisdictional conflicts and confusions which have done serious harm to innumerable children, a court in one state must assume major responsibility to determine who is to have custody of a particular child; that this court must reach out for help of courts in other states in order to arrive at a fully informed judgment which transcends state lines and considers all claimants, residents and nonresidents, on an equal basis and from the standpoint of the welfare of the child. If this can be achieved, it will be less important *which* court exercises jurisdiction but that courts of the several states involved act in partnership to bring about the best possible solution for a child's future.

The Act is not a reciprocal law. It can be put into full operation by each individual state regardless of enactment of other states. But its full benefits will not be reaped until a large number of states have enacted it, and until the courts, perhaps aided by regional or national conferences, have come to develop a new, truly "inter-state" approach to child custody litigation. The general policies of the Act and some of its specific provisions apply to international custody cases.

SECTION 1. (*Purposes of Act; Contruction of Provisions.*)
(a) The general purposes of this Act are to:

(1) avoid jurisdictional competition and conflicts with courts of other states in matters of child custody which have in the past resulted in the shifting of children from state to state with harmful effects on their well-being;

(2) promote cooperation with the courts of other states to the end that a custody decree is rendered in that state which can best decide the case in the interest of the child;

(3) assure that litigation concerning the custody of a child take place ordinarily in the state with which the child and his family have the closest connection and where significant evidence concerning his care, protection, training, and personal relation-

ships is most readiliy available, and that courts of this state decline the exercise of jurisdiction when the child and his family have a closer connection with another state;

(4) discourage continuing controversies over child custody in the interest of greater stability of home environment and of secure family relationships for the child;

(5) deter abductions and other unilateral removals of children undertaken to obtain custody awards;

(6) avoid re-litigation of custody decisions of other states in this state insofar as feasible;

(7) facilitate the enforcement of custody decrees of other states;

(8) promote and expand the exchange of information and other forms of mutual assistance between the courts of this state and those of other states concerned with the same child; and

(9) make uniform the law of those states which enact it.

(b) This Act shall be construed to promote the general purposes stated in this section.

COMMENT

Because this uniform law breaks new ground not previously covered by legislation, its purposes are stated in some detail. Each section must be read and applied with these purposes in mind.

SECTION 2. (*Definitions.*) As used in this Act:

(1) "contestant" means a person, including a parent, who claims a right to custody or visitation rights with respect to a child;

(2) "custody determination" means a court decision and court orders and instructions providing for the custody of a child, including visitation rights; it does not include a decision relating to child support or any other monetary obligation of any person;

(3) "custody proceeding" includes proceedings in which a custody determination is one of several issues, such as an action for divorce or separation, and includes child neglect and dependency proceedings;

(4) "decree" or "custody decree" means a custody determination contained in a judicial decree or order made in a custody proceeding, and includes an initial decree and a modification decree;

(5) "home state" means the state in which the child immediately preceding the time involved lived with his parents, a parent, or a person acting as parent, for at least 6 consecutive

months, and in the case of a child less than 6 months old the state in which the child lived from birth with any of the persons mentioned. Periods of temporary absence of any of the named persons are counted as part of the 6-month or other period;

(6) "initial decree" means the first custody decree concerning a particular child;

(7) "modification decree" means a custody decree which modifies or replaces a prior decree, whether made by the court which rendered the prior decree or by another court;

(8) "physical custody" means actual possession and control of a child;

(9) "person acting as parent" means a person, other than a parent, who has physical custody of a child and who has either been awarded custody by a court or claims a right to custody; and

(10) "state" means any state, territory, or possession of the United States, the Commonwealth of Puerto Rico, and the District of Columbia.

COMMENT

Subsection (3) indicates that "custody proceeding" is to be understood in a broad sense. The term covers habeas corpus actions, guardianship petitions, and other proceedings available under general state law to determine custody. See Clark, Domestic Relations 576-582 (1968).

Other definitions are explained, if necessary, in the comments to the sections which use the terms defined.

SECTION 3. (*Jurisdiction.*)

(a) A court of this State which is competent to decide child custody matters has jurisdiction to make a child custody determination by initial or modification decree if:

(1) this State (i) is the home state of the child at the time of commencement of the proceeding, or (ii) had been the child's home state within 6 months before commencement of the proceeding and the child is absent from this State because of his removal or retention by a person claiming his custody or for other reasons, and a parent or person acting as parent continues to live in this State; or

(2) it is in the best interest of the child that a court of this State assume jurisdiction because (i) the child and his parents, or the child and at least one contestant, have a significant connection with this State, and (ii) there is available in this State substantial evidence concerning the child's present or future care,

protection, training, and personal relationships; or

(3) the child is physically present in this State and (i) the child has been abandoned or (ii) it is necessary in an emergency to protect the child because he has been subjected to or threatened with mistreatment or abuse or is otherwise neglected (or dependent); or

(4) (i) it appears that no other state would have jurisdiction under prerequisites substantially in accordance with paragraphs (1), (2), or (3), or another state has declined to exercise jurisdiction on the ground that this State is the more appropriate forum to determine the custody of the child, and (ii) it is in the best interest of the child that this court assume jurisdiction.

(b) Except under paragraphs (3) and (4) of subsection (a), physical presence in this State of the child, or of the child and one of the contestants, is not alone sufficient to confer jurisdiction on a court of this State to make a child custody determination.

(c) Physical presence of the child, while desirable, is not a prerequisite for jurisdiction to determine his custody.

COMMENT

Paragraphs (1) and (2) of subsection (a) establish the two major bases for jurisdiction. In the first place, a court in the child's home state has jurisdiction, and secondly, if there is no home state or the child and his family have equal or stronger ties with another state, a court in that state has jurisdiction. If this alternative test produces concurrent jurisdiction in more than one state, the mechanisms provided in sections 6 and 7 are used to assure that only one state makes the custody decision.

"Home state" is defined as section 2(5). A 6-month period has been selected in order to have a definite and certain test which is at the same time based on a reasonable assumption of fact. See Ratner, Child Custody in a Federal System, 62 Mich. L. Rev. 795, 818 (1964) who explains:

> "Most American children are integrated into an American community after living there six months; consequently this period of residence would seem to provide a reasonable criterion for identifying the established home."

Subparagraph (ii) of paragraph (1) extends the home state rule for an additional six-month period in order to permit suit in the home state after the child's departure. The main objective is to protect a parent who has been left by his spouse taking the child along. The provision makes clear that the stay-at-home parent, if he acts promptly, may start proceedings in his own state if he desires, without the necessity of attempting to base jurisdiction on paragraph (2). This changes the law in those states which required presence of the child as a condition for jurisdiction and consequently forced the person left behind to follow the departed person to another state, perhaps to several states in succession. See also subsection (c).

Paragraph (2) comes into play either when the home state test cannot be met or as an alternative to that test. The first situation arises, for example, when a family has moved frequently and there is no state where the child has lived for 6 months prior to suit, or if the child has recently been removed from his home state and the person who was left behind has also moved away. See paragraph (1), last clause. A typical example of alternative jurisdiction is the case in which the stay-at-home parent chooses to follow the departed spouse to state 2 (where the child has lived for several months with the other parent) and starts proceedings there. Whether the departed parent also has access to a court in state 2, depends on the strength of the family ties in that state and on the applicability of the clean hands provision of section 8. If state 2, for example, was the state of the matrimonial home where the entire family lived for two years before moving to the "home state" for 6 months, and the wife returned to state 2 with the child with the consent of the husband, state 2 might well have jurisdiction upon petition of the wife. The same may be true if the wife returned to her parents in her former home state where the child had spent several months every year before. Compare Willmore v. Willmore, 273, Minn. 537, 143 N.W. 2d 630 (1966), cert. denied 385 U.S. 898 (1966). While jurisdiction may exist in two states in these instances, it will not be *exercised* in both states. See sections 6 and 7.

Paragraph (2) of subsection (a) is supplemented by subsection (b) which is designed to discourage unilateral removal of children to other states and to guard generally against too liberal an interpretation of paragraph (2). Short-term presence in the state is not enough even though there may be an intent to stay longer, perhaps an intent to establish a technical "domicile" for divorce or other purposes.

Paragraph (2) perhaps more than any other provision of the Act requires that it be interpreted in the spirit of the legislative purposes expressed in section 1. The paragraph was phrased in general terms in order to be flexible enough to cover many fact situations too diverse to lend themselves to exact description. But its purpose is to limit jurisdiction rather than to proliferate it. The first clause of the paragraph is important; jurisdiction exists only if it is in the *child's* interest, not merely the interest or convenience of the feuding parties, to determine custody in a particular state. The interest of the child is served when the forum has optimum access to relevant evidence about the child and family. There must be maximum rather than minimum contact with the state. The submission of the parties to a forum, perhaps for purposes of divorce, is not sufficient without additional factors establishing close ties with the state. Divorce jurisdiction does not necessarily include custody jurisdiction. See Clark, Domestic Relations 578 (1968).

Paragraph (3) of subsection (a) retains and reaffirms *parens patriae* jurisdiction, usually exercised by a juvenile court, which a state must assume when a child is in a situation requiring immediate protection. This jurisdiction exists when a child has been abandoned and in emergency cases of child neglect. Presence of the child in the state is the only prerequisite. This extraordinary jurisdiction is reserved for extraordinary circumstances. See Application of Lang, 9 App. Div. 2d 401, 193 N.Y.S. 2d 763 (1959). When there is child neglect without emergency or abandonment, jurisdiction cannot be based on this paragraph.

Paragraph (4) of subsection (a) provides a final basis for jurisdiction which is subsidiary in nature. It is to be resorted to only if no other state could, or would, assume jurisdiction under the other criteria of this section.

Subsection (c) makes it clear that presence of the child is not a jurisdictional requirement. Subsequent sections are designed to assure the appearance of the child before the court.

This section governs jurisdiction to make an initial decree as well as a modificational decree. Both terms are defined in section 2. Jurisdiction to modify an initial or modification decree of another state is subject to additional restriction contained in sections 8(b) and 14(a).

SECTION 4. *(Notice and Opportunity to be Heard.)* Before making a decree under this Act, reasonable notice and opportunity to be heard shall be given to the contestants, any parent whose parental rights have not been previously terminated, and any person who has physical custody of the child. If any of these persons is outside this State, notice and opportunity to be heard shall be given pursuant to section 5.

COMMENT

This section lists the persons who must be notified and given an opportunity to be heard to satisfy due process requirements. As to persons in the forum state, the general law of the state applies; others are notified in accordance with section 5. Strict compliance with sections 4 and 5 is essential for the validity of a custody decree within the state and its recognition and enforcement in other states under sections 12, 13, and 15. See Restatement of the Law Second, Conflict of Laws, Proposed Official Draft, sec. 69 (1967); and compare Armstrong v. Manso, 380 U.S. 545, 85 S. Ct. 1187, 14 L. Ed. 2d 62 (1965).

SECTION 5. *(Notice to Persons Outside this State; Submission to Jurisdiction.)*

(a) Notice required for the exercise of jurisdiction over a person outside this State shall be given in a manner reasonably calculated to give actual notice, and may be:

(1) by personal delivery outside this State in the manner

prescribed for service of process within this State;

(2) in the manner prescribed by the law of the place in which the service is made for service of process in that place in an action in any of its courts of general jurisdiction;

(3) by any form of mail addressed to the person to be served and requesting a receipt; or

(4) as directed by the court (including publication, if other means of notification are ineffective).

(b) Notice Under this section shall be served, mailed or delivered, (or last published) at least (10,20) days before any hearing in this State.

(c) Proof of service outside this State may be made by affidavit of the individual who made the service, or in the manner prescribed by the law of this State, the order pursuant to which the service is made, or the law of the place in which the service is made. If service is made by mail, proof may be a receipt signed by the addressee or other evidence of delivery to the addressee.

(d) Notice is not required if a person submits to the jurisdiction of the court.

COMMENT

Section 2.01 of the Uniform Interstate and International Procedure Act has been followed to a large extent. See 9B U.L.A. 315 (1966). If at all possible, actual notice should be received by the affected persons; but efforts to impart notice in a manner reasonably calculated to give actual notice are sufficient when a person who may perhaps conceal his whereabouts, cannot be reached. See Mullane v. Central Hanover Bank and Trust Co., 339 U.S. 306, 70 S. Ct. 652, 94 L. Ed. 865 (1950) and Schroeder v. City of New York, 371 U.S. 208, 83 S. Ct. 279, 9 L. Ed. 2d 255 (1962).

Notice by publication in lieu of other means of notification is not included because of its doubtful constitutionality. See Mullane v. Central Hanover Bank and Trust Co., *supra;* and see Hazard, A General Theory of State-Court Jurisdiction, 1965 Supreme Court Rev. 241, 277, 286-87. Paragraph (4) of subsection (2) lists notice by publication in brackets for the benefit of those states which desire to use published notices *in addition to* the modes of notification provided in this section where these modes prove ineffective to impart actual notice.

The provisions of this section, and paragraphs (2) and (4) of subsection (2) in particular, are subject to the caveat that notice and opportunity to be heard must always meet due process requirements as they exist at the time of the proceeding.

SECTION 6. *(Simultaneous Proceedings in Other States).*

(a) A court of this State shall not exercise its jurisdiction under this Act if at the time of filing the petition a proceeding concerning the custody of the child was pending in a court of another state exercising jurisdiction substantially in conformity with this Act, unless the proceeding is stayed by the court of the other state because this State is a more appropriate forum or for other reasons.

(b) Before hearing the petition in a custody proceeding the court shall examine the pleadings and other information supplied by the parties under section 9 and shall consult the child custody registry established under section 16 concerning the pendency of proceedings with respect to the child in other states. If the court has reason to believe that proceedings may be pending in another state it shall direct an inquiry to the state court administrator or other appropriate official of the other state.

(c) If the court is informed during the course of the proceeding that a proceeding concerning the custody of the child was pending in another state before the court assumed jurisdiction it shall stay the proceeding and communicate with the court in which the other proceeding is pending to the end that the issue may be litigated in the more appropriate forum and that information be exchanged in accordance with sections 19 through 22. If a court of this state has made a custody decree before being informed of a pending proceeding in a court of another state it shall immediately inform that court of the fact. If the court is informed that a proceeding was commenced in another state after it assumed jurisdiction it shall likewise inform the other court to the end that the issue may be litigated in the more appropriate forum.

COMMENT

Because of the havoc wreaked by simultaneous competitive jurisdiction which has been described in the Prefatory Note, this section seeks to avoid jurisdictional conflict with all feasible means, including novel methods. Courts are expected to take an active part under this section in seeking out information about custody proceedings concerning the same child pending in other states. In a proper case jurisdiction is yielded to the other state either under this section or under section 7. Both sections must be read together.

When the courts of more than one state have jurisdiction under sections 3 or 14, priority in time determines which court will proceed with the action, but the application of the inconvenient forum principle of section 7 may result in the handling of the case by the other court.

While jurisdiction need not be yielded under subsection (a) if the other court would not have jurisdiction under the criteria of this Act, the policy against simultaneous custody proceedings is so strong that it might in a particular situation be appropriate to leave the case to the other court even under such circumstances. See subsection (3) and section 7.

Once a custody decree has been rendered in one state, jurisdiction is determined by sections 8 and 14.

SECTION 7. *(Inconvenient Forum).*

(a) A Court which has jurisdiction under this Act to make an initial or modification decree may decline to exercise its jurisdiction any time before making a decree if it finds that it is an inconvenient forum to make a custody determination under the circumstances of the case and that a court of another state is a more appropriate forum.

(b) A finding of inconvenient forum may be made upon the court's own motion or upon motion of a party of a guardian ad litem or other representative of the child.

(c) In determining if it is an inconvenient forum, the court shall consider if it is in the interest of the child that another state assume jurisdiction. For this purpose it may take into account the following factors, among others:

(1) if another state is or recently was the child's home state;

(2) if another state has a closer connection with the child and his family or with the child and one or more of the contestants;

(3) if substantial evidence concerning the child's present or future care, protection, training, and personal relationships is more readily available in another state;

(4) if the parties have agreed on another forum which is no less appropriate; and

(5) if the exercise of jurisdiction by a court of this state would contravene any of the purposes stated in section 1.

(d) Before determining whether to decline or retain jurisdiction the court may communicate with a court of another state and exchange information pertinent to the assumption of jurisdiction by either court with a view to assuring that jurisdiction will be exercised by the more appropriate court and that a forum will be available to the parties.

(e) If the court finds that it is an inconvenient forum and that a court of another state is a more appropriate forum, it may dismiss the proceedings, or it may stay the proceedings upon condition that a custody proceeding be promptly commenced in another named state or upon any other conditions which may be just as proper, including the condition that a moving party stipulate his consent and submission to the jurisdiction of another forum.

(f) The court may decline to exercise its jurisdiction under this Act if a custody determination is incidental to an action for divorce or another proceeding while retaining jurisdiction over the divorce or other proceeding.

(g) If it appears to the court that it is clearly an inappropriate forum it may require the party who commenced the proceedings to pay, in addition to the costs of the proceedings in this State, necessary travel and other expenses, including attorneys' fees, incurred by other parties or witnesses. Payment is to be made to the clerk of the court for remittance to the proper party.

(h) Upon dismissal or stay of proceedings under this section the court shall inform the court found to be the more appropriate forum of this fact, or if the court which would have jurisdiction in the other state is not certainly known, shall transmit the information to the court administrator or other appropriate official for forwarding to the appropriate court.

(i) Any communication received from another state informing this State of finding of inconvenient forum because a court of this State is the more appropriate forum shall be filed in the custody registry of the appropriate court. Upon assuming jurisdiction the court of this State shall inform the original court of this fact.

COMMENT

The purpose of this provision is to encourage judicial restraint in exercising jurisdiction whenever another state appears to be in a better position to determine custody of a child. It serves as a second check on jurisdiction once the test of sections 3 or 14 has been met.

The section is a particular application of the inconvenient forum principle, recognized in most states by judicial law, adapted to the special needs of child custody cases. The terminology used follows section 84 of the Restatement of the Law Second, Conflict of Laws, Proposed Official Draft (1967). Judicial restrictions or exceptions to the inconvenient forum rule made in some states do not apply to this statutory scheme which is limited to child custody cases.

The section is a particular application of the inconvenient forum principle, recognized in most states by judicial law, adapted to the special needs of child custody cases. The terminology used follows section 84 of the Restatement of the Law Second, Conflict of Laws, Proposed Official Draft (1967). Judicial restrictions or exceptions to the inconvenient forum rule made in some states do not apply to this statutory scheme which is limited to child custody cases.

Like section 6, this section stresses interstate judicial communication and cooperation. When there is doubt as to which is the more appropriate forum, the question may be resolved by consultation and cooperation among the courts involved.

Paragraphs (1) through (5) of subsection (c) specify some, but not all, considerations which enter into a court determination of inconvenient forum. Factors customarily listed for purposes of the general principle of the inconvenient forum (such as convenience of the parties and hardship to the defendant) are also pertinent, but may under the circumstances be of secondary importance because the child who is not a party is the central figure in the proceedings.

Part of subsection (e) is derived from Wis. Stat. Ann., sec. 262.19(1). Subsection (f) makes it clear that a court may divide a case, that is dismiss part of it and retain the rest. See section 1.05 of the Uniform Interstate and International Procedure Act. When the custody issue comes up in a divorce proceeding, courts may have frequent occasion to decline jurisdiction as to that issue (assuming that custody jurisdiction exists under sections 3 or 14).

Subsection (g) is an adaptation of Wis. Stat. Ann., sec. 262.20. Its purpose is to serve as a deterrent against "frivolous jurisdiction claims," as G.W. Foster states in the Revision Notes to the Wisconsin provision. It applies when the forum chosen is seriously inappropriate considering the jurisdictional requirements of the Act.

SECTION 8. *(Jurisdiction Declined by Reason of Conduct.)*

(a) If the petitioner for an initial decree has wrongfully taken the child from another state or has engaged in similar reprehensible conduct the court may decline to exercise jurisdiction if this is just and proper under the circumstances.

(b) Unless required in the interest of the child, the court shall not exercise its jurisdiction to modify a custody decree of another state if the petitioner, without consent of the person entitled to custody, has improperly removed the child from the physical custody of the person entitled to custody or has improperly retained the child after a visit or other temporary relinquishment of physical custody. If the petitioner has violated any other provision of a custody decree of another state the court may decline to exercise its jurisdiction if this is just and proper under the circumstances.

(c) In appropriate cases a court dismissing a petition under this section may charge the petitioner with necessary travel and other expenses, including attorneys' fees, incurred by other parties or their witnesses.

COMMENT

This section incorporates the "clean hands doctrine," so named by Ehrenzweig, Interstate Recognition of Custody Decrees, 51, Mich. L. Rev. 345 (1953). Under this doctrine courts refuse to assume jurisdiction to reexamine an out-of-state custody decree when the petitioner has abducted the child or has engaged in some other objectionable scheme to gain or retain physical custody of the child in violation of the decree. See Fain, Custody of Children, The California Family Lawyer 1, 539, 546 (1961); Ex. Parte Mullins, 26 Wash. 2d 419, 174 P. 2d 790 (1946); Crocker v. Crocker, 122 Colo. 49, 219 P. 2d 311 (1950); and Leathers v. Leathers, 162 Cal. App. 2d

768, 328 P. 2d 853 (1958). But when adherence to this rule would lead to punishment of the parent at the expense of the wellbeing of the child, it is often not applied. See Smith v. Smith, 135 Cal. App. 2d 100, 286 P. 2d 1009 (1955) and In Re Guardianship of Rodgers, 100 Ariz. 269, 413 P. 2d 744 (1966).

Subsection (a) extends the clean hands principle to cases in which a custody decree has not yet been rendered in any state. For example, if upon a de facto separation the wife returned to her own home with the children without objection by her husband and lived there for two years without hearing from him, and the husband without warning forcibly removes the children one night and brings them to another state, a court in that state although it has jurisdiction after 6 months may decline to hear the husband's custody petition. "Wrongfully" taking under this subsection does not mean that a "right" has been violated - both husband and wife as a rule have a right to custody until a court determination is made - but that one party's conduct is so objectionable that a court in the exercise of its inherent equity powers cannot in good conscience permit that party access to its jurisdiction.

Subsection (b) does not come into operation unless the court has power under section 14 to modify the custody decree of another state. It is a codification of the clean hands rule, except that it differentiates between (1) a taking or retention of the child and (2) other violations of custody decrees. In the case of illegal removal or retention refusal of jurisdiction is mandatory unless the harm done to the child by a denial of jurisdiction outweighs the parental misconduct. Compare Smith v. Smith and In Re Guardianship of Rodgers, *supra*; and see In Re Walter, 228 Cal. App. 2d 217, 39 Cal. Rpts. 243 (1964) where the court assumed jurisdiction after both parents had been guilty of misconduct. The qualifying word "improperly" is added to exclude cases in which a child is withheld because of illness or other emergency or in which there are other special justifying circumstances.

The most common violation of the second category is the removal of the child from the state by the parent who has the right to custody, thereby frustrating the exercise of visitation rights of the other parent. The second sentence of subsection (b) makes refusal of jurisdiction entirely discretionary in this situation because it depends on the circumstances whether non-compliance with the court order is serious enough to warrant the drastic sanction of denial of jurisdiction.

Subsection (c) adds a financial deterrent to child stealing and similar reprehensible conduct.

SECTION 9. *(Information under Oath to be Submitted to the Court.)*

(a) Every party in a custody proceeding in his first pleading or in an affidavit attached to that pleading shall give information under oath as to the child's present address, the places where the child has lived within the last 5 years, and the names and present addresses of the persons with whom the child has lived during that period. In this pleading or affadavit every party shall further declare under oath whether:

(1) he has participated (as a party, witness, or in any other capacity) in any other litigation concerning the custody of the same child in this or any other state;

(2) he has information of any custody proceeding concerning the child pending in a court of this or any other state; and

(3) he knows of any person not a party to the proceedings who has physical custody of the child or claims to have custody or visitation rights with respect to the child.

(b) If the declaration as to any of the above items is in the affirmative the declarant shall give additional information under oath as required by the court. The court may examine the parties under oath as to details of the information furnished and as to other matters pertinent to the court's jurisdiction and the disposition of the case.

(c) Each party has a continuing duty to inform the court of any custody proceeding concerning the child in this or any other state of which he obtained information during this proceeding.

COMMENT

It is important for the court to receive the information listed and other pertinent facts as early as possible for purposes of determining its jurisdiction, the joinder of additional parties, and the identification of courts in other states which are to be contacted under various provisions of the Act. Information as to custody litigation and other pertinent facts occurring in other countries may also be elicited under this section in combination with section 23.

SECTION 10. *(Additional Parties.)* If the court learns from information furnished by the parties pursuant to section 9 or from other sources that a person not a party to the custody proceeding has physical custody of the child or claims to have custody or visitation rights with respect to the child, it shall order that person to be joined as a party and to be duly notified of the pendency of the proceeding and of his joinder as a party. If the person joined as a party is outside this State he shall be served with process or otherwise notified in accordance with section 5.

COMMENT

The purpose of this section is to prevent re-litigations of the custody issue when these would be for the benefit of third claimants rather than the child.

If the immediate controversy, for example, is between the parents, but relatives inside or outside the state also claim custody or have physical custody which may lead to a future claim to the child, they must be brought into the proceedings. The courts are given an active role here as under other sections of the Act to seek out the necessary information from formal or informal sources.

SECTION 11. *(Appearance of Parties and the Child.)*

(a) The court may order any party to the proceeding who is in this State to appear personally before the court. If that party has physical custody of the child the court may order that he appear personally with the child.

(b) If a party to the proceeding whose presence is desired by the court is outside this State with or without the child the court may order that the notice given under section 5 include a statement directing that party to appear personally with or without the child and declaring that failure to appear may result in a decision adverse to that party.

(c) If a party to the proceeding who is outside this State is directed to appear under subsection (b) or desires to appear personally before the court with or without the child, the court may require another party to pay to the clerk of the court travel and other necessary expenses of the party so appearing and of the child if this is just and proper under the circumstances.

COMMENT

Since a custody proceeding is concerned with the past and future care of the child by one of the parties, it is of vital importance in most cases that the judge has an opportunity to see and hear the contestants and the child. Subsection (a) authorizes the court to order the appearance of these persons if they are in the state. It is placed in brackets because states which have such a provision - not only in their juvenile court laws - may wish to omit it. Subsection (b) relates to the appearance of persons who are outside the state and provides one method of bringing them before the court; sections 19(b) and 20(b) provide another. Subsection (c) helps to finance travel to the court which may be close to one of the parties and distant from another; it may be used to equalize the expense if this is appropriate under the circumstances.

SECTION 12. *(Binding Force and Res Juducata Effect of Custody Decree.)* A custody decree rendered by a court of this State which had jurisdiction under section 3 binds all parties who have been

served in this State or notified in accordance with section 5 or who have submitted to the jurisdiction of the court, and who have been given an opportunity to be heard. As to these parties the custody decree is conclusive as to all issues of law and fact decided and as to the custody determination made unless and until that determination is modified pursuant to law, including the provisions of this Act.

COMMENT

This section deals with the intra-state validity of custody decrees which provides the basis for their interstate recognition and enforcement. The two prerequisites are (1) jurisdiction under section 3 of this Act and (2) strict compliance with due process mandates of notice and opportunity to be heard. There is no requirement for technical personal jurisdiction, on the traditional theory that custody determinations, as distinguished from support actions (see section 2(2) *supra*), are proceedings in rem or proceedings affecting status. See Restatement of the Law Second, Conflict of Laws, Proposed Official Draft, sections 69 and 79 (1967); and James, Civil Procedure 613 (1965). For a different theory reaching the same results, see Hazard, A. General Theory of State-Court Jurisdiction, 1965 Supreme Court Review 241. The section is not at variance with May v. Anderson, 345 U.S. 528, 73 S. Ct. 840, 97 L. Ed. 1221 (1953), which relates to interstate recognition rather than in-state validity of custody decrees. See Ehrenzweig and Louisell, Jurisdiction in a Nutshell 76 (2d ed. 1968); and compare Reese, Full Faith and Credit to Foreign Equity Decrees, 42 Iowa L. Rev. 183, 195 (1957). On May v. Anderson, *supra*, see comment to section 13.

Since a custody decree is normally subject to modification in the interest of the child, it does not have absolute finality, but as long as it has not been modified, it is as binding as a final judgment. Compare Restatement of the Law Second, Conflict of Laws, Proposed Official Draft, section 109 (1967).

SECTION 13. *(Recognition of Out-of-State Custody Decrees.)* The courts of this State shall recognize and enforce an initial or modification decree of a court of another state which had assumed jurisdiction under statutory provisions substantially in accordance with this Act or which was made under factual circumstances meeting the jurisdictional standards of the Act, so long as this decree has not been modified in accordance with jurisdictional standards substantially similar to those of this Act.

COMMENT

This section and sections 14 and 15 are the key provisions which guarantee a great measure of security and stability of environment to the "interstate child" by discouraging relitigations in other states. See Section 1, and see Ratner, Child Custody in a Federal System, 62 Mich. L. Rev. 795, 828 (1964).

Although the full faith and credit clause may perhaps not require the recognition of out-of-state custody decrees, the states are free to recognize and enforce them. See Restatement of the Law Second, Conflict of Laws, Proposed Official Draft, section 109 (1967), and see the Prefatory Note, *supra*. This section declares as a matter of state law, that the custody decrees of sister states will be recognized and enforced. Recognition and enforcement is mandatory if the state in which the prior decree was rendered 1) has adopted this Act, 2) has statutory jurisdictional requirements substantially like this Act, or 3) would have had jurisdiction under the facts of the case if this Act had been the law in the state. Compare Comment, Ford v. Ford: Full Faith and Credit to Child Custody Decrees? 73 Yale L.J. 134, 148 (1963).

"Jurisdiction" or "jurisdictional standards" under this section refers to the requirements of section 3 in the case of initial decrees and to the requirements of sections 3 and 14 in the case of modification decrees. The section leaves open the possibility of discretionary recognition of custody decrees of other states beyond the enumerated situations of mandatory acceptance. For the recognition of custody decrees of other nations, see section 23.

Recognition is accorded to a decree which is valid and binding under section 12. This means, for example, that a court in the state where the father resides will recognize and enforce a custody decree rendered in the home state where the child lives with the mother if the father was duly notified and given enough time to appear in the proceedings. Personal jurisdiction over the father is not required. See comment to section 12. This is in accord with a common interpretation of the inconclusive decision in May v. Anderson, 345 U.S. 528, 73 S. Ct. 840, 97 L. Ed. 1221 (1953). See Restatement of the Law Second, Conflict of Laws, Proposed Official Draft, section 79 and comment thereto, p. 298 (1967). Under this interpretation a state is permitted to recognize a custody decree of another state regardless of lack of personal jurisdiction, as long as due process requirements of notice and opportunity to be heard have been met. See Justice Frankfurter's concurring opinion in May v. Anderson; and compare Clark, Domestic Relations 323-26 (1968), Goodrich, Conflict of Laws 274 (4th ed. by Scoles, 1964); Stumberg, Principles of Conflict of Laws 325 (3rd ed. 1963); and Comment, The Puzzle of Jurisdiction in Child Custody Actions, 38 U. Colo. L. Rev. 541 (1966). The Act emphasizes the need for the personal appearance of the contestants rather than any technical requirement for personal jurisdiction.

The mandate of this section could cause problems if the prior decree is a punitive or disciplinary measure. See Ehrenzweig, Inter-state Recognition of Custody Decrees, 51 Mich. L. Rev. 345, 370 (1953). If, for example, a court grants custody to the mother and after 5 years of continuous life with the mother the child is awarded to the father by the same court for the sole reason that the mother who has moved to another state upon remarriage had not lived up to the visitation requirements of the decree, courts in other states may be reluctant to recognize the changed decree. See Berlin v. Berlin, 21 N.Y. 2d 371, 235 N.E. 2d 109 (1967); and Stout v. Pate, 120 Cal. App. 2d 699, 261 P. 2d 788 (1953); Compare Moniz v. Moniz, 142 Cal. App. 2d 527, 298 P. 2d 710 (1956). Disciplinary decrees of this type can be avoided under this Act by enforcing the visitation provisions of the decree directly in another state. See Section 15. If the original plan for visitation does not fit the new conditions, a petition for modification of the visiting arrangements would be filed in a court which has jurisdiction, that is, in many cases the original court. See section 14.

SECTION 14. *(Modification of Custody Decree of Another State.)*
(a) If a court of another state has made a custody decree, a court of this State shall not modify that decree unless (1) it appears to the court of this State that the court which rendered the decree does not now have jurisdiction under jurisdictional prerequisites substantially in accordance with this Act or has declined to assume jurisdiction to modify the decree and (2) the court of this State has jurisdiction.

(b) If a court of this State is authorized under subsection (a) and section 8 to modify a custody decree of another state it shall give due consideration to the transcript of the record and other documents of all previous proceedings submitted to it in accordance with section 22.

COMMENT

Courts which render a custody decree normally retain continuing jurisdiction to modify the decree under local law. Courts in other states have in the past often assumed jurisdiction to modify the out-of-state decree themselves without regard to the preexisting jurisdiction of the other state. See People ex rel. Halvey v. Halvey, 330 U.S. 610, 67 S. Ct. 903, 91 L. Ed. 1133 (1947). In order to achieve greater stability of custody arrangements and avoid forum shopping, subsection (a) declares that other states will defer to the continuing jurisdiction of the court of another state as long as that state has jurisdiction under the standards of this Act. In other words, all petitions for modification are to be addressed to the prior state if that state has sufficient contact with the case to satisfy section 3. The fact that the court

69

had previously considered the case may be one factor favoring its continued jurisdiction. If, however, all the persons involved have moved away or the contact with the state has otherwise become slight, modification jurisdiction would shift elsewhere. Compare Ratner, Child Custody in a Federal System, 62 Mich. L. Rev. 795, 821-2(1964).

For example, if custody was awarded to the father in state 1 where he continued to live with the children for two years and thereafter his wife kept the children in state 2 for 6-1/2 months (3-1/2 months beyond her visitation privileges) with or without permission of the husband, state 1 has preferred jurisdiction to modify the decree despite the fact that state 2 has in the meantime become the "home state" of the child. If, however, the father also moved away from state 1, that state loses modification jurisdiction interstate, whether or not its jurisdiction continues under local law. See Clark, Domestic Relations 322-23 (1968). Also, if the father in the same case continued to live in state 1, but let his wife keep the children for several years without asserting his custody rights and without visits of the children in state 1, modification jurisdiction of state 1 would cease. Compare Brengle v. Hurst, 408 S.W. 2d 418 (Ky. 1966). The situation would be different if the children had been abducted and their whereabouts could not be discovered by the legal custodian for several years. The abductor would be denied access to the court of another state under section 8(b) and state 1 would have modification jurisdiction in any event under section 3(a) (4). Compare Crocker v. Crocker, 122 Colo. 49, 219 P. 2d 311 (1950).

The prior court has jurisdiction to modify under this section even though its original assumption of jurisdiction did not meet the standards of this Act, as long as it would have jurisdiction *now*, that is, at the time of the petition for modification.

If the state of the prior decree declines to assume jurisdiction to modify the decree, another state with jurisdiction under section 3 can proceed with the case. That is not so if the prior Court dismissed the petition on its merits.

Respect for the continuing jurisdiction of another state under this section will serve the purposes of this Act only if the prior court will assume a corresponding obligation to make no changes in the existing custody arrangement which are not required for the good of the child. If the court overturns its own decree in order to discipline a mother or father, with whom the child had lived for years, for failure to comply with an order of the court, the objective of greater stability of custody decree is not achieved. See Comment to section 13 last paragraph, and cases there cited. See also Sharpe v. Sharpe, 77 Ill. App. 295, 222 N.E. 2d 340 (1966). Under section 15 of this Act an order of a court contained in a custody decree can be directly enforced in another state.

Under subsection (b) transcripts of prior proceedings if received under section 22 are to be considered by the modifying court. The purpose is to give the judge the opportunity to be as fully informed as possible before making a custody decision. "One court will seldom have so much of the story that another's inquiry is unimportant," says Paulsen, Appointment of a Guardian in the Conflict of Laws, 45 Iowa L. Rev. 212, 226 (1960). See also

Ehrenzweig, the Interstate Child and Uniform Legislation: A Plea for Extra-Litigious Proceedings, 64 Mich. L. Rev. 1, 6-7 (1965); and Ratner, Legislative Resolution of the Interstate Custody Problem: A Reply to Professor Currie and a Proposed Uniform Act, 38 S. Cal. L. Rev. 183, 202 (1965). How much consideration is "due" this transcript, whether or under what conditions it is received in evidence, are matters of local, internal law which are not affected by this interstate act.

SECTION 15. *(Filing and Enforcement of Custody Decree of Another State.)*

(a) A certified copy of a custody decree of another state may be filed in the office of the clerk of any (District Court, Family Court) of this State. The clerk shall treat the decree in the same manner as a custody decree of the (District Court, Family Court) of this State. A custody decree so filed has the same effect and shall be enforced in a like manner as a custody decree rendered by a court of this State.

(b) A person violating a custody decree of another state which makes it necessary to enforce the decree in this State may be required to pay necessary travel and other expenses, including attorney's fees, incurred by the party entitled to the custody or his witnesses.

COMMENT

Out-of-state custody decrees which are required to be recognized are enforced by other states. See section 13. Subsection (a) provides a simplified and speedy method of enforcement. It is derived from section 2 of the Uniform Enforcement of Foreign Judgments Act of 1964, 9A U.L.A. 486 (1965). A certified copy of the decree is filed in the appropriate court, and the decree thereupon becomes in effect a decree of the state of filing and is enforceable by any method of enforcement available under the law of that state.

The authority to enforce an out-of-state decree does not include the power to modify it. If modification is desired, the petition must be directed to the court which has jurisdiction to modify under section 14. This does not mean that the state of enforcement may not in an emergency stay enforcement if there is danger of serious mistreatment of the child. See Ratner, Child Custody in a Federal System, 62 Mich. L. Rev. 795, 832-33 (1964).

The right to custody for periods of visitation and other provisions of a custody decree are enforceable in other states in the same manner as the primary right to custody. If visitation privileges provided in the decree have been impractical upon moving to another state, the remedy against automatic enforcement in another state is a petition in the proper court to modify visitation arrangements to fit the new conditions.

Subsection (b) makes it clear that the financial burden of enforcement of a custody decree may be shifted to the wrongdoer. Compare 2 Armstrong, California Family Law 328 (1966 Suppl.), and *Crocker v. Crocker*, 195 F. 2d 236 (1952).

SECTION 16. *(Registry of Out-of-State Custody Decrees and Proceedings.)* The clerk of each (District Court, Family Court) shall maintain a registry in which he shall enter the following:

(1) certified copies of custody decrees of other states received for filing;

(2) communications as to the pendency of custody proceedings in other states;

(3) communications concerning a finding of inconvenient forum by a court of another state; and

(4) other communications or documents concerning custody proceedings in another state which may affect the jurisdiction of a court of this State or the disposition to be made by it in a custody proceeding.

COMMENT

The purpose of this section is to gather all information concerning out-of-state custody cases which reaches a court in one designated place. The term "registry" is derived from section 35 of the Uniform Reciprocal Enforcement of Support Act of 1958, 9C U.L.A. 61 (1967 Suppl.) Another term may be used if desired without affecting the uniformity of the Act. The information in the registry is usually incomplete since it contains only those documents which have been specifically requested or which have otherwise found their way to the state. It is therefore necessary in most cases for the court to seek additional information elsewhere.

SECTION 17. *(Certified Copies of Custody Decree.)* The Clerk of the (District Court, Family Court) of this State, at the request of the court of another state or at the request of any person who is affected by or has a legitimate interest in a custody decree, shall certify and forward a copy of the decree to that court or person.

SECTION 18. *(Taking Testimony in Another State.)* In addition to other procedural devices available to a party, any party to the proceeding or a guardian ad litem or other representative of the child may adduce testimony of witnesses, including parties and the child, by deposition or otherwise, in another state. The court on its own motion may direct that the testimony of a person be taken in another state and may prescribe the manner in which and the terms upon which the testimony shall be taken.

COMMENTS

Sections 18 to 22 are derived from sections 3.01 and 3.02 of the Uniform Interstate and International Procedure Act, 9B U.L.A. 305, 321, 326 (1966); from ideas underlying the Uniform Reciprocal Enforcement of Support Act; and from Ehrenzweig, the Interstate Child and Uniform Legislation: A Plea for Extralitigious Proceedings, 64 Mich. L. Rev. 1 (1965). They are designed to fill the partial vacuum which inevitably exists in cases involving an "interstate child" since part of the essential information about the child and his relationship to other persons is always in another state. Even though jurisdiction is assumed under sections 3 and 7 in the state where much (or most) of the pertinent facts are readily available, some important evidence will unavoidably be elsewhere.

Section 18 is derived from portions of section 3.01 of the Uniform Interstate and International Procedure Act, 9B U.L.A. 305, 321. The first sentence relates to depositions, written interrogatories and other discovery devices which may be used by parties or representatives of the child. The procedural rules of the state where the device is used are applicable under this sentence. The second sentence empowers the court itself to initiate the gathering of out-of-state evidence which is often not supplied by the parties in order to give the court a complete picture of the child's situation, especially as it relates to a custody claimant who lives in another state.

SECTION 19. *(Hearings and Studies in Another State; Orders to Appear.)*

(a) A court of this State may request the appropriate court of another state to hold a hearing to adduce evidence, to order a party to produce or give evidence under other procedures of that state, or to have social studies made with respect to the custody of a child involved in proceedings pending in the court of this State; and to forward to the court of this State certified copies of the transcript of the record of the hearing, the evidence otherwise adduced, or any social studies prepared in compliance with the request. The cost of the services may be assessed against the parties or, if necessary, ordered paid by the (County, State).

(b) A court of this State may request the appropriate court of another state to order a party to custody proceedings pending in the court of this State to appear in the proceedings, and if that party has physical custody of the child, to appear with the child.

73

The request may state that travel and other necessary expenses of the party and of the child whose appearance is desired will be assessed against another party or will otherwise be paid.

COMMENT

Section 19 relates to assistance sought by a court of the forum state from a court of another state. See comment to section 18. Subsection (a) covers any kind of evidentiary procedure available under the law of the assisting state which may aid the court in the requesting state, including custody in investigations (social studies) if authorized by the law of the other state. Under what conditions reports of social studies and other evidence collected under this subsection are admissible in the requesting state, is a matter of internal state law not covered in this interstate statute. Subsection (b) serves to bring parties and the child before the requesting court, backed up by the assisting court's contempt powers. See section 11.

SECTION 20. *(Assistance to Courts of Other States)*

(a) Upon request of the court of another state the courts of this State which are competent to hear custody matters may order a person in this State to appear at a hearing to adduce evidence or to produce or give evidence under other procedures available in this State (or may order social studies to be made for use in a custody proceeding in another state). A certified copy of the transcript of the record of the hearing or the evidence otherwise adduced (and any social studies prepared) shall be forwarded by the clerk of the court to the requesting court.

(b) A person within this State may voluntarily give his testimony or statement in this State for use in a custody proceeding outside this state.

(c) Upon request of the court of another state a competent court of this State may order a person in this State to appear alone or with the child in a custody proceeding in another state. The court may condition compliance with the request upon assurance by the other state that state travel and other necessary expenses will be advanced or reimbursed.

COMMENT

Section 20 is the counterpart of section 19. It empowers local courts to give help to out-of-state courts in custody cases. See comments to sections 18 and 19. The references to social studies have been placed in brackets so that states without authorization to make social studies outside of juvenile court proceedings may omit them if they wish. Subsection (b) reaffirms the existing freedom of persons within the United States to give evidence for use in proceedings elsewhere. It is derived from section 3.02 (b) of the Interstate and International Procedure Act, 9B U.L.A. 327 (1966).

SECTION 21. *(Preservation of Documents for Use in Other States.)* In any custody proceeding in this State the court shall preserve the pleadings, orders and decrees, any record that has been made of its hearings, social studies, and other pertinent documents until the child reaches (18, 21) years of age. Upon appropriate request of the court of another state the court shall forward to the other court certified copies of any or all such documents.

COMMENT

See comments to sections 18 and 19. Documents are to be preserved until the child is old enough that further custody disputes are unlikely. A lower figure than the ones suggested in the brackets may be inserted.

SECTION 22. *(Request for Court Records of Another State.)* If a custody decree has been rendered in another state concerning a child involved in a custody proceeding pending in a court of this State, the court of this State upon taking jurisdiction of the case shall request of the court of the other state a certified copy of the transcript of any court record and other documents mentioned in section 21.

COMMENT

This is the counterpart of section 21. See comments to sections 18, 19, and 14(b).

SECTION 23. *(International Application.)* The general policies of this Act extend to the international area. The provisions of this Act relating to the recognition and enforcement of custody decrees of other states apply to custody decrees and decrees involving legal institutions similar in nature to custody institutions rendered by appropriate authorities of other nations if reasonable notice and opportunity to be heard were given to all affected persons.

COMMENT

Not all of the provisions of the Act lend themselves to direct application in international custody disputes; but the basic policies of avoiding jurisdictional conflict and multiple litigation are as strong if not stronger when children are moved back and forth from one country to another by feuding relatives. Compare Application of Lang, 9 App. Div. 2d 401, 193 N.Y.S. 2d 763 (1959) and Swindle v. Bradley, 240 Ark. 903, 403 S.W. 2d 63 (1966).

The first sentence makes the general policies of the Act applicable to international cases. This means that the substance of section 1 and the principles underlying provisions like sections 6,7,8, and 14(a), are to be followed when some of the persons involved are in a foreign country or a foreign custody proceeding is pending.

The second sentence declares that custody decrees rendered in other nations by appropriate authorities (which may be judicial or administrative tribunals) are recognized and enforced in this country. The only prerequisite is that reasonable notice and opportunity to be heard was given to the persons affected. It is also to be understood that the foreign tribunal had jurisdiction under its own law rather than under section 3 of this Act. Compare Restatement of the Law Second, Conflict of Laws, Proposed Official Draft, sections 10, 92, 98, and 109(2) (1967). Compare also Goodrich, Conflict of Laws 390-93 (4th ed., Scoles, 1964).

SECTION 24. *(Priority.)* Upon the request of a party to a custody proceeding which raises a question of existence or exercise of jurisdiction under this Act the case shall be given calendar priority and handled expeditiously.

COMMENT

Judicial time spent in determining which court has or should exercise jurisdiction often prolongs the period of uncertainty and turmoil in a child's life more than is necessary. The need for speedy adjudication exists, of course, with respect to all aspects of child custody litigation. The priority requirement is limited to jurisdictional questions because an all encompassing priority would be beyond the scope of this act. Since some states may have or wish to adopt a statutory provision or court rule of wider scope, this section is placed in brackets and may be omitted.

SECTION 25. *(Severability.)* If any provision of this Act or the application thereof to any person or circumstance is held invalid, its invalidity does not affect other provisions or applications of the Act which can be given effect without the invalid provision or application, and to this end the provisions of this Act are severable.

MISSING CHILDREN ACT

SEPTEMBER 30, 1982 — Ordered to be printed

Mr. Edwards of California, from the committee of conference, submitted the following

CONFERENCE REPORT

(To accompany H.R. 6976)

The committee of conference on the disagreeing votes of the two Houses on the amendment of the Senate to the bill (H.R. 6976) to amend title 28, United States Code, to require the Attorney General to acquire and exchange information to assist Federal, State, and local officials in the identification of certain deceased individuals and in the location of missing persons (including unemancipated persons), having met, after full and free conference, have agreed to recommend and do recommend to their respective Houses as follows:

That the House recede from its disagreement to the amendment of the Senate and agree to the same with an amendment as follows:

In lieu of the matter proposed to be inserted by the Senate amendment insert the following:

That this Act may be cited as the "Missing Children Act".

SEC. 2, (a) Section 534(a) of title 28, United States Code, is amended . . .

. . . by inserting . . . the following new paragraphs:

"(2) acquire, collect, classify, and preserve any information which would assist in the identification of any deceased individual who has not been identified after the discovery of such deceased individual;

"(3) acquire, collect, classify, and preserve any information which would assist in the location of any missing person (including an unemancipated person as defined by the laws of the place of residence of such person) and provide confirmation

as to any entry for such a person to the parent, legal guardian, or next of kin that person (and the Attorney General may acquire, collect, classify, and preserve such information from such parent, guardian, or next of kin);" . . .

SEC. 3 (a) The heading for section 534 of title 28, United States Code, is amended to read as follows:

"§ 534. Acquisition, preservation, and exchange of identification records and information; appointment of officials".

(b) The table of sections at the beginning of chapter 33 of such title is amended by striking out the item relating to section 534 and inserting in lieu thereof the following new item:

"534 Acquisition, preservation and exchange of identification records and information; appointment of officials.".

And the Senate agree to the same.

DON EDWARDS
ROBERT W. KASTENMEIER,
PATRICIA SCHROEDER,
HAROLD WASHINGTON,
PAUL SIMON,
JAMES F. SENSENBRENNER, JR.,
DAN LUNGREN,
E. CLAY SHAW, JR.,
Managers on the Part of the House

STROM THURMOND
ORRIN G. HATCH,
ARLEN SPECTER,
PAULA HAWKINS,
JOSEPH R. BIDEN, JR.,
DENNIS DeCONCINI,
HOWELL HEFLIN,
Managers on the Part of the Senate

JOINT EXPLANATORY STATEMENT OF THE COMMITTEE OF CONFERENCE.

The managers on the part of the House and Senate at the conference on the disagreeing votes of the two Houses on the amendment of the Senate to the bill (H.R. 6976) to amend title 28, United States Code, to require the Attorney General to acquire and exchange information to assist Federal, State, and local officials in the identification of certain deceased individuals and in the location of missing persons (including unemancipated persons), submit the following joint statement to the House and the Senate in explanation of the effect of the action agreed upon by the managers and recommended in the accompanying conference report.

The Conference agreement restored the House language proposed to be stricken by the Senate amendment with the following additional language at the end of paragraph (3) of the amended section 534 of title 28.

At the end of paragraph (3), add these words: "and provide confirmation as to any entry for such a person to the parent, legal guardian, or next of kin of that person (and the Attorney General may acquire, collect, classify, and preserve such information from such parent, guardian, or next of kin)".

The conferees met and reached agreement on September 30, 1982.

> DON EDWARDS,
> ROBERT W. KASTENMEIER,
> PATRICIA SCHROEDER,
> HAROLD WASHINGTON,
> PAUL SIMON,
> JAMES F. SENSENBRENNER, JR.,
> DAN LUNGREN,
> E. CLAY SHAW, JR.,
> *Managers on the Part of the House.*

> STROM THURMOND,
> ORRIN G. HATCH,
> ARLEN SPECTER,
> PAULA HAWKINS,
> JOSEPH R. BIDEN, JR.,
> DENNIS DeCONCINI,
> HOWELL HEFLIN,
> *Managers on the Part of the Senate.*

MISSING PERSONS REPORT AND REQUEST FOR NATIONAL CRIME INFORMATION CENTER ENTRY

NAME _____

ADDRESS _____

D.O.B. _____ AGE _____ RACE _____ SEX ____ COMP _____

HEIGHT _____ WEIGHT _____ PHYSICAL BUILD _____

EYE COLOR _____ HAIR COLOR _____ HAIR STYLE _____

FACIAL HAIR AND STYLE, BEARD, MUSTACHE, ETC. _____

_____

SCARS _____

BIRTH MARKS _____

TATTOOS _____

CONDITION OF TEETH _____

EYE GLASSES _____ STYLE _____ CONTACT LENSES _____

FINGERPRINT CLASS _____

OTHER _____

CLOTHING LAST SEEN WORN _____

_____

JEWELRY WORN _____

DATE LAST SEEN _____ WHERE LAST SEEN _____

POSSIBLE DESTINATION _____

POSSIBLY TRAVELING WITH _____

REPORTING AGENCY _____ TELEPHONE _____

CASE NUMBER _____ DATE ENTERED N.C.I.C. _____

CAR INFORMATION _____

_____

This information sheet was prepared by Sgt. Dick Ruffino, Director, Missing Persons Bureau, Bergen County Sheriff's Office, 1 Court Street, Hackensack, New Jersey 07601, (201) 646-2192. Every question should be answered, even when the answer is "no".

SECTION V

PARENTAL KIDNAPPING PREVENTION ACT OF 1980

Public Law 96-611
96th Congress

PARENTAL KIDNAPPING PREVENTION ACT OF 1980

FINDINGS AND PURPOSES

42 USC 1305
note.

SEC. 7. (a) The Congress finds that —

(1) there is a large and growing number of cases annually involving disputes between persons claiming rights of custody and visitation of children under the laws, and in the courts, of different States, the District of Columbia, the Commonwealth of Puerto Rico, and the territories and possessions of the United States;

(2) the laws and practices by which the courts of those jurisdictions determine their jurisdiction to decide such disputes, and the effect to be given the decisions of such disputes by the courts of other jurisdictions, are often inconsistent and conflicting;

(3) those characteristics of the law and practice in such cases, along with the limits imposed by a Federal system on the authority of each such jurisdiction to conduct investigations and take other actions outside its own boundaries, contribute to a tendency of parties involved in such disputes to frequently resort to the seizure, restraint, concealment, and interstate transportation of children, the disregard of court orders, excessive relitigation of cases, obtaining of conflicting orders by the courts of various jurisdictions, and interstate travel and communication that is so expensive and time consuming as to disrupt their occupations and commercial activities; and

94 STAT. 3569

(4) among the results of those conditions and activities are the failure of the courts of such jurisdictions to give full faith and credit to the judicial proceedings of the other jurisdictions, the deprivation of rights of liberty and property without due process of law, burdens on commerce among such jurisdictions and with foreign nations, and harm to the welfare of children and their parents and other custodians.

(b) For those reasons it is necessary to establish a national system for locating parents and children who travel from one such jurisdiction to another and are concealed in connection with such disputes, and to establish national standards under which the courts of such jurisdictions will determine their jurisdiction to decide such disputes and the effect to be given by each jurisdiction to such decisions by the courts of other such jurisdictions. National system of locating parents, establishment.

(c) The general purposes of sections 6 to 10 of this Act are to—

(1) promote cooperation between State courts to the end that a determination of custody and visitation is rendered in the State which can best decide the case in the interest of the child;

(2) promote and expand the exchange of information and other forms of mutual assistance between States which are concerned with the same child;

(3) facilitate the enforcement of custody and visitation decrees of sister States;

(4) discourage continuing interstate controversies over child custody in the interest of greater stability of home environment and of secure family relationships for the child;

(5) avoid jurisdictional competition and conflict between State courts in matters of child custody and visitation which have in the past resulted in the shifting of children from State to State with harmful effects on their well-being; and

(6) deter interstate abductions and other unilateral removals of children undertaken to obtain custody and visitation awards.

FULL FAITH AND CREDIT GIVEN TO CHILD CUSTODY DETERMINATIONS

SEC. 8. (a) Chapter 115 of title 28, United States Code, is amended by adding immediately after section 1738 the following new section: 28 USC 1731 et seq.

"§1738A. Full faith and credit given to child custody determinations

"(a) The appropriate authorities of every State shall enforce according to its terms, and shall not modify except as provided in subsection (f) of this section, any child custody determination made consistently with the provisions of this section by a court of another State.

"(b) As used in this section, the term — Definitions.

"(1) 'child' means a person under the age of eighteen;

"(2) 'contestant' means a person, including a parent, who claims a right to custody or visitation of a child;

"(3) 'custody determination' means a judgment, decree, or other order of a court providing for the custody or visitation of a child, and includes permanent and temporary orders, and initial orders and modifications;

94 STAT. 3570

"(4) 'home State' means the State in which, immediately preceding the time involved, the child lived with his parents, a parent, or a person acting as parent, for at least six consecutive months, and in the case of a child less than six months old, the State in which the child lived from birth with any of such persons. Periods of temporary absence of any of such persons are counted as part of the six-month or other period;

"(5) 'modification' and 'modify' refer to a custody determination which modifies, replaces, supersedes, or otherwise is made subsequent to, a prior custody determination concerning the same child, whether made by the same court or not;

"(6) 'person acting as a parent' means a person, other than a parent, who has physical custody of a child and who has either been awarded custody by a court or claims a right to custody;

"(7) 'physical custody' means actual possession and control of a child; and

"(8) 'State' means a State of the United States, the District of Columbia, the Commonwealth of Puerto Rico, or a territory or possession of the United States.

85

"(c) A child custody determination made by a court of a State is consistent with the provisions of this section only if —

"(1) such court has jurisdiction under the law of such State;
and

"(2) one of the following conditions is met:

"(A) such State (i) is the home State of the child on the date of the commencement of the proceeding, or (ii) had been the child's home State within six months before the date of the commencement of the proceeding and the child is absent from such State because of his removal or retention by a contestant or for other reasons, and a contestant continues to live in such State;

"(B)(i) it appears that no other State would have jurisdiction under subparagraph (A), and (ii) it is in the best interest of the child that a court of such State assume jurisdiction because (I) the child and his parents, or the child and at least one contestant, have a significant connection with such State other then mere physical presence in such State, and (II) there is available in such State substantial evidence concerning the child's present or future care, protection, training, and personal relationships;

"(C) the child is physically present in such State and (i) the child has been abandoned, or (ii) it is necessary in an emergency to protect the child because he has been subjected to or threatened with mistreatment or abuse;

"(D)(i) it appears that no other State would have jurisdiction under subparagraph (A), (B), (C), or (E), or another State has declined to exercise jurisdiction on the ground that the State whose jurisdiction is in issue is the more appropriate forum to determine the custody of the child, and (ii) it is in the best interest of the child that such court assume jurisdiction; or

"(E) the court has continuing jurisdiction pursuant to subsection (d) of this section.

"(d) The jurisdiction of a court of a State which has made a child custody determination consistently with the provisions of this section continues as long as the requirement of subsection (c)(1) of this section continues to be met and such State remains the residence of the child or of any contestant.

"(e) Before a child custody determination is made, reasonable notice and opportunity to be heard shall be given to the contestants, any parent whose parental rights have not been previously terminated and any person who has physical custody of a child.

"(f) A court of a State may modify a determination of the custody of the same child made by a court of another State, if —

"(1) it has jurisdiction to make such a child custody determination; and

"(2) the court of the other State no longer has jurisdiction, or it has declined to exercise such jurisdiction to modify such determination.

"(g) A court of a State shall not exercise jurisdiction in any proceeding for a custody determination commenced during the pendency of a proceeding in a court of another State where such court of that other State is exercising jurisdiction consistently with the provisions of this section to make a custody determination.".

(b) The table of sections at the beginning of chapter 115 of title 28, United States Code, is amended by inserting after the item relating to section 1738 the the following new item:

"1738A. Full faith and credit given to child custody determinations.".

(c) In furtherance of the purposes of section 1738A of title 28, United States Code, as added by subsection (a) of this section, State courts are encouraged to —

(1) afford priority to proceedings for custody determinations; and

(2) award to the person entitled to custody or visitation pursuant to a custody determination which is consistent with the provisions of such section 1738A, necessary travel expenses, attorneys' fees, costs of private investigations, witness fees or expenses, and other expenses incurred in connection with such custody determination in any case in which —

(A) a contestant has, without the consent of the person entitled to custody or visitation pursuant to a custody determination which is consistent with the provisions of such section 1738A, (i) wrongfully removed the child from the physical custody of such person, or (ii) wrongfully retained the child after a visit or other temporary relinquishment of physical custody; or

(B) the court determines it is appropriate.

USE OF FEDERAL PARENT LOCATOR SERVICE IN CONNECTION WITH THE ENFORCEMENT OR DETERMINATION OF CHILD CUSTODY AND IN CASES OF PARENTAL KIDNAPPING OF A CHILD

SEC. 9. (a) Section 454 of the Social Security Act is amended —

42 USC 654.

(1) by striking out "and" at the end of paragraph (15);

(2) by striking out the period at the end of paragraph (16) and inserting in lieu thereof "; and"; and

(3) by inserting after paragraph (16) the following new paragraph:

"(17) in the case of a State which has in effect an agreement with the Secretary entered into pursuant to section 463 for the use of the Parent Locator Service established under section 453, to accept and transmit to the Secretary requests for information authorized under the provisions of the agreement to be furnished by such Service to authorized persons, and to impose and collect (in accordance with regulations of the Secretary) a fee sufficient to cover the costs to the State and to the Secretary incurred by reason of such requests, to transmit to the Secretary from time to time (in accordance with such regulations) so much of the fees collected as are attributable to such costs to the Secretary so incurred, and during the period that such agreement is in effect, otherwise to comply with such agreement and regulations of the Secretary with respect thereto.".

Post, p. 3572.
42 USC 653.

94 STAT. 3572

(b) Part D of title IV of the Social Security Act is amended by adding at the end thereof the following new section:

42 USC 651.

USE OF FEDERAL PARENT LOCATOR SERVICE IN CONNECTION WITH THE ENFORCEMENT OR DETERMINATION OF CHILD CUSTODY AND IN CASES OF PARENTAL KIDNAPPING OF A CHILD

"SEC. 463. (a) The Secretary shall enter into an agreement with any State which is able and willing to do so, under which the services of the Parent Locator Service established under section 453 shall be made available to such State for the purpose of determining the whereabouts of any absent parent or child when such information is to be used to locate such parent or child for the purpose of —

42 USC 663.

"(1) enforcing any State or Federal law with respect to the unlawful taking or restraint of a child; or

"(2) making or enforcing a child custody determination.

"(b) An agreement entered into under this section shall provide that the State agency described in section 454 will, under procedures prescribed by the Secretary in regulations, receive and transmit to the Secretary requests from authorized persons for information as to (or useful in determining) the whereabouts of any absent parent or child when such information is to be used to locate such parent or child for the purpose of —

42 USC 654.

"(1) enforcing any State or Federal law with respect to the unlawful taking or restraint of a child; or

"(2) making or enforcing a child custody determination.

"(c) Information authorized to be provided by the Secretary under this section shall be subject to the same conditions with respect to disclosure as information authorized to be provided under section 453, and a request for information by the Secretary under this section shall be considered to be a request for information under section 453 which is authorized to be provided under such section. Only information as to the most recent address and place of employment of any absent parent or child shall be provided under this section.

42 USC 653.

"(d) For Purposes of this section —

Definitions

"(1) the term 'custody determination' means a judgment, decree, or other order of a court providing for the custody or visitation of a

89

child, and includes permanent and temporary orders, and initial orders and modification;

(2) the term 'authorized person' means —

"(A) any agent or attorney of any State having an agreement under this section, who has the duty or authority under the law of such State to enforce a child custody determination;

"(B) any court having jurisdiction to make or enforce such a child custody determination, or any agent of such court; and

"(C) any agent or attorney of the United States, or of a State having an agreement under this section, who has the duty or authority to investigate, enforce, or bring a prosecution with respect to the unlawful taking or restraint of a child.".

94 STAT. 3573

(c) Section 455(a) of such Act is amended by adding after paragraph (3) the following: "except that no amount shall be paid to any State on account of amounts expended to carry out an agreement which it has entered into pursuant to section 463.".

42 USC 655.

(d) No agreement entered into under section 463 of the Social Security Act shall become effective before the date on which section 1738A of title 28, United States Code (as added by this title) becomes effective.

Ante, p. 3572
Effective date.
42 USC 663 note.
Ante., p. 3569

PARENTAL KIDNAPPING

SEC. 10.(a) In view of the findings of the Congress and the purposes of sections 6 to 10 of this Act set forth in section 302, the Congress hereby expressly declares its intent that section 1073 of title 18, United States Code, apply to cases involving parental kidnapping and interstate or international flight to avoid prosecution under applicable State felony statutes.

18 USC 1073 note.
42 USC 502.

(b) The Attorney General of the United States, not later than 120 days after the date of the enactment of this section (and once every 6 months during the 3-year period following such 120-day period), shall submit a report to the Congress with respect to steps taken to comply with the intent of the Congress set forth in subsection (a). Each such report shall include —

    (1) data relating to the number of applications for complaints under section 1073 of title 18, United States Code, in cases involving parental kidnapping;

    (2) data relating to the number of complaints issued in such cases; and

    (3) such other information as may assist in describing the activities of the Department of Justice in conformance with such intent.

Approved December 28, 1980.

1. Legislative History

CONGRESSIONAL RECORD, VOL. 126 (1980):
Dec. 5, considered and passed House.
Dec. 13, considered and passed Senate, amended; House agreed to Senate amendments.

2. Findings and Purposes

Congress enacted this legislation based upon findings that child stealing has harmful effects on children and that states have inherent difficulties in resolving the jurisdictional conflicts in custody contests that often ensue.

The findings and purposes set forth in section 7 of Pub. L. 96-611 bear a striking similarity to those contained in the Uniform Child Custody Jurisdiction Act, namely, to promote cooperation among the states in the recognition and enforcement of custody and visitation orders, to discourage continuing interstate controversies and conflicts, and to deter abductions. The novelty of this law lies in the fact that Congress has for the first time assumed a role in facilitating the resolution of the conflicts between states which are inherent in interstate child custody disputes.

3. Honoring Sister State Custody Determinations

On the date of passage of the PKPA, only forty-three states had adopted the UCCJA. Because the laws of the remaining jurisdictions did not close their courts to abductor-parents, these states had become, however unintentionally, havens for child snatching parents. Section 8 of the PKPA, 28 U.S.C. 1738A, was designed to make these and all other states unavailable and unreceptive to child stealers by requiring all states -- UCCJA and non-UCCJA states alike -- to respect sister state decrees which were made in conformity with the federal jurisdictional criteria. Specifically, section 8 requires appropriate authorities in every state to enforce and not modify, except in limited specified circumstances, child custody determinations made by courts of other states consistently with the jurisdictional criteria enumerated in the law. The jurisdictional criteria are similar, although not identical, to those contained in the Uniform Child Custody Jurisdiction Act.

The key difference between the federal jurisdictional criteria and those contained in the UCCJA may be explained in the following manner. In contrast to the UCCJA which enumerates alternative bases of initial jurisdiction, the federal law, for purposes of interstate recognition and enforcement of custody determinations, priorities "home state" decrees over those made by "significant connection" states. 28 U.S.C. 1738A (c) (2) (A) and (B). Thus, if State X, the child's home state, issues a custody decree, it is entitled to recognition and enforcement nationwide, while a decree concerning the custody of the same child made by State Y, a significant connection state, would not be entitled to the full protection of the federal law in sister states. This variation from the UCCJA is intended to have the indirect effect of encouraging courts having significant connections to a child to defer to home state courts for purposes of rendering initial decrees. Lawyers retained in custody cases should carefully analyze section 8 of the federal law and assess its impact on, and relationship to, the applicable sections of the UCCJA.

The law further provides that the jurisdiction of a court which renders a custody determination consistently with the federal standards continues, provided at least one contestant or the child remain in that state and the court would have jurisdiction under state law. For as long as that jurisdiction continues, no other state may modify the custody determination unless the court declines to exercise its jurisdiction. 28 U.S.C. 1738A(d) and (f).

Although federal court jurisdiction is not expressly foreclosed by the new law, the history of the legislation indicates that Congress intended for child custody litigation to continue in the state courts. The express language compels appropriate state authorities to enforce and refrain from modifying out-of-state decrees. 28 U.S.C. 1738A(a).

This provision of federal law is not self-executing. Lawyers representing clients in interstate cases must plead the applicable sections of the PKPA as a basis for the desired relief.

As a practical matter, family lawyers representing left-behind parents in pre-decree abduction situations should promptly act pursuant to section 3 (a) (1) (ii) of the UCCJA to invoke the jurisdiction of the child's "home state" court for a determination of custody. The absence of the child from the state does not preclude the court from adjudicating the custody issue, provided the notice requirements of the UCCJA and of the PKPA have been satisfied. By filing in the home state court for temporary or permanent custody, the left-behind parent has a sound basis for moving to dismiss any subsequent action instituted by the abductor-parent in either a non-UCCJA state or any other: the "home state" decree would be entitled to enforcement by the haven state under the federal law even if no comparable duty exists under state law. Note, too, that 28 U.S.C. 1738A(g) directs a court not to exercise jurisdiction in any custody proceeding commenced during the pendency of an action in another court which is exercising jurisdiction consistently with the federal criteria. Thus, an action brought in a "home state" could preclude proceedings being later filed or maintained elsewhere. It nevertheless remains imperative for courts to communicate with one another pursuant to the UCCJA to avoid simultaneous proceedings and/or divergent results.

4. Parent Locator Service

The second major provision of the Parental Kidnapping Prevention Act is found at Section 9 of the new law (42 U.S.C. 663). This section authorizes the Federal Parent Locator Service (FPLS) of the Department of Health and Human Services to locate children in connection with civil and criminal custody proceedings. This includes proceedings to determine custody and visitation rights, as well as actions brought to enforce or modify existing rights. It also covers the investigation and/or prosecution of state or federal criminal law violations such as custodial interference, parental kidnapping, criminal restraint, etc.

Every state currently operates a parent locator service as part of its child support enforcement program, mandated under Title IV-D of the Social Security Act. Consequently, the state agency which administers the service is often referred to as the "IV-D Agency" because of its legislative parent. (See, sections 451-462 of the Social Security Act; 42 U.S.C. 651 et seq.; 45 CFR Parts 300-305.)

The new law amends the Social Security Act to allow states to expand their existing parent locator services to include the transmission of requests for the location of abducted children by the FPLS. Any state may enter into an agreement with the FPLS to establish such relationship; it is not mandatory. The Department of Health and Human Services in Washington is in the final stages of drafting the model agreement and accompanying guidelines which will be forwarded to each of the states for their consideration and approval.

The FPLS will respond to requests made by persons authorized in the statute. Those persons include any agent or attorney in a state having an agreement with the FPLS who has the duty or authority under state law to enforce a child custody determination; any court or agent of a court having jurisdiction to make or enforce a child custody determination; and any agent or attorney of the United States, or of a State, who has the duty or authority to investigate, enforce, or bring a prosecution for the wrongful taking or restraint of a child.

Parents cannot apply directly to the parent locator service for assistance, nor can their legal representatives. A parent or attorney for the parent may, however, petition a court to request the FPLS to locate the absconding parent and missing child. While in some cases this may be burdensome, in many others, particularly pre-litigation abduction situations, it will have the beneficial effect of bringing the aggrieved party promptly before a court in the child's "home state," thus establishing that forum as the proper one to adjudicate the custody issue and undercutting any legal action the abductor-parent might initiate in a sister state. Similarly, a parent can request the local prosecutor or law enforcement official to make a location request, provided the state has a law covering the wrongful taking or restraint of a child. Note that a fee may be charged to cover the cost of processing a location request. It is estimated that the fee for each request will range from $10 to $15. The precise sum and procedures for collecting the fee will be spelled out in the Department's regulations.

For a number of reasons, the FPLS will not be one hundred percent successful in locating abducted children. First, the search for missing parents and children is **not** done by field investigators. Rather, it is a computer search which utilizes Social Security numbers as the principal tool for obtaining home and employer addresses from all FPLS data sources. These sources include the Social Security Administration, the Veterans Administration, the Internal Revenue Service, the Department of Defense, the Department of Transportation (Coast Guard), and the National Personnel Records Center of the General Services Administration. Thus, if an abductor-parent changes his or her identity and obtains a new Social Security number, an FPLS search would be futile. Secondly, even where the FPLS is successful, the service probably will not produce results as quickly as one would like. This is so because of a legislated change in the requirements for wage reporting by employers; addresses are now updated annually instead of quarterly. Consequently, the information obtained from the Social Security Administration may not accurately reflect the parent's or child's current address. Hence, a parent should be advised not to depend upon the FPLS as an exclusive tool for finding the missing child, nor should law enforcement authorities abandon their investigations merely because a computer search is being run by the FPLS. Indeed, when police are immediately notified of an abduction, a prompt investigation is imperative, since that is when the trail is hot and the likelihood of tracing the absconding parent the greatest.

5. Fugitive Felon Act

The third major provision of the Parental Kidnapping Prevention Act, Section 10 of the new law, declares that the Fugitive Felon Act, 18 U.S.C. 1073, is applicable in state felony parental kidnapping cases involving interstate or international flight. The original bill, S.105, proposed a federal misdemeanor offense for interstate child abductions. House-Senate conferees rejected this approach in favor of revitalizing the Fugitive Felon Act in serious state felony child abduction cases.

The primary purpose of the Fugitive Felon Act is to permit the federal government to assist in the location and apprehension of fugitives from state justice. Normally, once the fugitive is apprehended, the federal complaint is dismissed and state proceedings are instituted. Although the statute by its terms applies to all state offenses, the Justice Department historically carved out an exception for parental kidnapping/custodial interference cases in all but the rarest instances, based upon an analogy to the federal kidnapping law, 18 U.S.C. 1201, which specifically exempts parents from its purview.

The new law is intended to change this administratively decided policy so that states with felony parental kidnapping laws can obtain F.B.I. assistance in cases involving interstate or international flight to avoid prosecution. Congress specifically rejected the standards for federal involvement that were previously applied and which resulted in infrequent F.B.I. assistance in parental kidnapping cases, e.g., threat of serious, imminent physical injury to the child, or pattern of harmful conduct (drinking, drugs, etc.) by the abductor parent. Practically speaking, the Department of Justice is required by the

PKPA to revise the guidelines contained in the U.S. Attorney's Manual to reflect the newly announced policy.

If implemented according to congressional design, this section of the law would work as follows. Where a state felony parental kidnapping statute is violated and the alleged perpetrator has fled from the state for purposes of avoiding prosecution, the state or local prosecutor could apply to the U.S. Attorney for a fugitive warrant. (To facilitate the application process, the state prosecutor should provide the U.S. Attorney with a certified copy of the state complaint, warrant, indictment, information, or other document evidencing that the state prosecution has been commenced.) Upon a showing that the state is determined to take all steps necessary to secure the return of the fugitive and that it is their intention to bring the fugitive to trial on the state charge for which he or she is sought, the U.S. Attorney could issue a warrant, whereupon the F.B.I. would be called in to investigate. When the alleged fugitive is located and apprehended, he or she would be extradited to the requesting state where state proceedings would go forward. (While this may help to locate the child, it should be noted that extraditing the parent does not automatically mean that the child will be returned. Following applicable state procedures, the custodial parent must take prompt, lawful action pursuant to the UCCJA, the PKPA or other applicable statutes for the return of the child. To initiate appropriate procedures for the return of the child in a timely manner, it is imperative that the complainant-parent be notified when an arrest in the case is imminent.)

There has been resistance to the new law at the Justice Department and in the F.B.I. According to the first report submitted to Congress June 26, 1981 regarding the implementation by the Department of the Fugitive Felon provision of Pub. L. 96-611, the guidelines have been revised to permit F.B.I. involvement in felony child stealing cases, subject to prior approval from Washington, where there is "independent credible information that the child is in physical danger or is then in a condition of abuse or neglect." Concerned that this statement of new policy is essentially a restatement of pre-Pub. L. 96-611 policy, the House Judiciary Subcommittee on Crime has scheduled an oversight hearing in early fall to press the Justice Department for full and effective implementation of the new law in accordance with congressional intent. Ultimately, the sponsors of the legislation would like to see greater cooperation between federal investigators and state law enforcement officials in the investigation and prosecution of parental kidnapping cases, which hopefully will deter other parents from engaging in this conduct.

However, even with maximum cooperation from the Department of Justice, the effectiveness of this provision will nevertheless be irregular. States with felony child stealing laws already have the statutory tools to activate federal assistance. However, in the two states that do not have felony laws governing custodial interference, F.B.I. assistance will be unavailable unless the abductor parent can be charged under some other state felony statute, or new laws are enacted.

News release sent by United States Senator Paula Hawkins,
January 3, 1983

FBI TO EXPAND SEARCH EFFORTS FOR PARENTAL KIDNAP VICTIMS . . .
Hawkins calls decision "dramatic breakthrough"

WASHINGTON, D.C. . . . .The FBI will expand its efforts to find victims of parental kidnapping by suspending for one year requirements thought by many to cripple the effectiveness of the federal parental kidnapping prevention act, U.S. Senator Paula Hawkins of Florida said today.

Senator Hawkins, who was notified of the one-year trial program by Assistant Attorney General Robert A. McConnell, said she was elated by the decision. "This policy is evidence of a new and farsighted attitude toward the tragic dimensions of the missing children problem in America. It will provide a dramatic breakthrough in the FBI's ability to find and return missing children to their homes," she said.

Under the new program, the FBI will suspend two controversial enforcement requirements of the Parental Kidnapping Prevention Act of 1980: (1) proof that the child is in physical danger or the victim of abuse or neglect, and (2) authorization to prosecute parental kidnapping complaints from the Justice Department's Criminal Division.

These two requirements, McConnell said in a letter to Senator Hawkins, "have provoked controversy as they are felt to restrict very substantially federal involvement in such cases."

"The effect of this policy change will be to increase the number of cases in which fugitive felon warrants will be obtained by United States Attorneys and fugitive investigations initiated by the Federal Bureau of Investigation," McConnell said.

Senator Hawkins, who sponsored the Missing Children Act recently signed into law by President Reagan, said the new law and the FBI's new policy together provide tremendous potential to find missing children. The Missing Children Act establishes a national clearing house of information, using the FBI's crime information computer, to assist law enforcement officers in tracing missing children.

"Until now, the effectiveness of the parental kidnapping act has been hamstrung by overly restrictive enforcement provisions. When a child is kidnapped, it's usually impossible to present tangible evidence of danger or abuse, yet we know that any child who disappears from home faces dangers. This is particularly true of parental kidnapping cases, which are often motivated by revenge instead of love. We have learned that in too many cases the estranged parent who kidnaps a child has a history of instability or violence, and it is the child who suffers," Senator Hawkins said.

"Removing the requirements for Criminal Division authorization returns the decision-making to U.S. Attorneys in the state field offices and cuts through a great deal of red tape. It opens what until now has been a bureaucratic bottleneck," she said.

"The statistics speak for themselves. In 1981, the FBI evaluated 141 complaints and investigated only 40. During the first three months of 1982, the FBI evaluated 28 complaints and investigated 7," Senator Hawkins said. "Yet it is estimated that 100,000 children in this country are the victims of parental kidnapping. Loosening the restrictions of the parental kidnapping act is great news for the parents of missing children and a real breakthrough in the crackdown on parental kidnapping."

February 18, 1983

Honorable Paula Hawkins
United States Senate
Washington, D.C. 20510

Dear Senator Hawkins:

I understand that at the hearing on February 2, 1983, before the Subcommittee on Juvenile Justice, Committee on the Judiciary, you and Chairman Specter raised several questions about the policy of the FBI in investigating the disappearance of young children. You focused your attention on apparent inconsistencies in the application of the FBI's kidnaping policies.

To avoid any further misunderstanding by FBI personnel, I have sent all field offices a communication clarifying the FBI's jurisdiction and responsibility in these cases. A copy of this communication has also been furnished to Senator Arlen Specter, Chairman of the Subcommittee on Juvenile Justice. In addition, FBI Headquarters personnel are analyzing the need for further communications or manual changes.

Your work in bringing this problem to my attention is appreciated. I assure you that the FBI is sensitive to the concerns you raised and is taking actions to address and remedy those concerns. If I can be of any further assistance, please do not hesitate to contact me.

Sincerely yours,

William H. Webster
Director,
Federal Bureau of Investigation

FM DIRECTOR FBI
TO ALL FBI FIELD OFFICES   PRIORITY
      PERSONAL ATTENTION SACS

BT
UNCLAS E F T O SECTION 1 OF 2

KIDNAPING MATTERS; PERSONAL CRIMES PROGRAM.

AT THE REQUEST OF CONGRESS, ASSISTANT DIRECTOR OLIVER B. REVELL, CRIMINAL INVESTIGATIVE DIVISION (CID), TESTIFIED BEFORE THE SUBCOMMITTEE ON JUVENILE JUSTICE, COMMITTEE ON THE JUDICIARY, UNITED STATES SENATE, ON FEBRUARY 2, 1983. MEMBERS OF CONGRESS AND THE PARENTS OF MISSING, MURDERED AND KIDNAPED CHILDREN ALSO TESTIFIED BEFORE THE SUBCOMMITTEE.

THE RECORD DEVELOPED BY THE SUBCOMMITTEE UNEQUIVOCALLY REVEALS THAT THE FBI PERSONNEL HAVE FAILED TO ACCURATELY AND ADEQUATELY ARTICULATE FBI NATIONAL POLICY IN KIDNAPING MATTERS AS SET FORTH IN THE MANUAL OF INVESTIGATIVE OPERATIONS AND GUIDELINES (MIOG), PART I, SECTION 7, KIDNAPING, PARTICULARLY SECTIONS 7-1 THROUGH AND INCLUDING 7-2.2.

IN LIGHT OF INFORMATION PRESENTED TO THE SUBCOMMITTEE AND DEVELOPED THROUGH CID ANALYSES, THE FOLLOWING AREAS OF CONCERN ARE PARAMOUNT.

I.   KIDNAPINGS INVOLVING MINOR CHILDREN, MIOG, 7-2.2

CID, BASED UPON A REVIEW OF 200 MAIN KIDNAPING FILES AND 53 7-0 MATTERS RECEIVED AT FBIHQ DURING 1982, ASCERTAINED THAT MINORS WERE THE PRIMARY VICTIMS IN 101 OF THE 253 MATTERS REVIEWED.

IN VIEW OF THIS AND OTHER DATA DEVELOPED BY THE SUBCOMMITTEE, YOU ARE INSTRUCTED TO PERSONALLY INSURE THAT THE FBI'S NATIONAL POLICY IS THOROUGHLY UNDERSTOOD, FOLLOWED AND ACCURATELY ARTICULATED BY REPRESENTATIVES OF YOUR DIVISION. IN ACCORD WITH EXISTING INSTRUCTIONS, THE FOLLOWING IS SET FORTH:

A.   WHEN REPORTS ARE BROUGHT TO YOUR ATTENTION, WITHOUT REGARD FOR THE MEANS OF REFERRAL, OF MINORS ABDUCTED OR MISSING UNDER CIRCUMSTANCES INDICATING A POSSIBLE ABDUCTION, UNACCOMPANIED BY A

RANSOM DEMAND OR EVIDENCE OF INTERSTATE TRANSPOR-TATION OR TRAVEL, INSURE THE FOLLOWING:

1. ADVISE FBIHQ IMMEDIATELY.
2. FURNISH A TELETYPE SETTING FORTH SPECIFIC DE-TAILS BEARING UPON ABDUCTION OR CIRCUMSTANCES INDICATING A POSSIBLE ABDUCTION, ANY RANSOM DE-MAND, INTERSTATE TRANSPORTATION AND YOUR ACTION. MERE STATEMENTS THAT "LOCAL AUTHORITIES ADVISE NO EVIDENCE OF ABDUCTION EXISTS" ARE NOT ACCEPTABLE.
3. DETERMINE WHETHER IT IS NECESSARY TO INSTITUTE A PRELIMINARY INQUIRY IMMEDIATELY IN ORDER TO ASCER-TAIN THE NEED FOR A FULL INVESTIGATION.
4. RESOLVE QUESTIONS PERTAINING TO THE ABDUCTION, SEIZURE, CONFINEMENT, INVEIGLEMENT, DECOY, KIDNAP OR CARRYING AWAY BY ANY MEANS WHATSOEVER, THROUGH THE CONDUCT OF A PRELIMINARY INQUIRY IN ACCORD WITH EXISTING ATTORNEY GENERAL GUIDELINES.
5. NOTE THAT NO RANSOM DEMAND IS REQUIRED.
6. NOTE THAT INTERSTATE TRAVEL CAN BE PRESUMED AFTER 24 HOURS FROM THE TIME THE MINOR WAS ABDUCT-ED OR MISSING UNDER CIRCUMSTANCES INDICATING A POSSIBLE ABDUCTION.

B. COMPLETE DOCUMENTATION IS REQUIRED AS TO THE FACTS AND CIRCUMSTANCES WHICH CAUSE YOU TO CON-DUCT OR NOT CONDUCT A FULL INVESTIGATION. INCLUDE ANY UNITED STATES ATTORNEY'S OPINION AND THE SPECI-FIC LIAISON EFFECTED WITH LOCAL AUTHORITIES TOGETH-ER WITH ANY REQUESTS THAT LOCAL AUTHORITIES, CITI-ZENS OR FAMILY MEMBERS MAY MAKE AND YOUR ACTION THEREAFTER.

II. LIAISON WITH STATE OR LOCAL AUTHORITIES.

EXPEDITIOUSLY CAUSE ALL STATE AND LOCAL LAW ENFORCEMENT AGENCIES IN YOUR TERRITORY TO BE CON-TACTED AND SPECIFICALLY AND ACCURATELY ADVISED OF THE FBI'S EXISTING NATIONAL POLICY WITH REGARD TO THE KIDNAPING OF MINORS. INSURE THAT THESE CONTACTS ARE DOCUMENTED AND AVAILABLE FOR RETRIEVAL. YOUR CON-TACTS SHOULD BE CONDUCTED IN SUCH A MANNER AS TO INSURE FUTURE NOTIFICATIONS OR REFERRALS ARE MADE TO THE FBI OF MATTERS POSSIBLY COMING WITHIN OUR INVESTIGATIVE JURISDICTION.

III. FBI INTERACTION WITH PARENTS, GUARDIANS AND FAMILY MEMBERS OF MINOR KIDNAP VICTIMS.

THE FBI MUST CONTINUE TO DEMONSTRATE THE UTMOST CONCERN FOR AND EMPATHY WITH THE EMOTIONAL TRAUMA WHICH A VICTIM'S PARENTS, GUARDIANS OR FAMILY MEMBERS UNDERGO. ADDRESS ALL SITUATIONS IN AN ENTIRELY PROFESSIONAL MANNER CONSISTENT WITH OUR ROLE AS SERVANTS OF THE PUBLIC. INSURE THAT SUCH PERSONS, UNLESS DETERMINABLE AND ARTICULABLE FACTS PRECLUDE DOING SO, ARE KEPT ADVISED OF THOSE INVESTIGATIVE DEVELOPMENTS WHICH YOU DETERMINE CAN BE DISSEMINATED WITHOUT JEOPARDIZING THE INTEGRITY OF YOUR INVESTIGATION. WHILE YOU REMAIN BOUND TO THE PROHIBITION AGAINST DIVULGING PENDING CASE MATTERS TO THE PUBLIC, YOUR ATTENTION IS DRAWN TO THE SPECIAL CONCERN OF AN IDENTIFIED PARENT, GUARDIAN OR FAMILY MEMBER AND THE DUE REGARD FOR SAME WHICH THE FBI SHOULD EXHIBIT.

IV. USE OF THE POLYGRAPH IN INVESTIGATIONS OF KIDNAPED MINORS.

IN ACCORD WITH EXISTING INSTRUCTIONS CONTAINED IN MIOG, PART II, SECTION 13-22.2 THROUGH AND INCLUDING 13-22.4, THE FOLLOWING APPLIES:

1. THE POLYGRAPH IS TO BE USED SELECTIVELY AS AN INVESTIGATIVE AID.

2. RESULTS ARE TO BE CONSIDERED WITHIN THE CONTEXT OF A COMPLETE INVESTIGATION.

3. RESULTS ARE NOT TO BE RELIED UPON TO THE EXCLUSION OF OTHER EVIDENCE OR KNOWLEDGE OBTAINED DURING THE COURSE OF A COMPLETE INVESTIGATION.

4. USE OF THE POLYGRAPH AS A SUBSTITUTE FOR LOGICAL INVESTIGATION BY CONVENTIONAL MEANS IS STRICTLY PROHIBITED.

YOU OR THE PERSON ACTING FOR YOU WILL BE HELD ACCOUNTABLE FOR THE APPROPRIATE USE OF THE POLYGRAPH. THIS TECHNIQUE IS NOT TO BE ROUTINELY APPLIED TO THE PARENTS, GUARDIANS OR FAMILY MEMBERS OF A MINOR VICTIM. IF USE OF THE POLYGRAPH IS QUESTIONABLE, THIS SHOULD BE REFERRED TO FBIHQ BY COMMUNICATION. ATTENTION: PERSONAL CRIMES UNIT, WITH A COPY DESIGNATED FOR THE LABORATORY DIVISION. ATTENTION: POLYGRAPH SUBUNIT.

V. NCIC MISSING PERSON FILE.

INSURE THAT ALL INVESTIGATIVE AND APPROPRIATE SUPPORT PERSONNEL, WHO DEAL WITH THE PUBLIC, ARE THOROUGHLY CONVERSANT WITH THE RECENT MODIFICA-

TIONS REGARDING THE ENTRY OF MISSING, UNEMANCIPAT-
ED CHILDREN RECORDS INTO NCIC. THE MISSING CHILDREN
ACT, SIGNED INTO LAW BY THE PRESIDENT, REQUIRES FBI
FIELD OFFICES TO CONFIRM THE EXISTENCE OF A MISSING
PERSON RECORD IN NCIC WHEN REQUESTED BY A PARENT,
LEGAL GUARDIAN OR NEXT OF KIN. ADDITIONALLY, WHERE
LOCAL POLICE REFUSE TO COOPERATE WITH A PARENT OR
GUARDIAN, THE FBI IS REQUIRED TO ENTER THE INFOR-
MATION.

BT

2/7/83   UNCLAS E F T O   PRIORITY

FM DIRECTOR FBI
TO ALL FBI FIELD OFFICES   PRIORITY
  PERSONAL ATTENTION SACS

BT

UNCLAS E F T O SECTION 2 OF 2

KIDNAPING MATTERS; PERSONAL CRIMES PROGRAM.

   NOTE THAT THE NCIC OPERATING MANUAL, PART 8,
MISSING PERSON FILE, SECTION I, SETS FORTH INFORMATION
REGARDING THE CATEGORY OF "A PERSON OF ANY AGE WHO
IS MISSING UNDER CIRCUMSTANCES INDICATING THAT THE
DISAPPEARANCE WAS NOT VOLUNTARY, I.E., ABDUCTION OR
KIDNAPING." WITH REGARD TO THIS CATEGORY AND MI-
NORS ENTERED INTO THIS CATEGORY BY STATE AND LOCAL
AUTHORITIES IN YOUR TERRITORIES, INSURE THAT YOUR
LIAISON CONTACTS DEVELOP PROCEDURES FACILITATING
STATE AND LOCAL NOTIFICATION OF SUCH ENTRIES TO YOUR
OFFICE.
   VI. PRIORITY OF INVESTIGATIONS INVOLVING THE KID-
NAPING OF MINOR CHILDREN.

INSURE THAT INVESTIGATIONS INITIATED UNDER THE FEDERAL KIDNAP STATUTE INVOLVING KIDNAPED MINOR CHILDREN ARE ASSIGNED THE APPROPRIATE PRIORITY. NECESSARY RESOURCES ARE TO BE COMMITTED TO GAIN THE SAFE RETURN OF THE VICTIM(S) AND, CONCOMMITANTLY, TO IDENTIFY, APPREHEND AND PROSECUTE THE SUBJECT(S).

VII. ACTION UPON RECEIPT OF THIS TELETYPE.

IN ADDITION TO ANY OTHER ACTION UNDERTAKEN IN ACCORD WITH ALL THE ABOVE, DOCUMENT THAT ALL SPECIAL AGENTS AND SUPPORT EMPLOYEES, WHO ARE IN CONTACT WITH THE PUBLIC, HAVE READ AND UNDERSTAND THE CONTENTS OF THIS COMMUNICATION. YOUR DOCUMENTATION OF SAME SHOULD INCLUDE, AT THE LEAST, THE INITIALS OF ALL EMPLOYEES YOU IDENTIFY. THIS DOCUMENTATION SHOULD BE RETAINED FOR RETRIEVAL AS MAY BE NECESSARY.

YOU WILL BE PROVIDED A COPY OF ASSISTANT DIRECTOR REVELL'S OPENING STATEMENT TO THE SUBCOMMITTEE, WHICH SHOULD BE SIMILARLY DISSEMINATED.

BT

NOTE: THIS COMMUNICATION RESTATES EXISTING POLICY AND HAS BEEN PREPARED TO ADVISE AND INSTRUCT THE FIELD WITH REGARD TO INVESTIGATIONS OF KIDNAPINGS INVOLVING MINORS. IT HAS BEEN COORDINATED WITH NCIC SECTION, TECHNICAL SERVICES DIVISION; OFFICE OF CONGRESSIONAL AND PUBLIC AFFAIRS; AND THE POLYGRAPH SUBUNIT, LABORATORY DIVISION.

A GENERAL OVERVIEW OF A SYSTEM
FOR RESPONSE TO A PARENTAL KIDNAPPING
AND DELEGATION OF RESPONSIBILITIES

A GENERAL OVERVIEW OF A SYSTEM FOR RESPONSE TO A PARENTAL KIDNAPPING THAT MIGHT INCLUDE THE FOLLOWING FEATURES AND DELEGATION OF RESPONSIBILITIES.

POLICE

A specific unit of the police department, whose officers are familiar with applicable statutes and procedures, should be designated to receive initial complaints. Their assigned duties should include the gathering of necessary legal documentation to support the charge, obtaining witness statements and, often in consultation with the prosecutor, evaluating the nature of the case of parental kidnapping. Less serious incidences can frequently be resolved with limited intervention by the police, although referral for a conference with the prosecutor to avoid repetition is often advisable.

Referral of the case for charges or to seek a warrant is, of course, the responsibility of the police. Once official intervention occurs, the police collaborate with prosecutor and parent in investigating the perpetrators' whereabouts. In this regard, perhaps the most important function of the police is proper warrant entry and official communications with other police departments and public agencies.

PROSECUTOR

In parental kidnapping cases, the role of the prosecutor will reach far beyond the ordinary review of cases brought to him or her by police, and the prosecution of those cases if charges result. Because of the complicated legal elements involved in parental kidnapping cases, together with consequent police reticence to act on their own, the decision to arrest a perpetrator will ordinarily rest in the discretion of the prosecutor. Even in exigent circumstances requiring immediate arrest without a warrant, police ordinarily will seek the direction of a prosecutor before attempting to apprehend. Since flight or concealment most often attend serious instances of parental kidnapping, an arrest warrant obtained through the auspices of the prosecutor will most frequently trigger official involvement.

Additionally, whether during the initial review or after the official intervention, the prosecutor should make efforts to "educate" relatives and friends of a perpetrator who may be supporting the criminal effort. The issuance of legal process necessary in the investigation, together with requests for investigative assistance from other public agencies, are the responsiblity of the prosecutor as well.

Also, as will be discussed shortly, the role of the prosecutor in the arrest of a perpetrator and recovery of a victim is absolutely central.

At the outset of the investigation or prosecution of a custodial interference case it may be useful for the prosecutor to distinguish for the complainant the role and responsibilities of the prosecutor from those of the private lawyer representing that parent, since many parents mistakenly believe that the district attorney becomes their personal advocate once criminal charges are filed. While assuring the complainant-victim that the case will be given serious and prompt attention, it is recommended that the following points be covered:

(1) Typically, the parent's attorney institutes civil proceedings to enforce custody determinations and thereby to secure the return of the child. Such civil actions often run concurrently with criminal proceedings brought by the prosecutor on behalf of the State to redress cases of unlawful child abduction and restraint. The petitioner parent in the civil proceeding normally is the complainant in, and driving force behind, the criminal proceeding. However, the State's interest in a particular case and the parent's private interest are not necessarily identical: civil proceedings protect the parent's personal interest in the uninterrupted custody of a minor child, while criminal proceedings protect the public interest in deterring potential child snatchings, in protecting the integrity of judicial determinations, and in safeguarding the welfare of children.

(2) In the course of a criminal proceeding, prosecutive decisions may be made without regard to the complainant's wishes. For instance, a case will not necessarily be dropped at the request of a complainant who has reconciled with the defendant, or, conversely, a criminal prosecution will not necessarily be commenced upon the filing of a complaint. Consequently, a parent cannot and must not rely on the criminal process for vindication of custody rights; civil remedies should be pursued whether or not criminal proceedings are underway.

(3) Even when a criminal prosecution has been commenced, the return of the child is not necessarily automatic. The lawful custodian should be prepared to file an action in a court in the state in which the child is located to obtain an order compelling the child's return in the event the

defendant does not voluntarily relinquish possession. This may require hiring a lawyer in the state in which the defendant has been arrested. The legal basis for such an order may be the UCCJA, the PKPA, both of these laws or other state law. Upon the arrest of the alleged abductor the child would then be returned pursuant to the court order to his or her lawful custodian. Note that several states' criminal laws expressly require the defendant to return the child to the lawful custodian. In those states, separate civil proceedings of the kind suggested immediately above may not be needed. In other states, the sheriff or police officers may return the child to the lawful custodian on the basis of the original court order and appropriate identification without further legal proceedings.

(4) If the defendant is convicted of, or pleads guilty to, the offense of custodial interference, he or she may be incarcerated, fined, placed on probation, or otherwise punished. Sentencing will depend upon the facts of the case. However, conviction does not automatically terminate the convicted parent's rights of custody or of visitation. Therefore, a parent wishing to restrict or terminate visitation based upon the criminal conduct should consult his or her attorney to pursue appropriate civil legal actions. As a general rule, a criminal conviction or guilty plea will have a bearing on the judge's decision to curtail or cut off access between the offender and the child.

PARENT

The victimized parent will bear responsibility for gathering information and pursuing leads to establish the location of an absconding parent and victimized child. The parent will be required to gather all personal information referred to herein and, usually at the direction of the prosecutor, will be required to establish contacts with friends and family of the perpetrator.

Because a parent is far better equipped to understand information obtained, that party must bear the responsibility of correlating information obtained, developing leads therefrom and pursuing those leads to the extent he or she is legally able, seeking the assistance of the prosecutor where roadblocks arise.

FORMAL INTERVENTION

The speed with which police and prosecutors respond to a complaint of parental kidnapping relates directly to the time a child is likely to be absent from a custodial parent. Serious parental kidnapping cases which do not end in arrest within the first two weeks are likely to be extended for substantial periods and demand greater commitment of time and resources on the part of the police and prosecutors.

However, an equally important determination for police or prosecutors is the need for intervention in the form of criminal charges. The issuance of charges in instances in which resolution was possible through alternative means adds irrationality to a previously irrational situation and can escalate a relatively minor incident into a serious episode.

Less serious instances, on the other hand, ordinarily are evidenced by refusals to return a child after visitation wherein the perpetrator is reacting to a real or perceived wrong. No flight or threat of flight ordinarily occurs, and the perpetrator almost without exception communicates his or her intentions, including the intention to pursue legal remedies, to the victim.

In less serious instances, a sensitive prosecutor can often resolve the episode short of formal intervention. A phone call, in which the perpetrator is apprised of the repercussions of his or her conduct and the legal remedies available for redress of his or her perceived grievance, will often bring a child home.

However, in any instance in which prior threats of flight and concealment are involved, or violent abduction and flight have occurred, immediate intervention in the form of a felony arrest warrant, properly entered in the National Crime Information Center Computer, and the commencement of investigative activities is imperative.

INVESTIGATIVE TECHNIQUES AND ALTERNATIVES

F.B.I. INVESTIGATION

Section 10 of Pub. L. No. 96-611 (94 Stat. 3573) expressly declares congressional intent that the Fugitive Felon Act, 18 U.S.C.

1073, applies in state felony parental kidnapping cases involving interstate or international flight to avoid prosecution. By making the F.B.I. available to investigate felony child stealing cases, this statute aids the state prosecutor who would otherwise be handicapped in pursuing the fugitive across state lines and thus in prosecuting the underlying state charge.

Under the Fugitive Felon Act, a case generally proceeds as follows. The state or local prosecutor applies to the U.S. Attorney for a "UFAP" (Unlawful Flight to Avoid Prosecution) warrant. To facilitate the application process, the state prosecutor provides the U.S. Attorney with a certified copy of the state complaint, warrant, indictment, information, or other document evidencing that the state felony prosecution has been commenced. Upon a showing by the prosecutor that all steps necessary to secure the return of the fugitive and to bring the fugitive to trial on the state charge will be taken, the U.S. Attorney may then issue a warrant. If a UFAP warrant issues, the F.B.I. then commences an investigation. If and when the alleged fugitive is located and apprehended by the F.B.I., he or she would either waive extradition or stand extradition back to the requesting state where the state criminal proceeding would go forward. In short, the Fugitive Felon Act is a vehicle in aid of the extradition process.

After the PKPA was passed in December, 1980, the Justice Department issued revised guidelines governing the issuance of UFAP warrants in parental kidnapping cases. Additionally, the Attorney General has submitted reports to Congress on the Department's implementation of the law. The guidelines and reports reflect an adherence to the Department's pre-Act policies which limited federal assistance to state prosecutors in parental kidnapping cases. Specifically, the guidelines require as a condition precedent to the issuance of a UFAP warrant "independent credible information that the child is in physical danger or is then in a condition of abuse or neglect." Prior approval must also be obtained from the Justice Department in Washington before a U.S. Attorney can issue a fugitive complaint.

The House Judiciary Subcommittee on Crime conducted an oversight hearing on the implementation of the PKPA on September 24, 1981. The committee indicated its disapproval of the current discriminatory guidelines and urged the Department to bring its policies into conformity with the public law, or face possible enactment of a new federal parental kidnapping statute. Specifically, the Committee reiterated Congress' intent that parental kidnapping

113

be treated in the same manner as all other felony offenses. Shortly after the hearing, bills were introduced in both houses -- S. 1759 and H.R. 5019 --to hasten compliance by the F.B.I. and Justice Department with the PKPA. These companion measures would require the Justice Department to eliminate all restrictive criteria relative to the issuance of UFAP warrants in parental kidnapping cases.

To summarize, a prosecutor wishing to obtain a UFAP warrant in a parental kidnapping case should:

(1) Write to the local U.S. Attorney requesting issuance of the warrant;

(2) attach a copy of the state criminal complaint;

(3) include explicit representations as to the good faith intention to extradite and prosecute the offender under state law;

(4) detail investigative efforts undertaken, without success, at the state, local and private levels;

(5) provide as much "independent credible information" as can be developed showing that the child is in danger, or is being abused or neglected. Include copies of psychological evaluations of the offender and of the child, information about medical problems experienced by the child requiring special care, evidence of dangerous behaviour patterns and/or chemical addictions of the accused, and any other evidence that might have a bearing on the child's welfare;

(6) if the warrent is issued and the suspect is arrested by the F.B.I., honor your commitment to extradite and to prosecute. Frivolous use of F.B.I. resources can be expected to make those services unavailable in future cases;

(7) if the warrant is denied without good cause, file the application a second time and seek appropriate assistance if necessary, including congressional inquiries of the Attorney General to ascertain why the warrant was refused. Congressional assistance may also be helpful in cases involving undue delay in issuing a warrant.

Laboratory and Indentification Division are available for use by state authorities in child abduction and restraint cases. Even if criminal charges are not filed, police can issue "Be on the Lookout" (BOLO) bulletins to police agencies throughout the country which may prove helpful in locating absconding parents.

FEDERAL PARENT LOCATOR SERVICE

Section 9 of Pub. L. No. 96-611 authorizes access to the Federal Parent Locator Service (FPLS) to locate missing parents and children for purposes of making or enforcing child custody determinations and for investigating or prosecuting parental kidnapping cases. Unlike the actual field investigation conducted by the F.B.I. pursuant to the issuance of a UFAP warrant under section 10 of Pub. L. No. 96-611, the FPLS search is done exclusively with computers keyed to Social Security Numbers. Employer and home addresses may be obtained from IRS, Social Security Administration, Veterans Administration, Coast Guard and other data banks.

Under the law and implementing regulations published in the Federal Register of November 3, 1981 beginning at page 54554, states have the option of entering into an agreement with the federal government to transmit requests from "authorized persons" for address information contained in the various data banks accessible to the FPLS. In states that do not have agreements in effect for use of the FPLS, federal agents who have the duty or authority to investigate, enforce or bring a prosecution with respect to the unlawful taking or restraint of a child may submit requests directly to the FPLS.

"Authorized persons" in the statute are:

(1) any agent or attorney of any state having an agreement under this section who has the duty or authority under the law of such state to enforce a child custody determination;

(2) any court having jurisdiction to make or enforce such a child custody determination, or any agent of such court; and

(3) any agent or attorney of the United States, or of a State having an agreement under this section, who has the duty or authority to investigate, enforce, or bring a criminal prosecution with respect to the unlawful taking or restraint of a child.

Parents are not authorized to submit location requests directly to the FPLS. They must work with and through authorized persons named in the law.

There is a fee for the computer searches undertaken pusuant to this statute. The fee for federal services is presently $10, with an additional charge of $4 when the Social Security Number of the missing adult is unknown. States are also authorized by the law and regulations to establish a fee to cover their expenses in transmitting location requests.

To summarize, any prosecutor wishing to obtain address information from the FPLS should ascertain from the Director of the State Office of Child Support Enforcement whether the state has an agreement for access to the FPLS in parental kidnapping cases. If so, follow state procedures for submission of requests. If not, request the F.B.I. or U.S. Attorney in your jurisdiction to submit a request on your behalf to the FPLS in Washington, D.C. The authority for such request is found at 45 CFR 303.69. The address and telephone number for the FPLS are:

Office of Child Support Enforcement
Department of Health & Human Services
Room 1010
6110 Executive Boulevard
Rockville, Maryland 20852
(301) 443-4950

This search may be done in addition to any field investigation undertaken by the F.B.I. pursuant to the Fugitive Felon Act.

STATE AND LOCAL RESOURCES AND RESPONSIBILITIES

Some or all of the following steps should be taken where a serious instance of parental kidnapping has arisen and formal intervention has occurred or is anticipated. As noted earlier, many of the indicated tasks can and should be performed by the victimized parent.

1. Alerts should be issued through the police to be on the lookout for the vehicle of the absconding parent. These can be issued interstate assuming a felony warrant is in the N.C.I.C. Lookout requests should be issued for local airports, train stations and bus terminals as well as for those locations in places where it is suspected the absconding parent is headed.

2. Phone records of the defendant should be obtained. Often a pattern of calls will appear which will indicate a likely destination and suggests other parties who may be involved. A subpoena may or may not be necessary to obtain such.

3. The family and friends of a defendant should be contacted. If their involvement is suggested, phone records may be subject to subpoena. A mail cover on these individuals may also be initiated by a prosecutor by contacting the postal inspector. Finally, evidence may arise to support charges against those individuals as parties to a crime or for other charges.

4. Bank records of the defendant should be obtained, through subpoena if necessary. If accounts have been closed, determine how they were closed. Was an interbank transfer involved or an instrument subject to further tracing? If accounts have not been closed, are transactions occurring which

5. Determine the defendant's last place of employment. If checks are due and owing, what provisions have been made for those checks? The defendant may be in possession of employment checks which, when cashed, will indicate his or her location. Alert the employer to contact you regarding any communications pertaining to the defendant, for instance, work reference inquiries. All of these steps should be repeated with the offices of any union of which the defendant is a member, particularly with reference to union benefits.

6. Contact the postal service to determine the defendant's mail status. Was a hold placed on the mail and, if so, who is authorized to receive it? Request contact if any communication is received pertaining to the defendant's mail.

7. Obtain information from any credit card companies pertaining to transactions which the defendant conducted immediately prior to or after the abduction. In cases of joint accounts, these are available without subpoena.

8. Determine whether school records were obtained or have been requested from the school in which the child was enrolled. Also determine whether a birth certificate was obtained or requested.

9. Contact the branch of military service in which the defendant served. All branches are extremely helpful to law enforcement authorities in locating fugitives.

10. State tax, unemployment compensation or welfare information can be extremely beneficial in any investigation and are ordinarily subject to subpoena. Employer and home address information contained in federal tax returns and social security records can be accessed through the federal Parent Locator Service.

11. Support groups are available to consult with and advise victimized parents. Child Find, located in New Paltz, New York, is among the largest of these groups. They can be reached by calling (914) 255-1848.

12. If a parent decides to retain a private investigator to help locate the missing child, it is advisable to contact the Better Business Bureau or Consumer Protection Office to make sure that the detective is reputable. Ask the detective for references and check them out. Avoid any detective who promises to perform a "snatch back:" this is potentially disruptive and traumatic to the child, and may prejudice the legal situation against the parent who authorizes such conduct. Once the child is located, it is far better to seek a voluntary return from the abductor and/or to petition a court to enforce the out-of-state decree, usually with the help of a local custody lawyer.

ARREST AND RECOVERY

While a victimized parent can often effectively investigate an absconding parent's location with limited direction and assistance from a prosecutor or police, it is essential in the arrest and recovery process that the prosecutor, a member of his or her staff or an experienced police officer commit his or her time, energy and resources in the last stages of the efforts to locate the child and absconding parent.

When the absconding parent's likely position is localized, some or all of the following procedures should be utilized.

1. Contact local school authorities to determine whether a school-aged victim has been enrolled in school. Problems in determining an alias can be avoided by reference to dates of birth and dates of enrollment.

2. Determine what relatives and/or friends live in the community.

3. Local utility companies will ordinarily assist law enforcement officials in efforts to locate a fugitive.

Once the location is certain, it is imperative that the prosecutor or police establish phone contact with the shift commander or a member of the staff in the local prosecutor's office. Official communications through police channels confirming the existence of the warrant and requesting assistance should be forwarded simultaneously. However, phone contact will assure that the importance of the request is understood and that efforts to apprehend and recover are underway.

Phone contact should also involve investigation of the possibility of making an arrest outside the presence of the child, and of the child being taken into temporary custody by Protective Service workers pending arrival of the lawful custodian, if necessary. Every effort should be made to limit the additional trauma the child will suffer in the recovery process. Clarification of the legal processes to be utilized by police and/or Protective Service respecting the temporary custody of the victimized child should be clearly conveyed to the parent-victim.

At the same time, the activities of the victimized parent should be coordinated with officials from the arresting jurisdiction, the prosecutor's office and his or her legal counsel. To limit the child's trauma, and to obviate the need for temporary placement of the child in the custody of the Child Protective Service, the parent should arrive as quickly after arrest as possible. That parent should be equipped with certified or exemplified copies of the custody order and the child's birth certificate, as well as photographs of the child together with the victimized parent. It is often advisable for a victimized parent to have contacted local legal counsel in the area where the child is recovered to commence legal proceedings if necessary.

119

TRIAL

Guilty verdicts are often difficult to obtain in instances of parental kidnapping because of a natural tendency on the part of a juror to focus on the relationship of the defendant and victim, and fail to recognize the substantial adverse impact such conduct has on the child. Therefore, voir dire and trial strategy should focus on the following:

1. Establish that the crime is a serious offense against the child, interfering with his or her fundamental right to enjoy the love and support of both parents. Focus sympathy on the child and not the defendant.

2. Try only the criminal action and not the custody issue. Attacks on the character of the parent-victim are common but ordinarily not material.

3. Prepare your victimized parent carefully. Any hint of vindictiveness which appears in his or her testimony can be fatal.

4. For the child's well-being, avoid if at all possible using the child as a witness.

CONCLUSION

Parental kidnapping cannot be categorically dismissed as a "domestic dispute." It is a serious crime against children which has long-lasting harmful effects on its young victims. These children, so vulnerable at the hands of a divorced or divorcing parent, must not be subjected to the indifference and passivity of police officers, prosecutors, extradition officials, F.B.I. agents or judges. They deserve nothing less than full protection from the personnel who comprise our civil and criminal justice systems. Hopefully the foregoing discussion will assist prosecutors and police in fashioning effective responses to parental kidnapping cases.

Other Remedies: Tort Actions*

Abducting parents and any persons, including relatives, known or believed to have aided in the removal or retention of a child may be liable in compensatory and punitive damages for false imprisonment, intentional infliction of emotional distress, unlawful enticement, civil conspiracy to abduct a child, or similar causes of action recognized under state law. Suits of this kind may have the beneficial side effect of compelling disclosure of the child's location. This is true because defendants, particularly relatives of the absconding parent, would often rather disclose the location of the child than incur the emotional and financial expenses of defending a law suit.

Ethical Considerations*

Several lawyers and at least two judges have been disciplined for their roles in child custody cases involving wrongful removals or retentions of children. Lawyers representing clients in custody disputes are absolutely obliged to conform to the rules of conduct in effect in their states. Three examples of conduct deemed unacceptable follow.

1. An attorney may not counsel a client to snatch a child in violation of a court order.

In the case of Attorney Grievance Commission of Maryland vs. Leonard J. Kerpelman, Misc. Docket (Subtitle BV) No. 1, September Term, 1980, attorney Kerpelman was suspended from the practice of law for two years for violating several of Maryland's disciplinary rules in the course of representing clients in custody matters.

2. Attorneys should not end run a custody decision entered after full blown litigation under the UCCJA by seeking jurisdiction of the juvenile courts.
Judges will not tolerate such overzealousness; those who do permit such abuse of process may be sanctioned.

In an opinion well worth reading, the Supreme Court of Indiana held two judges, one private attorney, and a county prosecuting attorney in indirect criminal contempt for willfully and intentionally disobeying orders of the state Supreme Court and the mandate of the Court of Appeals entered in an appeal of an interstate custody case

*Condensed

decided under the Uniform Child Custody Jurisdiction Act (UCCJA). (See, In re the matter of Michelle Lemond), 413 N.E. 2d 228 (1980). Each of the judges and lawyers was fined $500 and charged with the costs of the case.

3. Lawyers should maintain a professional relationship with clients and should not let distractions impair their judgement.

For a custody case involving truly outrageous attorney misconduct see, Sixth District Committee of the Virginia State Bar v. Albert C. Hodgson, Respondent, Docket No. 80-18, April 1, 1981. Attorney Hodgson was permanently disbarred for using his attorney-client privilege to influence his female client to have sexual relations with him, and for advising his client that he could make arrangements to have her former husband killed in lieu of a child custody suit, the court having found that said advice was given in a non-jesting manner!

Excerpted or condensed from INTERSTATE AND INTERNATIONAL CHILD CUSTODY DISPUTES: A COLLECTION OF MATERIALS, 2nd Edition, A Monograph by the Child Custody Project, Patricia M. Hoff, Esq., Director, American Bar Association, Fund for Public Education, Washington, D.C. This section on prosecutors and police was co-authored by Ms. Hoff and Christopher Foley, Assistant District Attorney, Milwaukee, Wisconsin, for The Prosecutor magazine, a publication of the National District Attorney's Association.

SECTION VII

FEDERAL PARENT LOCATOR SERVICE

DEPARTMENT OF HEALTH AND HUMAN SERVICES

Office of Child Support Enforcement

45 CFR Parts 302, 303, and 304

Requests To Use the Federal Parent Locator Service in Parental Kidnapping and Child Custody Cases

Agency: Office of Child Support Enforcement (OCSE), HHS.

SUMMARY: Section 9 of Pub. L. 96-611, the Parental Kidnapping Prevention Act of 1980, provides that a State may enter into an agreement with the Office of Child Support Enforcement to obtain Federal Parent Locator Service (PLS) information for use in parental kidnapping and child custody cases.

Effective November 3, 1981.

FEDERAL PARENT LOCATOR SERVICE

Federal Parent Locator Service
Office of Child Support Enforcement
Department of Health & Human Resources
6110 Executive Blvd.
Rockville, Maryland 20850
(301) 443-4950
Attn: Naomi Marr
Internal Information, Systems Branch

SUPPLEMENTARY INFORMATION:

Statutory Provisions

Previously the Social Security Act provided for States to obtain information from the Federal PLS to locate absent parents only for the purposes of establishing paternity or establishing and enforcing child support obligations. Various Federal statutes and OCSE regulations expressly prohibited States from acquiring the information for any other purpose. Section 9 of Pub. L. 96-611 amends the

Social Security Act by amending sections 454 and 455 and adding a new section 463. The new section 463 provides that States may enter into an agreement with the Secretary to obtain information from the Federal PLS for use in locating a parent or child for the purposes of making or enforcing a child custody determination or in cases of parental kidnapping.

The new law amends section 454 by requiring the States amend their State IV-D plans to include whether or not they wish to perform this new function. Section 455 as amended precludes the payment of Federal matching funds for the costs of carrying out agreements under the new section 463.

Changes to Existing Regulations

Because OCSE already has regulations that govern State IV-D agency use of the Federal PLS, many of the new statutory requirements have been implemented simply by adding language to these existing regulations to extend use of the Federal PLS to parental kidnapping and child custody cases. Other minor changes have been made to these regulations to remove unnecessary or duplicate provisions and make the regulations easier to read. The regulations that have been amended in this manner are discussed below. One substantive change that is not required by the new statute has been made to 45 CFR 302.35. This change is also described below.

— 45 CFR 302.35, State parent locator service. The existing regulations provide for the establishment of a central State PLS office, as well as authorize the designation of additional IV-D offices that may submit requests for Federal PLS information. Currently IV-D agencies are permitted to designate up to two additional offices for this purpose. This provision has been changed to permit the IV-D agency to designate more than two additional offices if written approval is obtained from OCSE. Although this change is not required by the statute, we believe the flexibility it adds will benefit State management of the parent locator function.

Section 302.35 also lists types of individuals and entities from whom the State PLS offices may accept requests for Federal PLS information. In line with the requirements of Section 9 of Pub. L. 96-611, we have added to this list authorized persons who request information in connection with parental kidnapping or child custody cases. The term "authorized persons" is defined in Section 9 of the statute. We have incorporated the definition into a new regulation of 45 CFR 303.15, which is discussed later in this preamble under the heading "New Regulations on Agreements to Use the Federal PLS."

— 45 CFR 302.70, Requests for information from the Federal Parent Locator Service (PLS), redesignated as 45 CFR 303.70 and retitled Requests by the State parent locator service for information from the Federal Parent Locator Service (PLS). The existing regulations provide that the central State PLS office and any additional offices designated under §302.35 may submit requests for Federal PLS information. They also require that requests must be submitted in the manner and form prescribed by OCSE and that requests must contain the information that the regulations specify. These regulations further provide that requests must be accompanied by a statement attesting that (1) the information is being sought for a purpose that is authorized by law, and (2) the information will be treated as confidential. To the already authorized purposes of establishing paternity or securing child support, we have added as an authorized purpose use of the information in a parental kidnapping or child custody case.

The regulations also specify that States must collect or pay the fees required for processing requests made to the Federal PLS in connection with non-AFDC child support enforcement cases in which location was the only child support enforcement service being sought, as States have done in the past, and in connection with parental kidnapping and child custody cases, as required by the new statute. The reference to parental kidnapping and child custody cases has been added by these final rules.

Fees for processing requests for information in parental kidnapping and child custody cases cannot be collected as an offset to the quarterly IV-D grant awards as is done with the fees States collect for non-AFDC child support enforcement cases only in need of location services. This is because costs of processing the former requests are not eligible for Federal financial participation and, therefore, no Federal grant award is made with respect to these costs. The statute does require, however, that States collect fees to cover State and Federal expenses. As specified in §303.70(e), we will bill the State IV-D agency periodically to recover the Federal costs of processing requests. Paragraph (e) also requires the IV-D agency to transmit payment to the Federal government upon receipt of a bill. These fees must be paid to the Federal government even if no location information with respect to a particular individual can be found. OCSE will issue instructions that will specify in detail the procedures for billing and the appropriate methods of payment. Initially OCSE will charge a fee of $10 per request. A charge of $4 will be made to search for a social security number prior to an attempt to locate an individual. If the social security number cannot be found, a location request cannot be processed and the $10 fee will not be charged. We have not specified the amounts of the fees in the regulations. Subsection 454(17) of the Social Security Act explicitly requires that a fee be charged to cover Federal costs of processing requests for information in parental kidnapping and child custody cases. Since the Federal fee is tied to costs, which may vary periodically due to inflation, new processing techniques and so forth, it is impractical to specify these fees in regulations. In addition, since the fee must reflect costs, the Department has little discretion in establishing the amount of the fee. Instead, in advance of any revision to the fees, we will notify States of the new amounts and their effective date by action transmittal.

As noted above, these regulations on requests for information from the Federal Parent Locator Service have been moved from 45 CFR Part 302 to Part 303. This has been done as part of an overall effort to remove unnecessary State plan requirements from our regulations. As a result of this redesignation, failure to comply with the regulations will lead only to denial of the request for information, not noncompliance with the IV-D State plan.

— 45 CFR 304.20, Availability and rate of Federal financial participation. Paragraph (b) of this section has been amended to clearly indicate that Federal funding of parental kidnapping and child custody services is prohibited even though they are services performed under the IV-D State plan. Also see below 45 CFR 304.23.

— 45 CFR 304.23, Expenditures for which Federal financial participation is not available. As indicated by its title, this section specifies activities for which Federal funding is not available under the Child Support Enforcement program. To this list we have added expenditures made to carry out an agreement under 45 CFR 303.15. Section 303.15 is a new regulation which is discussed below under the preamble heading "New Regulation on Agreements to Use the Federal PLS".

New Regulation on Agreements To Use the Federal PLS

In implementing section 9 of Pub. L. 96-611, we have also added to the regulations a new 45 CFR 303.15, entitled "Agreements to Use the Federal Parent Locator Service (PLS) in Parental Kidnapping and Child Custody Cases". Section 303.15 provides that States must enter into an agreement with OCSE if they wish to use the Federal PLS to obtain information for locating absent parents or children in parental kidnapping or child custody cases. This agreement is required by the statute. In addition §303.15 specifies the type of information that OCSE will make available to the State under the agreement and sets forth the conditions that the State must agree to meet in requesting data and ensuring that the data are safeguarded.

Section 303.15 begins with two definitions taken from the statute. First, "authorized person" is defined to specify who may request Federal PLS information in parental kidnapping and child custody cases. In general, authorized persons are agents or attorneys of States that have agreements to use the Federal PLS, courts or agents of courts, and agents or attorneys of the United States as long as there is authority or jurisdiction to act in connection with a parental kidnapping or child custody case. Second, "custody determination" is defined as a judgement, decree, or other order of a court providing for custody or visitation of a child. It includes permanent and temporary orders and initial orders and modifications.

With regard to the contents of the agreement, §303.15 specifies that OCSE agrees to provide the most recent home address and place of employment of any absent parent or child if requested for the purpose of enforcing a State or Federal law with respect to the unlawful taking or restraint of a child or for the purpose of making or enforcing a child custody determination. The State must agree to make requests through the State PLS and to use the same format for requests that is normally used for child support enforcement cases.

Section 303.15 also requires that the State agree to distinguish parental kidnapping and child custody requests from child support enforcement requests. The purpose of this requirement is to enable OCSE to make proper billings for processing these requests, since the associated costs are not eligible for Federal matching funds. Because no Federal financial participation is available and because the statute requires it, the State must agree to impose, collect and account for fees to offset State and OCSE processing costs and must agree to transmit OCSE's portion of the fees when billed. The fee amounts are discussed above under the preamble heading "Changes to Existing Regulations."

Finally, the State must agree to restrict access to the data, store it securely, and otherwise ensure its confidentiality. Under this requirement, the State must agree to send the information directly to the requestor and make no other use of the information, as well as destroy any records related to the request that are confidential in nature. These provisions are necessary to ensure that the statutory requirements are met concerning access by authorized persons only, as discussed above.

The regulation at §303.15(d) provides that the agreement must be signed by the Governor of the State or the Governor's designee, as well as by the Attorney General of the State who must certify that the signing State official has the authority under State law to commit the

State to the agreement.

Appendix to New Regulations on Agreements
To Use the Federal PLS

In order to assist States in deciding whether to enter into an agreement to use the Federal PLS to obtain information in parental kidnapping and child custody cases, we have published the necessary agreement in the Federal Register as an appendix to the regulations at 45 CFR 303.15. We also expect that publishing the agreement will expedite State implementation of the agreement by making it readily available for use. The provisions of the agreement are based on the requirements of § 303.15 and specify both the duties of OCSE under the agreement and the conditions that the State must agree to meet in making requests and in safeguarding the information that the Federal PLS provides.

In addition to incorporating the provisions of § 303.15, the agreement contains a limitation of liability.

NOTE: Currently 22 states have agreements with the Department of Health and Human Resources to use the Federal Parent Locator Service in parental kidnapping and missing children cases. Please refer to page 125 for the address and telephone number where you may ask about the current status of the state in which you live.

SECTION VIII

STATE AGENCIES ADMINISTERING CHILD SUPPORT AND PARENT LOCATOR SERVICE PROGRAMS UNDER TITLE IV-D OF THE SOCIAL SECURITY PROGRAM

SURVEY OF STATE AGENCIES ADMINISTERING CHILD SUPPORT AND PARENT LOCATOR SERVICE PROGRAMS UNDER TITLE IV-D OF THE SOCIAL SECURITY ACT

IV-D AGENCY   **PARENT LOCATOR SERVICE**

ALABAMA

Mr. Paul Vincent, Director
Division of Child Support Activities
Bureau of Public Assistance
State Department of Pensions and Security
64 North Union Street
Montgomery, Alabama 36130
(205) 832-6236

ALASKA

Mr. Dan Copeland, Director
Child Support Enforcement Agency
Department of Revenue
201 East 9th Avenue, Room 202
Anchorage, Alaska 99501
(907) 276-3441

AMERICAN SAMOA

F.V. Vavoasa
Assistant Attorney General
Office of the Attorney General
P.O. Box 7
Pago Pago, American Samoa 96799
(684) 633-4163

ALABAMA

SAME

ALASKA

SAME

AMERICAN SAMOA

SAME

ARIZONA

Mr. John Ahl, Program Administrator
Child Support Enforcement Administration
Department of Economic Security
P.O. Box 6123 - Site Code 966C
Phoenix, Arizona 85005
(602) 255-3465

ARIZONA

SAME

ARKANSAS

Mr. Ed Baskin, Acting Director
Office of Child Support Enforcement
Arkansas Social Services
P.O. Box 3358
Little Rock, Arkansas 72203
(501) 371-2464

ARKANSAS

SAME
(501) 371-1614

CALIFORNIA

Mr. Robert A. Barton, Chief
Child Support Program Management
   Branch
Department of Social Services
744 P Street
Sacramento, California 95814

CALIFORNIA

CA Parent Locator
   Services
1800 I Street
Sacramento, Cali-
   fornia 95814
(916) 323-5192

COLORADO

Mr. James O. Galeotti, Director
Division of Child Support Enforcement
Department of Social Services
1575 Sherman Street - Room 423
Denver, Colorado 80203
(303) 866-2422
 866-5000 General Information

COLORADO

SAME

CONNECTICUT

Mr. Anthony DiNallo, Chief
Child Support Division
Department of Human Resources
110 Bartholemew Avenue
Hartford, Connecticut 06115
(203) 566-3053

CONNECTICUT

SAME
(203) 566-2522

DELAWARE

Mr. Rick Bennett, Director
Bureau of Child Support Enforcement
Department of Health & Social Services
920 Church Street
Wilmington, Delaware 19801
(302) 571-3620

DELAWARE

SAME
(302) 571-3024

DISTRICT OF COLUMBIA

Mr. Eugene Brown, Chief
Bureau of Paternity
Child Support Enforcement
Department of Human Services
601 Indiana Avenue, N.W., Room 1000
Washington, D.C. 20004
(202) 724-5610

DISTRICT OF COLUMBIA

Luis Rumbaut
SAME
(202) 724-5610

FLORIDA

Mr. Samuel G. Ashdown, Jr., Director
Office of Child Support Enforcement
Department of Health & Rehabilitative
   Services
1317 Winewood Boulevard
Tallahassee, Florida 32301
(904) 488-9900

FLORIDA

SAME
(904) 487-2097
(904) 488-9900

GEORGIA

Mr. Jesse Beck, Director
Child Support Recovery Unit
State Department of Human Resources
618 Ponce de Leon Avenue, N.E.
Atlanta, Georgia 30308
(404) 894-5194

GEORGIA

SAME
(404) 894-4832

GUAM

Ms. Julia Perez, Supervisor
Child Support Enforcement Unit
Division of Social Services
Dept. of Public Health & Social Services
Government of Guam
P.O. Box 2816
Agana, Guam 96910

GUAM

HAWAII

Mr. James O'Brien, IV-D Administrator
Child Support Enforcement Agency
770 Kapiolani Boulevard, Suite 403
Honolulu, Hawaii 96813
(808) 548-5779

HAWAII

Child Support Enf.
  Services
770 Kapiolani Blvd.
Honolulu, Hawaii
  96813
(808) 548-5779

IDAHO

Mrs. Pat Barrell, Chief
Bureau of Child Support Enforcement
Department of Health and Welfare
Statehouse Mail
Boise, Idaho 83720
(208) 344-4422

IDAHO

SAME

ILLINOIS

Mr. Gerald D. Slavens, Chief
Bureau of Child Support
Department of Public Aid
316 South Second Street
Springfield, Illinois 62762
(217) 782-1366

ILLINOIS

Bur. of Child Support
Ill. Dept. of Public Aid
225 S. 4th Street
2nd Floor
Springfield, IL 62762
(217) 785-8775
(217) 785-1365

INDIANA

Mr. Thomas W. McKean, Director
Child Support Enforcement Division
State Department of Public Welfare
141 S. Merridan Street, 4th Floor
Indianapolis, Indiana 46225
(317) 232-4903

INDIANA

SAME
(317) 232-4936

IOWA

Mr. Jack Baughman, Director
Child Support Recovery Unit
Iowa Department of Social Services
Hoover Building - 1st Floor
Des Moines, Iowa 50319
(515) 281-5580

IOWA

(515) 281-4692
Des Moines
(319) 324-3200
Davenport
(712) 328-7048
Council Bluffs

KANSAS

Ms. Betty Hummel, Director
Location and Support
Dept. of Social & Rehabilitation Services
2700 West 6th - Biddle Building, 2nd Floor
Topeka, Kansas 66606
(913) 296-4188

KANSAS

SAME
(913) 296-3409

KENTUCKY

Mr. Hanson Williams, Director
Division of Child Support Enforcement
Bureau of Social Insurance
Department of Human Resources
275 East Main Street, 6th Floor
Frankfort, Kentucky 40621
(502) 564-2285

KENTUCKY

Div. of Child Support
  Enforcement
Dept. of Human
  Resources
275 E. Main Street
Frankfort, KY 40621
(502) 564-2285
((502) 564-2836

LOUISIANA

Mr. P.M. Blakney, Director
Support Enforcement Services
P.O. Box 44276
Baton Rouge, LA 70804
(504) 342-4780

LOUISIANA

SAME
(504) 342-4786

MAINE

Mr. Colburn Jackson, Director
Support Enforcement and Location Unit
Bureau of Social Welfare
Department of Human Services
State House, Station 11
Augusta, Maine 04333
(207) 289-2886

MAINE

SAME

MARYLAND

Mr. John Williams, Chief
Bureau of Support Enforcement
Income Maintenance Administration
300 West Preston Street
5th Floor
Baltimore, Maryland 21201
(301) 669-8791 Ext. 498

MARYLAND

SAME
(301) 669-8791 Ext. 525

MASSACHUSETTS

Mr. Dennis Sullivan, Director
Child Support Enforcement Unit
Department of Public Welfare
600 Washington Street
Boston, Massachusetts 02111
(617) 727-7820

MASSACHUSETTS

Gertrude Linehan
SAME
(617) 426-5635

MICHIGAN

Mr. Jerrold Brockmyre, Director
Office of Child Support
Department of Social Services
300 South Capitol Avenue - Suite 621
Lansing, Michigan 48909
(517) 373-7570

MICHIGAN

SAME
(517) 373-8640

MINNESOTA

Mrs. Bonnie Becker, Director
Office of Child Support
Department of Public Welfare
Space Center Building
444 Lafayette Road
St. Paul, Minnesota 55101
(612) 296-2499

MINNESOTA

SAME
(612) 296-2542

MISSISSIPPI

Mr. Monte L. Barton, Director
Child Support Division
State Department of Public Welfare
P.O. Box 352
Jackson, Mississippi 39250
(601) 354-0341 Ext. 503

MISSISSIPPI

Child Support Division
State Department of
  Public Welfare
P.O. Box 4321
Fondren Station
Jackson, Mississippi
  39216
(601) 956-8713

MISSOURI

Mr. Paul Nelson, Administrator
Child Support Enforcement Unit
Division of Family Services
Department of Social Services
P.O. Box 88
Jefferson City, Missouri 65103
(314) 751-4301

MISSOURI

Central Registry
Dept. of Social Services
Div. of Family Services
P.O. Box 88
Jefferson City, Missouri
  65103
(314) 751-2769

MONTANA

Mr. Ray Linder, Bureau Chief
Child Support Enforcement Bureau
Montana Department of Revenue
P.O. Box 5955
Helena, Montana 59601
(406) 449-4614

MONTANA

SAME
(406) 449-4674

NEBRASKA

Mr. Bob Huston, Administrator
Child Support Enforcement Office
Department of Public Welfare
P.O. Box 95026
Lincoln, Nebraska 68509
(402) 471-3121 Ext. 221

NEBRASKA

Child Support
  Enforcement Office
301 Centennial Mall
  South
Lincoln, NE 68509
(402) 471-3121 Ext. 140

NEVADA

Mr. William Furlong, Chief
Child Support Enforcement
Nevada State Welfare Division
Department of Human Resources
251 Jeanell Drive
Carson City, Nevada 89710
(702) 885-4744

NEVADA

SAME

NEW HAMPSHIRE

Mr. Gray E. Thorn, Administrator
Office of Child Support Enforcement
  Services
Division of Welfare
Health and Welfare Building
Hazen Drive
Concord, New Hampshire 03301
(603) 271-4426

NEW HAMPSHIRE

SAME
(603) 271-4431

NEW JERSEY

Mr. Harry Wiggins, Chief
Child Support and Paternity Unit
Department of Human Services
P.O. Box 1627
3535 Quakerbridge Road
Trenton, New Jersey 08625
(609) 890-9500 Ext. 431

NEW JERSEY

SAME
(609) 890-9500 Ext. 388

NEW MEXICO

Mr. Ben Silva, Chief
Child Support Enforcement Bureau
Department of Human Services
P.O. Box 2348 - PERA Building
Santa Fe, New Mexico 87503
(505) 827-5591

NEW MEXICO

SAME

NEW YORK

Mr. Meldon F. Kelsey, Director
Office of Child Support Enforcement
New York State Department
  of Social Services
40 North Pearl Street
Albany, New York 12243
(518) 474-9081

NEW YORK

(518) 474-9091 Albany
(518) 474-3150 Albany
(212) 553-5114
  New York City

NORTH CAROLINA

Ms. Susan Jeffries, Chief
Child Support Enforcement Section
Division of Social Services
Department of Human Resources
443 N. Harrington Street
Raleigh, North Carolina 27603
(919) 733-4120

NORTH CAROLINA

SAME

NORTH DAKOTA

Mr. Thomas C. Tupa, Administrator
Child Support Enforcement Agency
Social Services Board of North Dakota
Russell Building - Highway 83 North
Bismarck, North Dakota 58505
(701) 224-3582

NORTH DAKOTA

SAME
(701) 224-3584

OHIO

Mr. Michael Seidemann, Chief
Bureau of Child Support
Department of Public Welfare
State Office Tower
30 East Broad Street - 31st Floor
Columbus, Ohio 43215
(614) 466-3233

OHIO

(614) 466-9510
Columbus
(216) 623-8883
Cleveland

OKLAHOMA

Mr. Robert Fulton, Director
Department of Human Services
Attention: Division of Child Support
P.O. Box 25352
Oklahoma City, Oklahoma 73125
(405) 424-5871

OKLAHOMA

ATTN: Robert Fulton
Central Locate Unit
P.O. Box 25352
Oklahoma City, Okla.
 73125
(405) 521-3641

OREGON

Mr. Leonard T. Sytsma, Manager
Support Service
Department of Human Resources
P.O. Box 14506
Salem, Oregon 97310
(503) 387-6093

OREGON

Department of Justice
Support Enforcement
  Division
100 State Office Bldg.
Central. Locate Unit
Salem, Oregon 97310
(503) 373-7300

PENNSYLVANIA

Ms. Linda Gunn, Director
Child Support Programs
Bureau of Claim Settlement
Department of Public Welfare
P.O. Box 8018
Harrisburg, Pennsylvania 17105
(717) 783-1779

PENNSYLVANIA

PA Parent Locator Serv.
P.O. Box 2675
Harrisburg, Penn. 17120
(717) 787-3669 Main Ofc.
(215) 686-8995
  Philadelphia

PUERTO RICO

Mr. Miguel Verdiales, Director
Child Support Enforcement Program
Department of Social Services
P.O. Box 11398, Fernandez Juncos Station
Santurce, Puerto Rico 00910
(809) 722-4731

PUERTO RICO

SAME

RHODE ISLAND

Mr. George Moriarty, Chief Supervisor
Bureau of Family Support
Dept. of Social & Rehabilitative Services
77 Dorance Street
Providence, Rhode Island 02903
(401) 277-2409

RHODE ISLAND

SAME
(401) 277-2847

SOUTH CAROLINA

Mr. Roy T. Loyd, Director
Division of Child Support
Public Assistance Division
Bureau of Public Assist. & Field Operations
Department of Social Services
P.O. Box 1520
Columbia, South Carolina 29202
(803) 758-3151

SOUTH CAROLINA

SAME
(803) 758-8860

SOUTH DAKOTA

Mr. Leland E. Swann, Program
  Administrator
Office of Child Support Enforcement
State Office Building #3 - Illinois Street
Pierre, South Dakota 57501
(605) 773-3641

SOUTH DAKOTA

Office of Child Support
  Enforcement
Richard F. Kniep Bldg.
Pierre, So. Dakota 57501
(605) 773-4641

TENNESSEE

Ms. Julia Alexander, Director
Child Support Services
Legal Services Division
Department of Human Services
111-19 7th Avenue N. - Sixth Floor
Nashville, Tennessee 37203
(615) 741-3288

TENNESSEE

SAME
(615) 741-7923

TEXAS

Mr. Barry Fredrickson,
  Assist. Commissioner
Child Support Enforcement Branch
Department of Human Resources
P.O. Box 2960
Austin, Texas 78769
(512) 835-0440 Ext. 2121

TEXAS

SAME
(512) 835-0440 Ext. 2025

144

UTAH

Mr. John P. Abbott, Director
Office of Recovery Services
Department of Social Services
P.O. Box 2500
150 West North Temple - Suite 250
Salt Lake City, Utah 84110
(801) 533-7439

UTAH

Parent Locator Service
3195 South Main
Salt Lake City, Utah
84115
(801) 533-7695

VERMONT

Mr. Paul Ohlson, Director
Child Support Division
Department of Social Welfare
103 S. Main Street
Waterbury, Vermont 05676
(802) 241-2868

VERMONT

SAME
(802) 241-2869

VIRGIN ISLANDS

Mr. Harry Biske, Director
Division of Paternity & Child Support
Insular Department of Social Welfare
P.O. Box 539
Charlotte Amalie
St. Thomas, Virgin Islands 00801
(809) 774-0930 Ext. 219

VIRGIN ISLANDS

SAME
(809) 774-0930 Ext. 279

VIRGINIA

Ms. Jean White, Director
Division of Support Enforcement
Department of Welfare
8004 Franklin Farms Drive
Richmond, Virginia 23288
(804) 281-9108

VIRGINIA

State Parent Locate
  Service
Bureau of Support
  Enforcement
8007 Discovery Drive
Richmond, Virginia 23288
(804) 281-9074

WASHINGTON

Mr. Robert Querry, Chief
Office of Support Enforcement
Department of Social & Health Services
P.O. Box 9162-FU-11
Olympia, Washington 98504
(206) 459-6481

WASHINGTON

SAME
(206) 753-1426

WEST VIRGINIA

Ms. Sandra K. Gilmore, Director
Office of Child Support Enforcement
Department of Welfare
1900 Washington Street , East
Charleston, West Virginia 25305
(304) 348-3780

WEST VIRGINIA

SAME
(304) 348-3780 Ext. 32

WISCONSIN

Mr. Duane Campbell, Director
Bureau of Child Support
Division of Economic Assistance
18 South Thornton Avenue
Madison, Wisconsin 53708
(608) 266-0528

WISCONSIN

Bureau of Child Support
P.O. Box 8913
Madison, Wisc. 53708
(608) 266-0252

WYOMING

Mrs. Shirley Kingston, Director
Child Support Enforcement Section
Division of Public Assistance
   and Social Services
State Dept. of Health & Social Services
Hathaway Building
Cheyenne, Wyoming 82002
(307) 777-6083

WYOMING

SAME
(307) 777-7561

SECTION IX

FORM FOR AGREEMENT BETWEEN A STATE AND THE OFFICE OF CHILD SUPPORT TO OBTAIN FEDERAL PARENT LOCATOR SERVICE

This is the form for the agreement between a state and the office of child support in order to obtain Federal Parent Locator Service information for use in parental kidnapping cases. If your state has not entered into this agreement, please encourage them to do so.

Use of the Federal Parent Locator Service of the Office
of Child Support Enforcement to Locate Persons Sought
in Connection with Child Custody and Parental Kidnapping
Cases
(Agreement with the State in accordance with section
463 of the Social Security Act (42 U.S.C. 663))

AGREEMENT

Between
The Director of the Office of Child Support Enforcement

and

The State of _____

The Director, Office of Child Support Enforcement, hereinafter referred to as the Director, and the State of _____ , hereinafter referred to as the State, in accordance with sections 454 (17) and 463 of the Social Security Act and the regulations promulgated thereunder hereby agree to the following:

Article I — Definitions

For the purposes of this agreement —

A.   The term "Act" means the Social Security Act.

B. The term "authorized person" means (1) any agent or attorney of any State having an agreement under this section, who has the duty or authority under the law of such State to enforce a child custody determination; (2) any court having jurisdiction to make or enforce such a child custody determination, or any agent of such court; and (3) any agent or attorney of the United States, or of a State having an agreement under this section, who has the duty or authority to investigate, enforce or bring a prosecution with respect to the unlawful taking or restraint of a child.

C. The term "custody determination" means a judgment, decree, or other order of a court providing for the custody or visitation of a child and includes permanent and temporary orders, and initial orders and modifications.

D. The term "Director" means the Director, Office of Child Support Enforcement, who is the Secretary's designee to administer the Child Support Enforcement program under title IV-D of the Act.

E. The terms "Federal Parent Locator Service" or "PLS" mean the Parent Locator Service operated by OCSE pursuant to section 452(a)(9) of the Act.

F. The "Office of Child Support Enforcement" or "OCSE" means the separate organizational unit within the Department of Health and Human Services with the responsibility for the administration of the Child Support Enforcement program.

Article II — Duties of the Director

A. The Director, through the Federal PLS, shall provide the State IV-D agency the data specified in part B of this Article for the purpose of determining the whereabouts of any absent parent or child when this data is to be used to locate such parent or child for the purpose of:

(1) Enforcing any State or Federal law with respect to the unlawful taking or restraint of a child; or

(2) Making or enforcing a child custody determination.

150

B.   Pursuant to Part A of this Article, the Director shall provide the State IV-D agency the most recent home address and place of employment of any absent parent or child.

Article III - Requests for Data

A.   The State shall make requests to the Director for the most recent home address and place of employment of a parent or child solely for the purpose of (1) enforcing any State or federal law with respect to the unlawful taking or restraint of a child; or (2) making or enforcing a child custody determination.

B.   The State shall make the requests for information defined in part A of this Article only on behalf of authorized persons to the Federal PLS through the State parent locator service that is operated by the State agency described in section 454 of the Act.

C.   The State shall submit requests for information defined in part A of this Article to the Federal PLS in the standard format and exchange media normally available to or used by the State parent locator service.

D.   The State shall identify all requests for information defined in part A of this Article in a manner prescribed by OCSE so that such requests can be distinguished from child support enforcement requests submitted to the Federal PLS in order that a proper accounting can be made of amounts due the Federal government under part E of this Article.

E.   The State shall impose, collect and account for fees to offset the costs to the State and OCSE incurred in processing requests under part A of this Article.

F.   The State shall periodically transmit the fees collected to cover the costs of the Federal PLS in processing requests for information defined in part A of this Article in the amount and in the manner prescribed by OCSE in instructions.

Article IV - Confidential Nature and Limitation on Use of Information and Records

The State shall adopt policies and procedures to ensure that information obtained from the Director under this agreement shall be used and disclosed solely as provided in section 463 of the Act. Under this requirement, the State shall:

(1) Restrict access to the data to authorized personnel whose duties or responsibilities require access in connection with child custody and parental kidnapping cases;

(2) Store the data during nonduty hours or when not in use, in a locked container, within a secure area that is safe from access by unauthorized persons;

(3) Process the data under the immediate supervision and control of authorized personnel, in a manner which will protect the confidentiality of the data, and in such a way that unauthorized persons cannot retrieve the data by computer, remote terminal, or other means;

(4) Brief all employees who will have access to the data on security procedures and instructions;

(5) Send the information directly to the requestor and make no other use of the information;

(6) After the information is sent to the requestor, destroy all confidential records and information related to the request.

Article V - Limitation of Liability

The Director shall not be responsible for any financial loss incurred by the State, whether directly or indirectly, through the use of any data furnished pursuant to this agreement.

Article VI - Term of Agreement

This agreement shall begin on _____ and end on _____ . It will automatically be renewed for successive periods of **one year** unless the State or the Director gives written notice not to renew at least 30 days before the end of the current period.

Article VII - Termination and Modification of Agreement

A.   This agreement may be terminated or modified in writing at any time by mutual consent of the parties hereto.

B.   The Director or the State may terminate this agreement at any time upon 30 days written notice to the other party.

In Witness Whereof, the parties hereby execute this agreement this

_____ day of _____ .

The Director, Office of Child Support Enforcement

BY _____

_____

_____

(TITLE) _____

_____

(STATE) _____

_____

BY _____

(TITLE) _____

_____

(ADDRESS) _____

I, _____ , certify that I am the Attorney General of the State of _____ ; that _____ , who signed this agreement on behalf of the State, was then _____ of said State; and that he is authorized to enter into this agreement on behalf of the State and that there is authority under the laws of the State of _____ to carry out all functions to be performed by the State as provided herein and comply with the terms of this agreement.

_____

Signature of the Attorney General

STATUS REPORT ON
PARENTAL KIDNAPPING AGREEMENTS

States with Approved Agreements

Alabama	New Mexico
Arizona	North Dakota
Arkansas	Oklahoma
California	Oregon
Colorado	Pennsylvania
Georgia	Rhode Island
Hawaii	South Dakota
Kentucky	Tennessee
Minnesota	Texas
Missouri	Virginia
Nevada	Washington
New Jersey	

SECTION X

RESPONSIBILITIES OF THE DEPARTMENT OF STATE

ISSUANCE AND DENIAL OF PASSPORTS TO MINOR CHILDREN

Passport Services frequently is asked by parents or guardians not to issue passports to minor children, or to revoke passports previously issued to such children. This Notice provides basic information on the policies and procedures applicable to such cases.

RESPONSIBILITY OF THE DEPARTMENT OF STATE

Every effort is made to assist parents. However, the Department cannot assume any legal responsibility if it is unable to carry out the wishes of parents or guardians in the issuance or denial of a passport to a minor. The laws governing parental rights vary from state to state and from country to country, and parents or guardians ultimately must look to the courts of those countries to enforce their rights.

DEFINITION OF A MINOR

Passport regulations define a minor as an unmarried person under 18 years of age. For that reason, parental objections do not provide a basis for denying a passport to a person 18 years or over.

PASSPORT APPLICATION PROCEDURES

Place of Application. Applications must be made in the country within which the minor is located at the time of application.

Who must Execute the Application. A parent or legal guardian must apply on behalf of a minor under the age of 13 years. Any other person making application on behalf of a minor must present written authorization from the parent or guardian. The minor may be required to appear before the official accepting the application if necessary to establish the minor's identity or confirm the minor's presence in the country where the application is made.

Minors 13 years of age or over should execute their own applications unless the accepting official determines that the circumstances warrant execution of the application by a parent or guardian. Such minors may be required to submit the written consent of a parent or guardian before a passport is issued.

PROCEDURES FOR REQUESTING DENIAL
OF A PASSPORT TO A MINOR

Form and Content of Denial Requests. Requests must be made in writing. At a minimum, the request must provide the complete name, date, and place of birth of the minor, and the minor's relationship to the person requesting that a passport not be issued.

Where to Send Passport Denial Requests. Requests should be addressed to the Office of Citizenship Appeals and Legal Assistance (PPT/C), Department of State, Washington, D.C. 20520, directly or through the nearest Passport Agency in the United States. If the minor is abroad, the request should be sent to the nearest American Embassy or consulate.

Action Taken Upon Receipt of Denial Requests. Upon receipt, a notice is entered in the name of the minor child so that the objecting parent or guardian can be notified if an application is received in the minor's name. The objecting parent will receive confirmation of this in writing. If a search of the files reveals that the minor already had been issued a passport, a parent or guardian will be informed and advised concerning any assistance which can be provided in such cases.

DURATION AND GEOGRAPHIC APPLICABILITY
OF DENIAL NOTICES

Duration of Notice. Notices recording objections to the issuance of passports to minors remain in effect until the minors become 18 years of age, unless withdrawn by the objecting parent or guardian before that date.

Applicability of Notice. Notices entered in the United States are applicable only within the limits of the United States. If a notice requests the denial of a passport to a child residing abroad, the notice will be applicable only within the country in which the child is located.

DENIAL OF PASSPORT WHEN CUSTODY
OF MINOR IS IN DISPUTE

Presumption as to Parental Consent. Absent prior notification to the contrary, an application executed by or with the consent of one parent is presumed to have the consent of the other parent. Unless there has been a judicial award of custody to the objecting parent or a restraining order prohibiting the child's departure from the particular jurisdiction, the parent's objection will not prevent issuance of a passport which was applied for with the consent of the other parent. Nevertheless, a notice can still be entered so that the objecting parent can be notified if a passport application is executed.

Denial Requests Where One Parent Has Been Awarded Custody. A request that a minor not be issued a passport without the consent of the custodial parent or legal guardian must be accompanied by a copy of the court order awarding custody of the minor to that parent or guardian. Passport Services will also deny a passport to a minor at the written request of a non-custodial parent if that parent submits a copy of a court order which prohibits the minor's departure from the particular jurisdiction. The court order must have been issued or recognized by a court in the country in which the minor is residing.

Conflicting Court Orders as to Custody of a Minor. In such cases, Passport Services will not attempt to resolve the conflict between court orders. The parent objecting to the issuance of the passport may be given a limited time in which to resolve the conflict through the courts or by agreement of the parties, otherwise, the passport application of the minor will be approved.

Enforcement of Visitation Rights. Except as noted, whether or not a passport will be issued to a minor is determined by whether or not the objecting parent has been awarded legal custody of the minor. Unless specifically provided for in a court order, visitation rights awarded to a non-custodial parent will not be enforced by either the issuance or denial of a passport to a minor.

Denial Requests in Country Other Than One in Which Custody Was Awarded. It is the Department's policy that no extraterritorial validity will be given to a court order involving custody of a minor. For that reason, it is not possible to deny a passport to a minor who is outside the country whose courts awarded custody of the minor to the objecting parent.

REVOCATION OF PASSPORTS ISSUED TO MINORS

Parental objections, or court orders or decrees concerning custody do not provide a basis under passport regulations for the revocation of passports. However, the regulations do not prevent the objecting parent or guardian from attempting to recover possession of a minor's passport, either directly or through order of a court.

PASSPORT REVOCATION TO ENFORCE NON-CUSTODY
PROVISIONS OF COURT ORDERS

Warrants of arrest, injunctions, or contempt of court citations issued
for the failure of a parent or guardian to abide by the provisions of
custody orders are enforceable by revocation of a passport only to
the extent that they would be enforced against the violators by
federal felony action in the Courts of the United States.

OTHER SERVICES - WELFARE/WHEREABOUTS OF MINORS
OUTSIDE THE UNITED STATES

Frequently, a parent or legal guardian will ask the assistance of the
Department in determining the whereabouts or welfare of a minor
child who is outside the United States. Such requests should be made
in writing and addressed to the Office of Citizens Consular Services,
Overseas Citizens Services, Department of State, Washington, D.C.
20520. All requests should include the telephone number of the
writer in case he or she must be contacted for further information.
Upon receipt of such a request, an effort will be made to establish the
minor's location or welfare and to provide information that may help
the concerned parent.

The Office of Citizens Consular Services has available on request a
Notice entitled "Assistance in Child Custody Disputes" which
contains more information about welfare/whereabouts services
offered by that office.

ASSISTANCE IN CHILD CUSTODY DISPUTES

The Department of State receives many requests for advice and
assistance from parents whose children have been taken from the
United States or prevented from returning to the United States by the
other parent. The Department and American Embassies and Con-
sulates will do whatever they can to assist parents who are involved in
child custody disputes; however, in most cases, the amount and type
of assistance which the Department and its Foreign Service posts can
offer is quite restricted. While the Department attempts to be of
assistance in these matters, it cannot assume responsibility for any
failure or inability to comply with the wishes of parents or guardians.

Consular Assistance

In child custody controversies which children have been taken to another country or have been kept abroad by one parent, the Department of State, through its Foreign Service posts, can attempt to locate the children, monitor their welfare upon the request of a parent, make available general information about child custody laws and procedures, and furnish a list of attorneys in the foreign country should the parents indicate the need for legal advice or assistance. The Department can provide information about the welfare of a child under the age of eighteen to either parent, regardless of custody. If it appears that a child is being abused or neglected, Department officers can alert the local authorities or social service agencies.

Requests for Assistance

Persons who desire the Department's assistance in ascertaining the welfare or whereabouts of a child should send the following information to the Office of Citizens Consular Service (CA/OCS/CCS), Department of State, Washington, D.C. 20520, or to the U.S. Embassy or Consulate nearest the child's foreign residence: the full name of the child; the child's date and place of birth; passport data, if known; any available information about the child's departure from the United States or destination; and the names and, if possible, the addresses and telephone numbers of persons with whom the child travelled or is believed to be staying. Information concerning the provisions which have been made for custody of the child or a copy of any pertinent court decree is helpful. Parents should include telephone numbers where they can be reached if the Department or a Foreign Service post needs further details. The Office of Citizens Consular Services can be reached by telephone at (202) 632-3444.

Jurisdictional Limitations and Legal Assistance

If an amicable settlement of a child custody dispute cannot be worked out by the parents, the only recourse may be a court action in the country where the child is located. The law of the country in which the child is physically present, even temporarily, is controlling.

Traditionally, the legal doctrine to which most countries have adhered is that the presence of a child within a particular country renders its courts competent to determine who should have custody of the child, regardless of any prior custody judgment issued by a court in another country. As a result, it is not unusual to find conflicting custody decisions in different jurisdictions. Courts in

161

some countries have honored American custody decrees, but on the whole the outcome is unpredictable. The United States Government cannot force a foreign country to honor any American court order regulating custody or visitation rights.

Although U.S. consular officers can provide lists of attorneys in their consular districts, they cannot recommend any particular attorney, offer legal advice, represent U.S. citizens in custody or other hearings before foreign courts, or attempt to influence the outcome of those hearings.

Consular officers have no legal authority to obtain physical custody of children and return them to the United States. They cannot assist a parent in acquiring physical custody of a child illegally or by force or deception. Officers cannot help a parent to leave a foreign country with a child whose custody is disputed if the departure would violate a court order or the laws of the foreign country. They can, however, provide a passport for the U.S. citizen child whose custody is disputed if the child appears in person and they have not received a court order issued by the foreign government barring the child's departure from the country or awarding custody to someone other than the parent accompanying the child.

Passport Denial

When there is controversy concerning the custody of a minor, a passport-issuing office in the United States or abroad may deny issuance of a passport to the minor if it receives a court order from a court within the country in which passport services are sought. The court order must give custody of the child to the person who has requested that passport services be denied or must specifically forbid the child's departure from the country without the court's permission. Even in cases where a passport cannot be denied, parents can be notified if passport applications are submitted in the names of their children. Generally, after a passport has been issued, it cannot be revoked merely because the bearer has become involved in a child custody dispute.

Persons interested in passport denial may write to the Office of Citizenship Appeals and Legal Assistance (PPT/C), Department of State, Washington, D.C. 20520.

SECTION XI

HAGUE CONVENTION OF THE CIVIL ASPECT OF INTERNATIONAL CHILD ABDUCTION

HAGUE CONVENTION OF THE CIVIL ASPECT OF INTERNATIONAL CHILD ABDUCTION

Final Act of the Fourteenth Session

The undersigned, Delegates of the Governments of Argentina, Australia, Austria, Belgium, Canada, Czechoslovakia, Denmark, the Arab Republic of Egypt, Finland, France, the Federal Republic of Germany, Greece, Ireland, Israel, Italy, Japan, Jugoslavia, Luxemburg, the Netherlands, Norway, Portugal, Spain, Surinam, Sweden, Switzerland, Turkey, the United Kingdom of Great Britain and Northern Ireland, the United States of America and Venezuela, and the Representatives of the Governments of Brazil, the Holy See, Hungary, Monaco, Morocco, the Union of Soviet Socialist Republics and Uruguay participating by invitation or as Observer, convened at The Hague on the 6th October 1980, at the invitation of the Government of the Netherlands, in the Fourteenth Session of the Hague Conference on Private International Law.

Following the deliberations laid down in the records of the meetings, have decided to submit to their Governments —

A   The following draft Conventions—

I

CONVENTION OF THE CIVIL ASPECTS OF INTERNATIONAL CHILD ABDUCTION

The State signatory to the present Convention,

Firmly convinced that the interests of children are of paramount importance in matters relating to their custody,

Desiring to protect children internationally from the harmful effects of their wrongful removal or retention and to establish procedures to ensure their prompt return to the State of their habitual residence, as well as to secure protection for rights of access,

Have resolved to conclude a Convention to this effect, and have agreed upon the following provisions—

CHAPTER 1 - SCOPE OF THE CONVENTION

Article 1

The objects of the present Convention are:

a   to secure the prompt return of children wrongfully removed to or retained in any Contracting State; and

b   to ensure that rights of custody and of access under the law of one Contracting State are effectively respected in the other Contracting States.

Article 2

Contracting States shall take all appropriate measures to secure within their territories the implementation of the objects of the Convention. For this purpose they shall use the most expeditious procedures available.

Article 3

The removal or the retention of a child is to be considered wrongful where:

a it is in breach of rights of custody attributed to a person, an institution or any other body, either jointly or alone, under the law of the State in which the child was habitually resident immediately before the removal or retention; and

b at the time of removal or retention those rights were actually exercised, either jointly or alone, or would have been so exercised but for the removal or retention.

The rights of custody mentioned in sub-paragraph *a* above, may arise in particular by operation of law or by reason of a judicial or administrative decision, or by reason of an agreement having legal effect under the law of that State.

Article 4

The Convention shall apply to any child who was habitually resident in a Contracting State immediately before any breach of custody or access rights. The Convention shall cease to apply when the child attains the age of 16 years.

Article 5

For the purposes of this Convention:

a 'rights of custody' shall include rights relating to the care of the person of the child and, in particular, the right to determine the child's place of residence;

b 'rights of access' shall include the right to take a child for a limited period of time to a place other than the child's habitual residence.

CHAPTER II - CENTRAL AUTHORITIES

Article 6

A Contracting State shall designate a Central Authority to discharge the duties which are imposed by the Convention upon such authorities.

Federal States, States with more than one system of law or States having autonomous territorial organizations shall be free to appoint more than one Central Authority and to specify the territorial extent of their powers. Where a State has appointed more than one Central Authority, it shall designate the Central Authority to which applications may be addressed for transmission to the appropriate Central

Authority within that State.

Article 7

Central Authorities shall co-operate with each other and promote co-operation amongst the competent authorities in their respective States to secure the prompt return of the children and to achieve the other objects of this Convention.

In particular, either directly or through any intermediary, they shall take all appropriate measures-

a to discover the whereabouts of a child who has been wrongfully removed or retained;

b to prevent further harm to the child or prejudice to interested parties by taking or causing to be taken provisional measures;

c to secure the voluntary return of the child or to bring about an amicable resolution of the issues;

d to exchange, where desirable, information relating to the social background of the child;

e to provide information of a general character as to the law of their State in connection with the application of the Convention;

f to initiate or facilitate the institution of judicial or administrative proceedings with a view to obtaining the return of the child and, in proper case, to make arrangements for organizing or securing the effective exercise of rights of access;

g where the circumstances so require, to provide or facilitate the provision of legal aid and advice, including the participation of legal counsel and advisors;

h to provide such administrative arrangements as may be necessary and appropriate to secure the safe return of the child;

i to keep each other informed with respect to the operation of this Convention and, as far as possible, to eliminate any obstacles to its application.

CHAPTER III - RETURN OF CHILDREN

Article 8

Any person, institution or other body claiming that a child has been removed or retained in breach of custody rights may apply either to the Central Authority of the child's habitual residence or to the Central Authority of any other Contracting State for assistance in securing the return of the child.

The application shall contain -

a information concerning the identity of the applicant, of the child and of the person alleged to have removed or retained the child;

b where available, the date of birth of the child;

c   the grounds on which the applicant's claim for return of the child is based;

d   all available information relating to the whereabouts of the child and the identity of the person with whom the child is presumed to be.

The application may be accompanied or supplemented by -

e   an authenticated copy of any relevant decision or agreement;

f   a certificate or an affidavit emanating from a Central Authority, or other competent authority of the State of the child's habitual residence, or from a qualified person, concerning the relevant law of that State;

g   any other relevant document.

Article 9

If the Central Authority which receives an application referred to in Article 8 has reason to believe that the child is in another Contracting State, it shall directly and without delay transmit the application to the Central Authority of that Contracting State and inform the requesting Central Authority, or the applicant, as the case may be.

Article 10

The Central Authority of the State where the child is shall take or cause to be taken all appropriate measures in order to obtain the voluntary return of the child.

Article 11

The judicial or administrative authorities of Contracting States shall act expeditiously in proceedings for the return of children.

If the judicial or administrative authority concerned has not reached a decision within six weeks from the date of commencement of the proceedings, the applicant or the Central Authority of the requested State, on its own initiative or if asked by the Central Authority of the requesting State, shall have the right to request a statement of the reasons for the delay. If a reply is received by the Central Authority of the requested State, that Authority shall transmit the reply to the Central Authority of the requesting State, or to the applicant, as the case may be.

Article 12

Where a child has been wrongfully removed or retained in terms of Article 3 and, at the date of the commencement of the proceedings before the judicial or administrative authority of the Contracting

State where the child is, a period of less than one year has elapsed from the date of the wrongful removal or retention, the authority concerned shall order the return of the child forthwith.

The judicial or administrative authority, even where the proceedings have been commenced after the expiration of the period of one year referred to in the preceding paragraph, shall also order the return of the child, unless it is demonstrated that the child is now settled in its new environment.

Where the judicial or administrative authority in the requested State has reason to believe that the child has been taken to another state, it may stay the proceedings or dismiss the application for the return of the child.

Article 13

Exceptions

Notwithstanding the provisions of the preceding Article, the judicial or administrative authority of the requested State is not bound to order the return of the child if the person, institution or other body which opposes its return establishes that:

a   the person, institution or other body having the care of the person of the child was not actually exercising the custody rights at the time of removal or retention, or had consented to or subsequently acquiesced in the removal or retention; or

b   there is a grave risk that his or her return would expose the child to physical or psychological harm or otherwise place the child in an intolerable situation.

The judicial or administrative authority may also refuse to order the return of the child if it finds that the child objects to being returned and has attained an age and degree of maturity at which it is appropriate to take account of its views.

In considering the circumstances referred to in this Article, the judicial and administrative authorities shall take into account the information relating to the social background of the child provided by the Central Authority or other competent authority of the child's habitual residence.

Article 14

In ascertaining whether there has been a wrongful removal or retention within the meaning of Article 3, the judicial or administrative authorities of the requested State may take notice directly of the law of, and of judicial or administrative decisions, formally recognized or not in the State of the habitual residence of the child without recourse to the specific procedures for the proof of that law or for the recognition of foreign decisions which would otherwise be applicable.

Article 15

The judicial or administrative authorities of a Contracting State may, prior to the making of an order for the return of the child, request that the applicant obtain from the authorities of the State of the habitual residence of the child a decision or other determination that the removal or retention was wrongful within the meaning of Article 3 of the Convention, where such a decision or determination may be obtained in that State. The Central Authorities of the Contracting States shall so far as practicable assist applicants to obtain such a decision or determination.

Article 16

After receiving notice of a wrongful removal or retention of a child in the sense of Article 3, the judicial or administrative authorities of the Contracting State to which the child has been removed or in which it has been retained shall not decide on the merits of rights of custody until it has been determined that the child is not to be returned under this Convention or unless an application under this Convention is not lodged within a reasonable time following receipt of the notice.

Article 17

The sole fact that a decision relating to custody has been given in or is entitled to recognition in the requested State shall not be a ground for refusing to return a child under this Convention, but the judicial or administrative authorities of the requested State may take into account of the reasons for that decision in applying this Convention.

Article 18

The provisions of this Chapter do not limit the power of a judicial or administrative authority to order the return of the child at any time.

Article 19

A decision under this Convention concerning the return of the child shall not be taken to be a determination on the merits of any custody issue.

Article 20

Exception

The return of the child under the provisions of Article 12 may be refused if this would not be permitted by the fundamental principles of the requested State relating to the protection of human rights and fundamental freedoms.

CHAPTER IV - RIGHTS OF ACCESS

Article 21

An application to make arrangements for organizing or securing the effective exercise of rights of access may be presented to the Central Authorities of the Contracting States in the same way as an application for the return of a child.

The Central Authorities are bound by the obligations of co-operation which are set forth in Article 7 to promote the peaceful enjoyment of access rights and the fulfillment of any conditions to which the exercise of those rights may be subject. The Central Authorities shall take steps to remove, as far as possible, all obstacles to the exercise of such rights.

The Central Authorities, either directly or through intermediaries, may initiate or assist in the institution of proceedings with a view to organizing or protecting these rights and securing respect for the conditions to which the exercise of these rights may be subject.

CHAPTER V - GENERAL PROVISION

Article 22

No security, bond or deposit, however described, shall be required to guarantee the payment of costs and expenses in the judicial or administrative proceedings falling within the scope of this Convention.

Article 23

No legalization or similar formality may be required in the context of this Convention.

Article 24

Any application, communication or other document sent to the Central Authority of the requested State shall be in the original language, and shall be accompanied by a translation into the official language or one of the official languages of the requested State or, where that is not feasible, a translation into French or English.

However, a Contracting State may, by making a reservation in accordance with Article 42, object to the use of either French or English, but not both, in any application, communication or other document sent to its Central Authority.

Article 25

Nationals of the Contracting States and persons who are habitually resident within those States shall be entitled in matters concerned with the application of this Convention to legal aid and advice in any other Contracting State on the same conditions as if they themselves were nationals of and habitually resident in that State.

Article 26

Each Central Authority shall bear its own costs in applying this Convention. Central Authorities and other public services of Contracting States shall not impose any changes in relation to applications submitted under this Convention. In particular, they may not require any payment from the applicant towards the costs and expenses of the proceedings or, where applicable, those arising from the participating of legal counsel or advisers. However, they may require the payment of the expenses incurred or to be incurred in implementing the return of the child.

However, a Contracting State may, by making a reservation in accordance with Article 42, declare that it shall not be bound to assume any costs referred to in the preceding paragraph resulting from the participation of legal counsel or advisors or from court proceedings, except insofar as those costs may be covered by its system of legal aid and advice.

Upon ordering the return of a child or issuing an order concerning rights of access under this Convention, the judicial or administrative authorities may, where appropriate, direct the person who removed or retained the child, or who prevented the exercise of rights of access, to pay necessary expenses incurred by or on behalf of the applicant, including travel expenses, any costs incurred or payments made for locating the child, the costs of legal representation of the applicant, and those of returning the child.

Article 27

When it is manifest that the requirements of this Convention are not fulfilled or that the application is otherwise not well founded, a Central Authority is not bound to accept the application. In that case, the Central Authority shall forthwith inform the applicant or the Central Authority through which the application was submitted, as the case may be, of its reasons.

Article 28

A Central Authority may require the application be accompanied by a written authorization empowering it to act on behalf of the applicant, or to designate a representative so to act.

Article 29

The Convention shall not preclude any person, institution or body who claims that there has been a breach of custody or access rights within the meaning of Article 3 or 21 from applying directly to the judicial or administrative authorities of a Contracting State, whether or not under the provisions of this Convention.

Article 30

Any application submitted to the Central Authorities or directly to the judicial or administrative authorities of a Contracting State in accordance with the terms of this Convention, together with documents and any other information appended thereto provided by a Central Authority, shall be admissible in the courts or administrative authorities of the Contracting States.

Article 31

In relation to a State which in matters of custody of children has two or more systems of law applicable in different territorial units-
a any reference to habitual residence in that State shall be construed as referring to habitual residence in a territorial unit of that State;
b any reference to the law of the State of habitual residence shall be construed as referring to the law of the territorial unit in that State where the child habitually resides.

173

Article 32

In relation to a State which in matters of custody of children has two or more systems of law applicable to different categories of persons, any reference to the law of that State shall be construed as referring to the legal system specified by the law of that State.

Article 33

A State within which different territorial units have their own rules of law in respect of custody of children shall not be bound to apply this convention where a State with a unified system of law would not be bound to do so.

Article 34

This Convention shall take priority in matters within its scope over the *Convention of 5 October 1961 concerning the powers of authorities and the law applicable in respect of the protection of minors,* as between Parties to both Conventions. Otherwise the present Convention shall not restrict the application of an international instrument in force between the State of origin and the State addressed or other law of the State addressed for the purposes of obtaining the return of a child who has been wrongfully removed or retained or of organizing access rights.

Article 35

This Convention shall apply as between Contracting States only to wrongful removals or retentions occurring after its entry into force in those States.

Where a declaration has been made under Article 39 or 40 the reference in the preceding paragraph to a Contracting State shall be taken to refer to the territorial unit or units in relation to which this Convention applies.

Article 36

Limit Exception

Nothing in this Convention shall prevent two or more Contracting States, in order to limit the restrictions to which the return of the child may be subject, from agreeing among themselves to derogate from any provisions of this Convention which may imply such a restriction.

CHAPTER VI - FINAL CLAUSES

Article 37

The Convention shall be open for signature by the States which were Members of the Hague Conference on Private International Law at the time of its Fourteenth Session. It shall be ratified, accepted or approved and the instruments of ratification, acceptance or approval shall be deposited with the Ministry of Foreign Affairs of the Kingdom of the Netherlands.

Article 38

Any other State may accede to the Convention.
The instrument of accession shall be deposited with the Ministry of Foreign Affairs of the Kingdom of the Netherlands.
The Convention shall enter into force for a State acceding to it on the first day of the third calendar month after the deposit of its instrument of accession.
The accession will have effect only as regards the relations between the acceding State and such Contracting States as will have declared their acceptance of the accession. Such a declaration will also have to be made by any Member State ratifying, accepting or approving the Convention after an accession. Such declaration shall be deposited at the Ministry of Foreign Affairs of the Kingdom of the Netherlands; this Ministry shall forward through diplomatic channels, a certified copy to each of the Contracting States.
The Convention will enter into force as between the acceding State and the State that has declared its acceptance of the accession on the first day of the third calendar month after the deposit of the declaration of acceptance.

Article 39

Any State may, at the time of signature, ratification, acceptance, approval or accession, declare that the Convention shall extend to all the territories for the international relations of which it is responsible, or to one or more of them. Such a declaration shall take effect at the time the Convention enters into force for that State.
Such declaration, as well as any subsequent extension, shall be notified to the Ministry of Foreign Affairs of the Kingdom of the Netherlands.

Article 40

If a Contracting State has two or more territorial units in which different systems of law are applicable in relation to matters dealt with in this Convention, it may at the time of signature, ratification, acceptance, approval or accession declare that this convention shall extend to all its territorial units or only to one or more of them and may modify this declaration by submitting another declaration at any time. Any such declaration shall be notified to the Ministry of Foreign Affairs of the Kingdom of the Netherlands and shall state expressly the territorial units to which the Convention applies.

Article 41

Where a Contracting State has a system of government under which executive, judicial and legislative powers are distributed between central and other authorities within that State, its signature or ratification, acceptance or approval of, or accession to this Convention, or its making of any declaration in terms of Article 40 shall carry no implication as to the internal distribution of powers within that State.

Article 42

Any State may, not later than the time of ratification, acceptance, approval or accession, or at the time of making a declaration in terms of Article 39 or 40, make one or both of the reservations provided for in Article 24 and Article 26, third paragraph. No other reservation shall be permitted.
Any State may at any time withdraw a reservation it has made. The withdrawal shall be notified to the Ministry of Foreign Affairs of the Kingdom of the Netherlands.
The reservation shall cease to have effect on the first day of the third calendar month after the notification referred to in the preceding paragraph.

Article 43

The Convention shall enter into force on the first day of the third calendar month after the deposit of the third instrument of ratification, acceptance, approval or accession referred to in Articles 37 and 38.

Thereafter the Convention shall enter into force-

1   for each State ratifying, accepting, approving or acceding to it subsequently, on the first day of the third calendar month after the deposit of its instrument of ratification, acceptance, approval or accession;

2   for any territory or territorial unit to which the Convention has been extended in conformity with Article 39 or 40, on the first day of the third calendar month after the notification referred to in that Article.

Article 44

The Convention shall remain in force for five years from the date of its entry into force in accordance with the first paragraph of Article 43 even for States which subsequently have ratified, accepted, approved it or acceded to it.
If there has been no denunciation, it shall be renewed tacitly every five years.
Any denunciation shall be notified to the Ministry of Foreign Affairs of the Kingdom of the Netherlands at least six months before the expiry of the five year period. It may be limited to certain of the territories or territorial units to which the Convention applies.
The denunciation shall have effect only as regards the State which has notified it. The Convention shall remain in force for the other Contracting States.

Article 45

The Ministry of Foreign Affairs of the Kingdom of the Netherlands shall notify the State Members of the Conference, and the States which have acceded in accordance with Article 38, of the following-

1   the signatures and ratifications, acceptances and approvals referred to in Article 37;

2   the accessions referred to in Article 38;

3   the date on which the Convention enters into force in accordance with Article 43;

4   the extensions referred to in Article 39;

5   the declarations referred to in Articles 38 and 40;

6   the reservations referred to in Article 24 and Article 26, third paragraph, and the withdrawals referred to in Article 42;

7   the denunciations referred to in Article 44.

In witness whereof the undersigned, being duly authorized thereto, have signed this Convention.

Done at The Hague, on the 6th day of October, 1980 in the English and French languages, both texts being equally authentic, in a single-copy which shall be deposited in the archives of the Government of the Kingdom of the Netherlands, and of which a certified copy shall be sent, through diplomatic channels, to each of the States Members of the Hague Conference on Private International Law at the date of its Fourteenth Session.

NOTE: To-date only seven countries have signed this document of Private International Law. The Member States of the conference that have acted on Child Abduction by signature or ratification are: Belgium, Canada, France, Greece, Portugal, Switzerland and the United States. Three countries must agree before it becomes effective. Though completing the following form may not get you immediate action, it will tell those Member States (or countries) that you, as an individual, have faith in this approach to Private International Law. If enough people register parentally kidnapped or missing children, perhaps this will become a factor in acquiring the support so desperately needed from the new international legal community.

The following Recommendation concerning the draft Convention on the civil aspects of international child abduction:

The Fourteenth Session.

Recommends to the States Parties to the *Convention on the Civil Aspects of International Child Abduction* that the following model form be used in making application for the return of wrongfully removed children:

Request for Return

Hague Convention of _____ on the Civil aspects of International Child Abduction

REQUESTING CENTRAL AUTHORITY OR APPLICANT	REQUESTED AUTHORITY

Concerns the following child: _____ who will attain the age of 16 on _____ 19 ____.

NOTE: The following particulars should be completed insofar as possible:

I IDENTITY OF THE CHILD AND ITS PARENTS

1   *Child*

name and first names   _____
date and place of birth   _____
habitual residence before removal
or retention   _____
passport or identity card No. if any   _____
description and photo, if possible   _____

2   *Parents*

2.1   Mother: name and first names   _____
       date and place of birth   _____
       nationality   _____
       occupation   _____
       habitual residence   _____
       passport or identity card No. if any   _____

2.2   Father: name and first names   _____
       date and place of birth   _____
       nationality   _____
       occupation   _____
       habitual residence   _____
       passport or identity card No. if any   _____

2.3   Date and place of marriage   _____

II REQUESTING INDIVIDUAL OR INSTITUTION (who actually exercised custody before the removal or retention)

3   name and first names   _____
          nationality of individual applicant   _____
          occupation of individual applicant   _____
          address   _____
          passport or identity card No. if any   _____
          relation to child   _____
          name and address of legal adviser, if any   _____

III PLACE WHERE THE CHILD IS THOUGHT TO BE

4.1   Information concerning the person alleged to have removed or
       retained the child

          name and first names   _____
          date and place of birth, if known   _____
          nationality, if known   _____
          occupation   _____
          last known address   _____
          passport or identity card No. if any   _____
          description and photo, if possible   _____

4.2   address of the child   _____

_____

_____

4.3   Other persons who might be able to supply
additional information relating to the   _____
whereabouts of the child   _____

_____

_____

IV - TIME, PLACE, DATE AND CIRCUMSTANCES OF THE WRONGFUL REMOVAL RETENTION

_____

_____

_____

_____

_____

V - FACTUAL OR LEGAL GROUNDS JUSTIFYING THE REQUEST

_____

_____

_____

_____

_____

VI - CIVIL PROCEEDING PROGRESS

_____

_____

_____

_____

_____

VII - CHILD IS TO BE RETURNED TO:

a   name and first names   _____
date and place of birth   _____
address   _____
telephone number   _____

b   proposed arrangements for return of child   _____

_____

_____

VIII - OTHER REMARKS

_____
_____
_____
_____
_____

IX - LIST OF DOCUMENTS ATTACHED

_____
_____
_____
_____
_____

Date _____
Place _____

Signature and/or stamp of the requesting Central Authority or applicant.

_____

SEND COMPLETED FORM TO:

The Central Authority
International Child Abduction Authority
THE HAGUE
Kingdom of the Netherlands

SECTION XII

BONUS BOOK — *"CHILD-SNATCHED"*

THE DANNY STRICKLAND CASE

CHILD-SNATCHED

BY
MARGARET STRICKLAND

CHILD-SNATCHED
By Margaret Strickland

Published by
RAINBOW BOOKS
P.O. Box 1069
Moore Haven, FL 33471

This story will be shocking to some, disturbing to others, and unbelievable to practically everybody. I know. Because I lived through twenty-two months of incredible apprehension, when my four-year-old son, Danny, was abducted from my custody by my ex-wife, Joan O'Brien Strickland Ng Fremo.

Danny's case is not a rarity. Statistics tell us some 25,000 to 150,000 child-snatchings occur each year. Those who observe court orders and follow the letter of the law risk being losers, and all too often child-snatching leads to death and tragedy. Only then, except in rare cases like mine, does it lead to nation wide newspaper headlines. But my family and I fought a long, hard, rough, rocky road for Danny, out of love, and at tremendous expense. Not only emotionally and mentally, but financially. Without the help of my wife, Sue, and my mother and father, Margaret and Dewey Strickland, none of it would have been possible.

Each of them sacrificed money and time, and suffered the anguish and despair, right along with me. Together we decided our story should be told. We feel it needs telling. And so, my mother Margaret Strickland, has put together the narrative that follows: *CHILD-SNATCHED*. This is a classic case of child-snatching, steeped in pettiness, frustration, at times bordering on the ridiculous, but always fraught with pain and danger. Every word is based on documented fact, courtroom records, and depositions, piles of legal paperwork weighing a total of 30 pounds and costing, to date, $25,000.

Our family feels this is a small price to pay for the life of my son, Danny Strickland, an innocent child caught in the web of legal jargon, without rules or regulations to protect his rights.

David Strickland
Merritt Island, Florida

1971

Joan wore a white street-length dress with a white veil and orchid corsage. David was attired in his father's best dark suit. They were a striking couple; David, a tall, strapping, dark-eyed, dark-haired young man in his second year as an art student at Florida's Brevard

Community College, and Joan, the proverbial girl next door, exceptionally pretty, exceptionally intelligent.

As I watched our son, David Strickland, and Joan O'Brien marry in the Cocoa Beach, Florida Catholic Church on April 24, 1971, I prayed not a little, but a lot. The kids were going to need great good fortune to see them through the future.

Joan was a high school drop-out. David had worked summers only for pocket money. But Joan was pregnant, and there was no turning back.

In retrospect, I suppose I was more numb than anything else as the wedding progressed into a champagne and cake reception in the company of a hundred relatives and close friends. There had been so many days when I was afraid to leave the house, afraid to leave David and Joan alone together. A blind person could have seen what was happening between them. It was that obvious.

My husband, Dewey, and I worried about it often. What to do? Well, I'd just have to hang around the old homestead as much as possible, keep an eye on the situation and hope for the best. But we could not stop it, and we knew it.

Joan would decide that she did not feel well enough to attend school on the days when David didn't have college classes. She suffered knee pains, sometimes necessitating the use of a wheel chair. But as David was free to swim, hunt and fish, Joan's pain lasted only long enough to keep her from school for the day and spend it with David. They were inseparable, together every waking hour.

Dewey and I faced the fact that Joan, petite, hazel-eyed, with dark silken hair, could charm the wings off a butterfly. David was only human. He could not resist her enticing ways any more than anyone else could.

Joan's father, Dan O'Brien, a small, quiet, retiring man, was away from home for weeks at a time in winter. He was a sound technician for The Jackie Gleason Show, Disney World and later Circus World through Vision Enterprises, Orlando, Florida. In summers, the family closed their Florida home and moved north to Long Island, New York, where Dan worked at Guy Lombardo's Jones Beach Theatre. So the raising of Joan fell mostly to Joan's mother, Eileen.

Eileen was talkative, attractive, stylish. We visited back and forth. Eileen tried to keep Joan in school. She tried hard. But Joan outwitted her mother consistently. If Joan did condescend to go to school, she lasted only an hour or so; then, Joan would phone her mother or David, claim she was too ill to continue, and ask one or the other to pick her up.

In conversations with Eileen and Joan, I learned that prior to moving to Merritt Island from Miami, Joan had run away from home twice. On one occasion, Joan had spent time in Miami Youth Hall. I could not understand Joan's need to run. She had a good home and respectable parents. But, there it was. Joan was talking again about running.

As Christmas 1970 came and went, Joan became more verbal on the subject. "I don't want to go to New York this summer." That was the gist of it; and if Joan had her way, she would not go to New York.

It was the last of March, 1971, when Joan telephoned our house and asked me to come to the O'Brien home. I was preparing the evening meal -- it was late afternoon -- but I put everything aside and went next door. Joan and Eileen were sitting at the dining room table having coffee. I joined them. The conversation idled along in no particular direction. I was puzzled, until Joan spoke up and said, "I'm pregnant;" just like that. No preliminary remarks, no building up to it; mainly, just getting it over and done.

I was not surprised, not really. But still, I wasn't prepared for it. I suppose nobody ever is. We held a family conference immediately. The kids wanted to be married as soon as possible. They were in love. We would all make the best of it; and, of course, the issue of whether Joan would move to New York during the coming summer was settled too.

Shortly after the wedding, the O'Briens packed up and went to New York. David and Joan occupied the O'Brien's home. David found a job working in a lumberyard. It wasn't much. But we helped out with extra money to keep them going.

They were happy. Joan's pregnancy seemed to be progressing normally. We were pleased the situation was falling into the realm of normal. Then, one day I looked out the window and saw Joan, dressed in a shirt and jeans, practically on her hands and knees, coming up the driveway, as if she was suffering immense pain. I rushed out to help her.

"What's wrong?" I demanded.

Joan gasped, "I'm afraid I'm going to lose the baby. I've been bleeding all night."

I ran inside the house, dropped my dish towel and telephoned Doctor Marling Abel, Joan's physician. Doctor Abel said, "Bring Joan in at once."

As we drove toward the doctor's office, I said, "Will it bother you if I go into the examining room, Joan? Should you miscarry, I'll need to know what the doctor says, so I can call your parents in New York."

"No," Joan managed. "Please do."

When we arrived at Doctor Abel's office, Joan and I were ushered into an examining room immediately. The competent Doctor Abel proceeded with a thorough examination. He said, "Mrs. Strickland, when were you bleeding?"

"All night," Joan said matter-of-factly.

"You're clean as can be," Doctor Abel said. "Everything is fine."

I am confident Joan believed what she told the doctor. I do not think she would have encouraged me to enter the examining room if she had not believed herself.

As we had come to know Joan intimately, we had realized she had difficulty discerning fact from fiction. When a fiction was told, it became fact quickly, and Joan could justify or dismiss it easily. This remarkable ability to manipulate the truth did not desert Joan as we drove homeward. She did not discuss what had happened in the doctor's office. It was as if nothing were amiss, nothing had gone awry to ruin the day. I tried to take the long view. Joan made it easy for me.

She said, "I'd like a vanilla ice cream cone."

We stopped at an ice cream store, Joan donned her dark glasses, and like the child she was, enjoyed her ice cream cone, the unsettling episode behind us. So simple.

In the fall, the O'Briens returned from New York. The kids needed a place to live. Dewey and I rented Joan and David a neat little three-room house on Merritt Island and agreed to pay the rent and bills, while David returned to school. David had decided that he must acquire a skill that would provide for his family as quickly as possible. He entered State Police School in October.

Danny was born November 23, 1971. He was a beautiful, healthy baby with brown eyes and a thatch of black hair. We loved him on sight. With everything settled and going well -- our daughter, Kathy, was on her own, a key punch operator in Texas, and our other son, Tom, was in high school and doing fine -- Dewey and I felt a sense of freedom we had not experienced in years. Dewey took a week's vacation from his position as an electrical engineer for Martin-Marietta at Kennedy Space Center. We headed for the Florida Keys. After the strain of these last months, we enjoyed ourselves beyond reason.

Upon our return, we discovered David had acquired a full-time job as a temporary guard at Kennedy Space Center, which he worked after completing Police School. When this job ended, he drove a tour bus. David was trying hard to assume the responsibilities of his family. He did not dwell on the past or his desires to follow a career in art. He had a firm grip on today and the future. We were proud of him.

After Christmas, Joan decided she was going back to school. She asked me, "Will you keep Danny?"

Since Dewey and I believe high school is an absolute basic minimum requirement for life, we accepted the responsibility of assisting in the care of Danny gladly, and Joan went off to school.

David and Joan's life together appeared to be progressing nicely. Never did we anticipate what was to be.

1972

Joan graduated from high school on July 28th. She had done exceptionally well, making straight A's throughout with seemingly little effort. We celebrated at our house with pizza. Joan called her parents long distance in New York and shared this glad evening with them.

Meanwhile, David had acquired a full-time job with Brevard Ambulance. He began work in September. Here he discovered a job he truly enjoyed. He enrolled at Brevard Community College in the emergency medical technician program. His schedule was full. He worked 24 hours on and 24 hours off. Those nights he did not work, he went to school. Somehow, in between, he put in his hours of hospital training.

We had no hint trouble was brewing. Far from it. But trouble was waiting in the wings.

Now Joan asked me, "Will you keep Danny, while I go to college?"

"I'll think about it," I told her.

Dewey and I discussed the matter. We decided it was time the kids learned to stand alone. We had managed to educate ourselves through hard word and some sacrifice. We believed they deserved the same privilege of responsibility and opportunity.

I told Joan, "I'm sorry, but I can't do it. Dewey and I think you and David must depend on one another. If you want to go to college, you and David should work out a schedule, so that one or the other is with Danny."

Joan didn't like it. She said as much, and it was as if the scales had been tipped in the wrong direction. Joan became increasingly restless. We tried to discount a series of well-meaning telephone calls, telling us that Joan had a boy friend, Leonard Savary -- he was married and his wife was pregnant -- who worked with David at Brevard Ambulance. We should have listened more carefully, more closely.

Joan appeared at Brevard Ambulance, while David was at work. She told David she had hired an attorney and had filed for divorce. "When you get off work tomorrow morning," she concluded, "come and get your clothes. They'll be in the yard."

Baffled, angry and heartsick, David picked up his clothes and moved home. He didn't know what else to do. There was no reasoning, no talking with Joan. And, she would not allow him to see Danny.

Now David began to get desperate. A couple of weeks passed. Joan arrived at Brevard Ambulance and told David, "If you'll sign papers giving Danny to me, I'll let you see him."

David agreed. He wanted to be with his son as much as possible. But David wasn't satisfied, mainly because he worried about the care Joan was giving Danny.

Dewey's brother, Shelton Strickland, went to Joan's home to pick up a fan he had loaned her. Shelton found a teenage girl baby-sitting Danny. The baby-sitter carried a shotgun. Why? To shoot David, if David should come to the house. This was our first inkling that the future might hold real problems. But many more such stories were to reach David's ears.

David's friend, Jerry Brown, reported to David that Joan was spending her nights in bars. Leonard Savary's pregnant wife, Susan, said that she had seen Danny alone in a parked car at 2:00 a.m. at the Savary home, while Joan was inside with Leonard. If that wasn't enough, David and his friend, Frank Demsky, stopped by Joan's house after class one night to visit with Danny, and the baby-sitter, David's fellow employee at Brevard Ambulance, Dick Reardon, was so drunk he could not get up to open the front door for them. David was growing more and more disillusioned, but he tried to keep a level head. He didn't want to lose the privilege of seeing his son.

In late October, Joan telephoned David. "Come over and meet Danny's new daddy, Billy Corbett," she taunted.

"What?" David demanded.

"That's right. We're going to get married and go to New York."

David didn't know what to think about Danny now. Someone gave him something to think about. He received an anonymous phone call, informing him that Joan and Billy Corbett planned to mutilate themselves physically and say David had beaten them up.

David was furious. He hopped into his car and tore out for Joan's house. I didn't know what might happen. Frantic, I telephoned my friend, Virginia Johns -- she lived across the street from Joan -- and said, "Get over to Joan's and do something. David's on his way. He's so mad, well, try to do something!"

Virginia got there ahead of David, intercepted him. She persuaded David to come home and calm down, which wasn't easy. David was feeling cornered. He told Dewey and me, "I've got to get Danny away from Joan. He doesn't stand a chance!"

David began to concentrate on one thing and one thing only: freeing Danny from the irresponsible environment in which it was evident Danny lived. Finally, David did something about it.

He picked up his friend, Danny Hutchinson, and drove over to Joan's house. He brought Danny home with him. When Joan came for Danny, David said, "No. You're not taking care of him."

Joan telephoned her attorney. The gist of it: "I want my child back!"

The result was a temporary custody hearing before Judge Volie Williams in Titusville, Brevard County, Florida in November.

After hearing testimony from Joan, David, Eileen O'Brien, Leonard Savary, Leonard Savary's wife, Susan, and me, Judge Williams awarded temporary custody to me, while a complete background check was made on David and Joan by the Brevard County Health Department.

We went shopping for baby clothes, a play pen and crib for Danny. David was a real help. Dewey and our son, Tom, were stable standbys. It had been a long while since I'd cared for a small child full time, but the knack of it returned quickly. The family took delight in Danny and his laughter. Joan went her irresponsible, irrational and merry way, as if she had the situation well in hand.

She cashed a check for $100 at The Island Bar on Merritt Island. The check had David's signature on it, but he had not signed the check. The bank refused payment. At work, he received a threatening phone call: "If you don't make good on that check, we're going to beat you up." The caller did not identify himself.

Throughout this period, too often David arrived home from work sad-faced and weary-eyed. His troubles multiplied in all directions. His car was being vandalized on a regular and relentless schedule, as if it might be intentional.

By now, David, Dewey and I sensed this was only the beginning. We could not have been more correct.

Our wonderful neighbor, next door to the south of us, Marion Chambers, called us at a dinner party and said breathlessly, "You'd better come home fast."

Since Marion is not given to the superfluous, Dewey and Kenny Coan, our host, jumped into a car and drove to our house. There was Joan and Eileen along with an automobile mechanic. David's car had been pushed into the street, and the mechanic was trying to get it started.

The car was registered in David's and Dewey's names. David owed more on the car than it was worth. Dewey was not about to let them take the car and have David continue to make payments. Dewey spelled out the not-so-pleasant facts of life to Joan and Eileen.

Eileen said, "If we can't take the car, I'm going to wreck it," whereupon she jumped into her car, started it, pressed the gas pedal to the floor and roared toward the offensive automobile, as if she meant what she said.

At the last minute, though, Eileen decided on the better part of valor and missed. After many more words that do not bear repeating, Joan and her mother departed. Dewey and Kenny returned to the dinner party, and all the neighborhood children, who had viewed the scene with enthusiasm, went home.

Now we enjoyed a few days of peace and quiet, and prayed the worst was behind us. No such luck.

The telephone rang on December 9th. It was the Brevard County Sheriff's Department, reporting to David that his wife, Joan, had been picked up for shoplifting. David followed through on the hearing out of courtesy to Danny. Policewoman Drucella Roberts testified that Joan had narcotics in her purse when she was arrested on the shoplifting charge. Joan was found guilty and placed on one year's self-probation.

None of these events inspired confidence in the future. Was there no end to it? Evidently not. We began to cringe everytime the telephone rang, as it did again on December 16th.

Olive Powers, Joan's landlady, was calling. She said, "Joan tried to commit suicide. She tore the phone out of her wall. The police have her outside right now, trying to make her vomit."

"I'm sorry," I said, and I meant it, "but I don't dare come and help. As it is, Joan accuses David, Dewey and me of continually being on her street to check on her. I don't want any more trouble than we have."

Then, came the night of December 20th. Very late our doorbell rang. Dewey and I were in bed. David answered the door.

A man's elevated voice began to raise hell with David. I slipped from bed and made my way into the living room. There was the short, muscular billiard player, Billy Corbett, Joan's boy friend.

It seemed Joan was visiting someone down the street. She had sent Billy along to tell David to stay away from her or he, Billy Corbett, would kill David. I didn't get it, since David had reconciled himself to Joan's behavior; he was interested only in preserving a decent home for Danny. I didn't have long to ponder the matter though. The telephone rang. It was Joan. She wanted David.

David took the phone in hand.

Joan said sweetly, "I'm at the Dobb's House. Please come and meet me."

David declined, since Billy Corbett had promised to do him in if David so much as laid eyes on Joan!

We began to suspect that all those who were not already crazy would become insane. Meanwhile, we were very anxious about Danny. Joan had visitation rights two week-ends a month. When she came to take Danny away, we worried throughout his absence. It was beyond us to imagine what Joan might do to herself or to Danny. Or, perhaps, it was beginning to dawn on us precisely how many problems we faced, and we were afraid to imagine.

1973

Our New Year's resolution: we will maintain control of ourselves and our destiny, and try to get through this mess with Joan without further turmoil.

I don't know what made us think we could do it, but we were not so wise then, so we gave it the old college try.

On January 12th, Joan came to get Danny for his week-end visit with her. She told me that the judge had dismissed her hearing on the shoplifting charge. I knew this to be untrue. She knew I knew it was untrue, but she said it anyway. She also stated that a court date had been set on the December hit and run charge. The hit and run charge was news to me. Later we learned the court found Joan guilty and fined her $100 on each count. Now Joan moved on to complain incoherently about us having the electricity in her house cut off.

So there would be no misunderstanding, I explained, "We paid the deposit and can no longer be responsible for your electric bills, since Billy Corbett testified in court that he is living at your address and is assuming responsibility for your welfare."

Joan took Danny and departed in a huff.

Then, Joan moved to the Kissimmee, Florida, area where Dan and Eileen were now living. In fact, she took up residence with the O'Brien's. This seemed to help. Matters improved, except for minor irritations.

On the 11th of February, when Joan brought Danny home after his week-end visit with her, she failed to return his clothing. Never mind. After the next visit on February 24th, Eileen delivered Danny and took after me personally, hammer and claw, about Dewey. Condensed, and with a bunch of bad words removed, it boiled down to this: Dewey was common and conscious only of his sex, and that's putting it lightly.

March rolled around. Joan and David's former landlady and neighbor, Olive Powers, phoned and asked me to visit her. Virginia Johns accompanied me to Mrs. Powers' home. Mrs. Powers had much to say.

An elderly lady, kind and thoughtful, Mrs. Powers had made up her mind to share her feelings about Joan, because of Danny. She hoped we were as concerned about Danny as she was. I reassured her.

Mrs. Powers said she had liked Joan tremendously. But, Joan had been a very big disappointment to her. Now with Danny in mind, she went over the subject of Joan's attempted suicide, about which she had called me. She said Joan had written a suicide note. Billy Corbett had found Joan -- and that's all that saved Joan. Further, Mrs. Powers remembered the day that Billy and Joan had replaced a headlamp on Joan's car, apparently evidence of the hit and run charge. Mrs. Powers said, "I don't like repeating these things, but I feel you should know about them in detail since a baby is at stake."

I thanked her and went home to the telephone. I reported the conversation to Family Services' Mary Rodon, our caseworker. Mrs. Rodon confirmed the conversation with Mrs. Powers herself. A few weeks later, Mrs. Powers phoned again and asked to see me on the same subject. Once more, Virginia Johns and I visited Mrs. Powers.

Mrs. Powers told us Eileen O'Brien and Joan had come to her home and forced her to go to Family Services with them and say, "I lied." Mrs. Powers was very apologetic, but she admitted frankly, "I'm afraid of them."

I said, "It's all right. Don't worry. I understand," and I did.

When Joan came for Danny next, she raised a fearful fuss over the tennis shoes Danny wore. She did not approve of tennis shoes. When Danny returned home, he was wearing no shoes.

Mrs. Rodon of Family Services arrived in April to check on Danny's home environment. She was most complimentary. We had a pleasant visit. Our spirits rose.

Then, after Danny's May visit with Joan, Danny returned with a severe bite on his arm. David drove Danny to Wuesthoff Hospital emergency room in Rockledge, Florida. It was a human bite and required several days' treatment. We wondered who could have been so cruel as to bite a small child.

I was not so apprehensive about Mrs. Rodon's second home visit. We got on famously, she liked children and enjoyed Danny. We took heart.

In July, our daughter, Kathy, came for a few days on her vacation. Kathy developed scarlet fever and was hospitalized. The entire family had to take preventive medicine, including Danny. Joan became very agitated about the medicine. I handed the bottle of medicine to her and said, "Danny must take the medication, Joan."

Back in Kissimmee, Joan wrote a letter to David, saying she was not going to bring Danny home again. Then, she telephoned and said to ignore the letter. She brought Danny home as scheduled, again without shoes.

In August, Joan and David gave depositions to the Brevard Circuit Court in connection with Danny's custody. The time passed quietly and again our spirits soared, but not for long.

September came. Eileen O'Brien warned me, "Tell Kathy to keep her filthy hands off Danny. Tell her to have a child of her own."

Beyond belief ... After Kathy's recovery from scarlet fever, she had gone back to her job. She was not living in Florida when Danny was born and she had not lived in Florida since Danny's birth. I shook my head to clear the cobwebs.

October proved to be a mild and pretty month. But, November lay in wait for us.

The custody hearing was set for November at the Rockledge Branch County Court House in Rockledge, Florida. Prior to this event, Joan asked Veronica Kuhne, who was renting the O'Brien house next door, to write a derogatory letter about David to the court. Eileen O'Brien asked Kathy to testify against her brother David. Dan O'Brien asked Eileen O'Brien to "Please shut up," which cheered us greatly. All requests were refused, except for Veronica Kuhne: she wrote a letter to the court, but it explained in detail Joan's request. If this is beginning to sound like a soap opera, take heart. It gets worse. Now for the hearing.

Judge Joe Cowart heard the testimony and reviewed the background information. He awarded David permanent custody of Danny, but Joan was allowed to have Danny one week out of every month. After visitation with Joan, Eileen brought Danny home and wanted to talk to David. I said, "David's not here."

Said Eileen, "I'd call back, but I know you don't allow David to use the phone."

Eileen was sinking fast; that's about all I could conclude, since David was a big boy and used the phone when he liked.

We looked to the New Year with a kind of wistful longing. But we weren't out of 1973.

After Christmas, Eileen and Dan came to get Danny for his visit with Joan. When Danny returned home, someone had given him a wild, choppy hair cut. It was months before his hair grew back to any semblance of reality.

Well, it was over. We celebrated the end of the year. It could have been better. But we had kept our equilibrium and our sense of humor, and a stable home base and environment for Danny.

We prayed for God's guidance and assistance in the difficult task ahead of us. We were walking a tightrope and we knew it.

1974

During the first two months of 1974, relative silence descended upon us. We thought we had died and gone to Heaven. But in March, Joan telephoned and said, "I can't come for Danny."

I didn't give it much thought. Danny was fine. Doing well. Really happy. Growing and laughing. A normal little boy.

Three days later, though, Joan called again and asked for Danny's immunization chart.

David was becoming accustomed to Joan's sudden whims. He replied quietly, "I'll get you a copy at once."

Now Joan said, "I'd like you to sign a statement and have it notarized, saying that Danny can be with me for more than a week."

David refused. The judge made the decision and it was not for David to change it.

David asked me to see that Joan received a copy of Danny's immunization chart. I got on it right away. We tried to comply with every reasonable request Joan made, no matter how small.

Again quiet. But we were learning to distrust these brief interludes.

In early April, Eileen was on our doorstep, abusing me personally and saying that our son, Tom, scared her. True, Tom is a tall, husky boy, but he's as gentle as a lamb. I didn't get it and said as much.

Well, it all went back to the March visit, when Eileen had called for Danny. On this occasion, Eileen had done her verbal worst on me -- which was the rule of thumb. Tom had come to the door, when he overheard Eileen's ravings, and said firmly, "Please quit giving Mom a hard time and go home."

David and I had grown so accustomed to receiving the brunt of these verbal outbursts -- and that's in the best sense of the word -- it all rolled off our backs like water from a duck in a rainstorm. We gave very little thought to any of it anymore. Regardless, we were off and running.

As Eileen took her departure, she raged, "It's all your fault!"

Joe Caruso, David's attorney, had told us, "Say nothing and mark it on the calendar." I had another entry for my calendar!

In May, Joan called. "I'd like to pick Danny up on Friday instead of Sunday --'

"Fine."

"My mother will come and get him --"

"Fine."

When Eileen showed up for Danny, Annette Blackmon, a friend, was in our home. Danny was ready. But he was feeling mule-headed stubborn. He didn't want to leave. Eileen made for the front door with Danny in tow. Our next door neighbor, Marion Chambers, was in her yard. As Eileen reached the front lawn, she turned and shouted at me vehemently, "You're teaching Danny to hate Joan. You're teaching him bad words," and on and on. An impossible scene.

Sometimes I felt as if we were playing out our lives on the streets of Merritt Island. It was embarrassing and discouraging.

The following day, June 1st, Joan phoned and talked to me, as though all was right in a rose-colored world. She was getting a new car; she had influential friends who were going to co-sign her note for the car; and she was riding a bike. None of it made a lick of sense. But I was happy for her, if she was happy. I marked the calendar and hung up.

Betty and Charles Rehiel, Daytona Beach, Florida, were our guests in June. Sherry Down, a neighbor on the block, was present, too. Eileen came to fetch Danny. Danny began to cry. He just did not want to leave.

Sherry suggested thoughtfully, "Perhaps it would be better if Joan came for Danny --"

Eileen screamed, "Mind your own damn business!"

The situation was becoming too much for me, especially now that Danny was beginning to protest leaving. I didn't know what had caused this change in his attitude. But Danny was a growing, thinking little boy with a tiny life of his own, much of which we knew nothing about. We had to allow for that. I suspected he had his reasons. I didn't know what they were. But I had reached the point where I could not be a helpless by-stander to these forced departures and watch the tears roll down his face. But I held my tongue and turned away. I had no other choice in the matter.

That fall, David registered Danny in the Baptist Church Kindergarten and Pre-School, which has a reputation for being the best of its kind on Merritt Island. David felt a three-year-old needed the company of other children his own age and would benefit from the learning experience.

Joan telephoned, "I'm picking Danny up on September 23rd."

I packed Danny's bag, so that he would be ready when she showed up. We waited all day. At six in the evening, we began to worry. I phoned the O'Brien home in Kissimmee. Joan wasn't home. Later she telephoned to say, "I'll pick Danny up tomorrow." This time she made it.

The whole family was looking forward to October 4th. An exciting day was ahead for us.

Months ago we had bought a houseboat hull. After thousands of hours of work, Dewey finished hooking up the steering on SEA-TREK. She was ready for her trial run.

The wind was blowing hard. White caps graced the Banana River that runs past our front door just across the street. The family went out to the end of our 250 foot-long dock on the river and climbed aboard SEA-TREK. She performed beautifully, but Dewey realized he had much more work to do. A fly-bridge with controls would be necessary to see the stern and bow, and facilitate docking. So Dewey had his spare-time planned for him. And Danny would not be out of a job; he was Dewey's assistant on SEA-TREK.

Meanwhile, Danny was learning colors, memorizing simple Bible verses, playing with other children, making new friends, developing nicely. David, Dewey and I looked forward each evening to dinner, when Danny would give his daily recital on the exciting events at school.

Children had been the missing ingredient in Danny's life. A house without other children is a very poor house indeed. Now Danny brought his new-found friends home. There was laughter and joy. But after his October visit with Joan, problems began to occur with alarming regularity.

Danny said, "I have two daddy's now."

David tried to explain, "No, you just have one daddy. Me."

But Danny insisted.

In David's behalf -- he was at work -- I asked Joan in November, if she would mind changing pick up days for Danny to Tuesday or Wednesday. If she would do this, Danny would not miss one whole week of school at a crack. The teaching was geared each week for a particular color or number.

She snapped, "Pre-School is nothing but baby-sitting!"

I did not dignify her remark with a reply.

All the while, David was trying to go on, create a new life for himself without Joan. He worked, watched over Danny and became president of the Brevard Wildlife Federation, where he played an active and important role in conservation.

When Christmas appeared on the horizon, our son, Tom, asked his father, "Can we use the houseboat, put a piano topside and take the 'Sound of Motion' choral group Christmas caroling through the canals of Cocoa Beach and Merritt Island?"

Dewey thought it was a great idea.

Girls from the group arrived to erect a Christmas tree with lights on the stern of SEA-TREK. Linda Ellis' electric piano and David's amplifier went topside. The director of the group, Natt Chambliss, was enjoying himself, as if he'd reached the apex of his career, and urged everyone onward. Danny was everywhere, enjoying this most marvelous and wonderous Christmas happening.

Linda Ellis and Jenny Head, members of the choral group, came over to our house. We made lots of sandwiches and dips, and laid in a huge supply of chips and soft drinks. We borrowed life jackets from Funtime Boats. When Debby Curry sat down at the piano that night, Dewey cast off from the dock.

We crossed the Banana River to Cocoa Beach. We stopped at an apartment house. Residents of the apartment came out to applaud our singing and request their favorite carols. As we cruised the canals other boats joined us. Everyone sang along. Danny clapped his hands and danced with joy. We had a wonderful time, so wonderful, that when we became too noisy or unruly, the inspired Mr. Chambliss made us sing JOY TO THE WORLD. Needless to say, JOY TO THE WORLD was heard often!

It was a memorable evening. We were glad we had Danny to share it with us. Suddenly the old year didn't seem so bad. We cheered up and looked ahead. But it was building, building, building, these petty, useless scenes with Joan and the O'Briens. Soon they would not seem so petty.

1975

January was upon us. Eileen arrived to take Danny home with her. Twice before they departed, Danny asked Eileen, "Are we going to Willie's house?"

We had heard Willie's name before. He was a part of Danny's life, that other part. But we assumed Willie must be a little playmate.

When Eileen brought Danny home from his stay, he wore no coat, no hat, no gloves. David bought Danny a new coat, new hat, new gloves. But that was the least of it.

During his short, one week stay with Joan, Danny had undergone a complete change of personality. He was no longer the normal, spirited boy we knew so well.

He would say, "I'm hot," and proceed to undress himself right down to his birthday suit, no matter where he was, in public or private. He would try to undress other people. When they protested, Danny kicked and screamed.

We attempted to explain to Danny why this was not acceptable behavior. But Danny would yell, "Willie does it and it's okay!"

David decided the time had come in which to put a few questions to Joan about Willie.

On February 23rd, Joan and Eileen came for Danny. David was waiting, "Who's Willie?" he demanded.

In that small voice that so insidiously undermined, Joan said, "He's one of Danny's playmates."

David was suspicious. "Joan, don't lie to me. Willie sounds more like one of your playmates."

"Oh, no, David. Really. He's Danny's playmate."

David wanted to believe Joan, but he couldn't; and he was right not to believe her.

At the end of Danny's March visit, Joan called and said, "I've hurt my back. I can't bring Danny home. If you want him, you'll have to meet me at McCoy Jet Port in Orlando."

David was working, so my sister Gladys Jones from Rocky

Mount, North Carolina, who was vacationing with us, and I drove to McCoy Jet Port. There was Danny. If his behavior had been unpredictable before, now it was beyond all reason.

Driving homeward, Danny described sex acts performed by Joan and his playmate, Willie, in his presence. The details were so vivid, so explicit, no child Danny's age could have invented them.

We pulled in our belts and tried to help Danny acquire more healthy interests. Tom's chorale entertained in concert at Brevard Community College. Danny was given a singing part. Our good neighbor, Norma Davis, made Danny a new suit. David bought him a new tie. Danny put aside his obsessions. He was so proud of his song and the chance to appear on stage with his Uncle Tom, that he sang like a bird!

We hoped for improvement. Although from time to time, Danny continued, both in school and at home, to speak of these sex acts, to talk of two fathers, to display unusual behavior patterns, we soothed him, tried to reason with him. Inevitably his behavior was worse the first three or four days after Danny had been in Joan's company. Then, everything would be all right again until the next visit. We attempted to carry on, as if we didn't know something was drastically wrong and didn't succeed, though we tried extra hard to help Danny over these disturbing periods in his life.

That summer Danny gave advice to Dewey as they worked together on SEA-TREK's fly-bridge. He basked in the glow of David's undivided attention as David walked with him along the beach, fished with him, swam with him. He tagged around after his Uncle Tom; they kidded back and forth. He asked me to cook his favorite foods, and I did. All in all, it was a fine summer with those intolerable exceptions.

Came fall and Danny entered school again. He loved school, the teachers, the children, the activities. He made a special friend of Jim Goodroe, Minister of Youth at the First Baptist Church. Then, everything fell apart or joined together, whichever view one cares to take.

On November 9th, Joan phoned and said, "I'm getting a divorce. My husband is irrational, crazy, not responsible for Danny and has an uncontrollable temper!"

I paused in thought. Billy Corbett had disappeared from the scene months ago. Finally I blurted out, "Is his name -- Willie?"

"Yes," she said, as if this was not news.

And suddenly I was sick. "Why didn't you tell us about Willie?" I said angrily.

"I didn't lie," Joan said. "Willie is little. He's Oriental. And he was

Danny's playmate,"

I had felt helpless before, but never so helpless as I felt now. "Oh, Joan!"

"Listen," Joan said. "I want to warn you about Willie. He's threatened Danny, and he could harm David."

Totally demoralized, I acknowledged the message and hung up the phone. When David came in from work, I related this incredible conversation.

Immediately David went up and down our street, asking friends and neighbors to watch for an Oriental, explaining the bizarre situation briefly. Next he drove to Danny's school and alerted the people there. He simply did not know what to expect.

But now we had to face reality. Danny had been telling us the truth.

Twice David had tried calling Joan during that week. He reached her on Sunday, November 16th. He was wild with worry.

"I don't know why," Joan said blandly.

"I won't allow Danny to visit you, Joan, until Family Services checks the matter out and assures me that it's safe for Danny."

"Don't worry. I've got a restraining order out on Willie. There'll be no trouble --"

"No, I have to be positive Danny will be safe." David could no longer trust Joan to tell the truth about anything, particularly when Joan had told me that Willie might harm Danny.

David's next step was to ask Mrs. Rodon of Family Services to request an investigation of Joan's home in Kissimmee.

Ten days later the Osceola County Health Department, where Kissimmee is located, had not returned a report. So David spoke with his attorney, Joe Caruso.

With Joe's advice under his belt, David phoned Joan and told her she could come and visit Danny at our house any time she wanted. But she could not take Danny away, until he was positive the home environment had changed for the better.

Now each time Danny went on one of his jags about what Joan and Willie did, we realized we were in over our heads. I recall one morning in particular.

Our friend, Grace Beck, had stopped by for a cup of coffee and a friendly chat. Danny was drawing pictures. Suddenly he jumped up and showed his drawing to Grace. I glanced at the drawing. It was an explicit sexual encounter. Quickly I grabbed the paper and crumpled it in my hand. Later I passed it on to attorney Joe Caruso for his files.

During Mrs. Rodon's next visit, I explained Danny's problem. "We need help," I told her. "Right now. What do you suggest?"

Mrs. Rodon had listened sympathetically. She recommended taking Danny to the Mental Health Clinic at Rockledge. David had me make an appointment for Danny.

Though the appointment was made, we were in the midst of coping with a problem that defied us. How did one go about handling a situation of this magnitude? If Danny didn't receive some constructive advice and assistance at this point, I couldn't imagine how this might warp his personality in days to come.

The alternative to a constructive solution was chilling. I realized there was no point in dwelling on the negative, but I couldn't help being worried and apprehensive. I prayed that the Mental Health Clinic would see us through this trying time. We were in dire need of a helping hand -- no two ways about it.

On December 1st, David and I took Danny to the Mental Health Clinic for the first of two sessions. At the end of the second session, Mental Health's advice: encourage Danny to say what he wanted to say, and listen.

We listened as instructed. But we did not comment on what he had to say. Danny did not dwell on the subject of Joan and Willie any longer. By our acceptance of what he said, Danny was removed from the position of one who must convince.

As a result of these visits to Mental Health, they made the recommendation that Joan should visit Danny at home with David. However, on Sunday, December 7th, Pearl Harbor Day, Joan and Dan drove up in Dan's truck to get Danny. Dan was laboring under the impression that Joan could now take Danny home for a visit. I directed him to the phone and Family Services.

Dan refused the use of our telephone and drove off in his truck. He made the call at a pay phone, I suppose. Shortly our phone rang. It was Mrs. Bell of Family Services, calling for Joan. "Sorry, but not so," Mrs. Bell told Joan. Joan slammed down the phone. Joan must visit with Danny in David's presence.

Dan returned in his truck. Dewey, ever level-headed and thoughtful, went out to meet him. Dan got out of the truck and began to beat his head on the side of the truck, as if life was too much for him. When he saw Dewey, Dan pulled himself together and asked, "Can we have a picnic on your dock together?"

Dewey said, "Sure. Why not? It's a good day for a picnic."

Again Dan drove off his his truck. Upon his return, he carried hamburgers, French fries and soft drinks. Joan and Danny joined him on our dock across the street. They seemed to enjoy themselves.

That was fine with David. He didn't mind. In fact, for now, he wanted to encourage these kinds of wholesome visits, since the

Health Department had said, "Until an investigation is made and completed, do not allow Joan to take Danny from the premises."

With Christmas upon us, though, the pressures increased. Joan wanted to see Danny during the holidays. Understandable. David talked with attorney Joe Caruso. "Would it be all right for Danny to visit with Joan, if her parents came for Danny, were responsible for Danny during his visit and returned Danny?"

Under the present circumstances, Joe thought David was being overly generous. But in the true spirit of Christmas, Joe encouraged David to go ahead and give it a try. Perhaps this thoughtful act on David's part would ease the tension.

Dewey telephoned Dan O'Brien and told him of this plan for visitation during the holidays. Dan said they would come for Danny on December 26th and return Danny the night of December 28th. Dan said, "I will be responsible."

Well, we had made it through another year. We looked off down the road and wondered where we were headed. Nothing was light; in fact, it seemed to be growing darker by the minute.

We contemplated the future uneasily.

1976

To get the year off on the right foot, in David's behalf, Dewey phoned Kissimmee and spoke to Dan O'Brien and Joan. He offered visitation to Joan two week-ends out of the month, if Dan would be totally responsible for Danny. Both Joan and Dan refused flatly. But Dewey did make an agreement with Dan for him to come for Danny on January 9th with these ground rules in mind. What happened was far from what Dan O'Brien had promised.

Joan, the perennial woman of the world and mystery -- she had taken to wearing dark glasses by day and by night -- came blowing the horn on the car, starting two blocks before she reached the house, and saying her mother was at Merritt Square Mall. We let Danny accompany her. When Joan returned, as usual the honking began two blocks away to insure herself an audience. I went out to get Danny. Danny jumped from the car, Joan pulled the door closed behind him and roared off without a parting word.

Danny had a huge knot on his head. The knot had a small, deep puncture wound in its center. Ten minutes later Joan telephoned and said, "That bump on Danny's head. He fell from the bed."

I had to cut Danny's shirt to slip it over his head. I said to Danny, "How did it happen?" since I could not believe Joan.

He didn't remember. But he began to plead, "Please don't make me go with Mama Joan again. They're going to keep me."

I gave him a kiss and said, "Nonsense! Nobody's going to keep you," and doctored the bump.

During the next few weeks, without warning, for no reason whatsoever, Danny would look at his father, at Dewey, at me, and say, "Please don't make me go anymore. They're going to keep me."

We tried to discount these words, ignore them. But we couldn't forget them.

Since David had refused to allow Danny visitation with Joan without some assurance that a responsible person would be present at all times, a court hearing was scheduled in Rockledge for February 12th before Judge Roger Dykes. The date was moved back to February 24th. Finally Judge Dykes decided he did not have time to hear the case. He handed down an order anyway. David must allow Danny to visit Joan. David told Danny that Joan would come for him on February 29th.

Danny said, "I won't go. They won't bring me back."

Finally we convinced Danny that Joan would bring him back. But he went off with Joan under protest. His return was scheduled for March 7th.

Joan called and said, "You'll have to come to the Pancake House in Cocoa, if you want Danny."

Dewey was replacing the tail pipes on my car. I went next door to Gerry Hipp -- she owned the O'Brien house now -- and asked her to drive me to Cocoa.

Joan and Danny were waiting. The moment Danny crawled into the car with us, and we drove away, he showed me his arm. A long row of raw, half-healed scabs were much in evidence.

"What happened?" I said.

"Mama Joan did it with a knife."

Gerry and I exchanged horrified glances.

That night when David gave Danny his bath, he discovered the same markings covered Danny's stomach. David was infuriated. "How did this happen, Danny?"

"Mama Joan did it with a knife."

After this visit and throughout March there was no containing

Danny. He was wild. He kept repeating, "They're going to keep me."
He begged his teacher at school, Ann Bair, to talk to the judge for
him. To add fuel to the already raging fire, Joan arrived on March
28th unexpectedly.

Danny flew into a panic and grabbed David around the legs.
"Don't make me go," he screamed.

Joan went to the phone and called her attorney. When she hung
up, David telephoned Joe Caruso. David listened, closed the
conversation and turned to Joan. "You can't take him."

Joan called her mother long distance. A remark she made to her
mother was to haunt us in the days to come: "I'll not be able to go on
my New York trip."

Why? We didn't know. But at the moment we didn't care.

For the remainder of the day, Danny clung to David. He was an
anxious and frightened child, afraid of the future, afraid of losing his
home.

To reassure Danny, David took him to the store and bought him
a fishing pole. Danny's favorite sport was netting crabs or shrimp
and fishing from our dock across the street on the Banana River. At
four and a half years old, Danny could not manage a rod and reel.
David thought a cane pole might work for Danny. Though Danny
and David spent the remainder of the day on the dock fishing, Danny
continued to beg, "Don't let me go, Daddy. They'll never bring me
back."

April 4th dawned beautiful and sparkling. David had to work. I
packed Danny's clothes and vitamins for his visit with Joan. I
explained exactly what I was doing and reassured him continuously.
After breakfast, Danny vanished.

Tom's friend, young Bill Chambers from next door, came outside
to help me look for Danny. We found Danny hidden in our banana
trees. "I'm not going," he yelled. "You can't make me. I won't go."

I took Danny inside the house and tried to quiet him. But he was
inconsolable. I gave him a bath. He dressed. It was close to 10:00 a.m.

Danny was so restless I allowed him to go two doors down the
street and visit his best adult friends, Norma and Walt Davis. Danny
was back in a few minutes. He paced the house like a caged animal.

I said to Dewey, "Why don't you take Danny over to the dock and
let him use his new cane pole? Maybe that'll help."

I followed Dewey and Danny through the front door of the house
and into the yard. I watched them away. They crossed the road and
walked to the end of the dock. The sun danced on the water. A perfect
day, I thought.

Dewey and Danny settled on the edge of the dock. Dewey helped

Danny bait his line. Danny dropped the line into the water and appeared to relax. I remember glancing at my watch: 10:30 a.m.

Our next door neighbors, Jim and Marion Chambers, appeared on their lawn. Norma and Walt Davis were already outside. Then, Grace Beck stopped by after Sunday School. It was a day nobody could resist.

Joan wasn't due until 11:00 a.m. We all stood around chatting, talking back and forth, commenting on the gorgeous day in general. Then, two cars came down the road slowly.

Grace and I paused in our conversation and took note.

The cars drove past our house, turned around in the driveway next door and returned. I recognized Dan O'Brien's car. It came to a halt at our driveway. The second car, a white Ford Torino, stopped directly behind Dan's car. Strange, I thought ... the second car had a red dash light. I guessed Joan had brought the police. But I didn't know why that should be necessary. Joan had every right to Danny today.

I walked out to the road. Joan was sitting in the back seat of Dan's car, wearing dark glasses, as usual; two men I didn't know were in the front seat. Still I wasn't alarmed.

Joan got out of the car. I said, "Oh, Joan. When you bring Danny back, try to remember his identification bracelet."

David insisted Danny wear an identification bracelet. From his work as an emergency medical technician, he had learned to respect the value and importance of being able to identify an injured individual, so that physicians may contact relatives and acquire proper medical background without delay.

Twice David had bought Danny new I.D. bracelets, because twice Danny had come home from Joan's with his missing.

This was the sum total of my conversation with Joan. I called for Dewey and Danny. In the doing, I glanced back. The two men in the front seat got out of Dan O'Brien's car. They did not speak.

The driver was a big fellow with dark hair slicked back into a duck-tail. He unbuckled his pants and tucked in the tail of his white shirt. The second man grew a long red beard half-way down his chest. He had bunches of muscles and flexed them mightily. Then, he pulled a pipe from his pocket and lit the pipe. He flexed his muscles some more, as if he expected to use them.

I remember hearing Jim Chambers comment, "What in the hell is that guy trying to prove?"

I shrugged. I didn't know. I returned my attention to Dewey and Danny on the dock. As I went toward the dock, I eyed the second car suspiciously. There was something funny-peculiar going on here.

The man in the second car had his hands propped on top of the steering wheel -- and he was pointing a gun directly at me!

I tried to rationalize what I was seeing . . . surely this was a law enforcement officer. The car was white with a red light and two radio antennas; then, there was the gun. But none of it made a lick of sense. Judge Dykes' court order was on hand. Danny was on hand. Why should Joan need an officer of the law?

Bewildered, I called to Dewey and Danny.

Danny came along the dock, dragging his heels behind him. He crossed the street and got into the car with Joan. The car door closed. The two men returned to the front seat of the O'Brien car, and both cars sped off down the street.

As the second car passed me, the driver, who had held the gun, busied himself, talking into a radio mike. I assumed that another third party or car was involved. I glanced around. What next?

Nothing. That was it.

But what had occurred was extraordinary, beyond explanation. Suddenly I was frightened. I yelled at Dewey on the dock, "Something's wrong!"

Dewey came running. I told him what had happened. He said, "Let's go."

"Where?"

"Follow them."

Grace Beck's car was handiest. The three of us piled into her car and tried to catch up with Joan's entourage.

Grace said, "I realized something was awfully wrong. I tried to get the tag number on the second car." But she had failed to remember the entire tag number. Several digits were missing.

We drove onward for about ten miles, until we reached the St. John's River. We didn't see anything of either car. We gave up and returned home.

Dewey mused aloud, "I'm concerned about the conversation Danny and I had."

"What?"

"Danny said, 'Papa, you better not let me go. They're going to keep me for sure this time.' I told him, 'No, they won't.' I explained that he was only going for a visit. Then Danny said to me, 'Papa, promise me you'll come and get me if they don't bring me back.' I promised."

We tried to think what we ought to be doing. Well, nothing. Joan had every legal right to Danny for a week, gun or no gun.

When David came in from work on Monday morning, I told him of Sunday's events. He got on the phone to Joe Caruso and said,

"Please check with Joan's attorney in Kissimmee. Be sure Danny's all right. I don't like what happened here yesterday."

Joe returned David's call. It seemed Joan's attorney was not at his desk when Joe called him. But he telephoned Joe at once. Joan's attorney told Joe that Joan had called him and said David might call, since she had brought friends with her when she came for Danny.

David thought it odd that Joan's attorney had seemed to expect the call and was ready with Joan's pat explanation about what had happened. But this was the end of that; and that and that alone was all that David could do. For now.

While we waited for Judge Dykes' court ordered visit to end, gun or no gun -- bear this in mind -- we could do nothing within the law. All our thoughts were for Danny. And Danny, we felt positive, was in terrible circumstances.

A week passed. An endless week. Sunday again. Finally. April 11th. We called Joe Caruso. Joe could do nothing about the legalities of the situation until Monday. Joe suggested David call Joan's parents. Perhaps, just perhaps, Joan was merely late in returning Danny.

David phoned the O'Briens. Dan O'Brien said he did not know where Danny or Joan were. He had not seen them all week. The last time Dan had seen Joan was early on April 4th. Then, he added, "But I'm not concerned. Don't bother me."

What a helpless feeling.

We sat down to think. We couldn't let the matter rest. David and Dewey called all hospitals in our own county of Brevard and the city of Kissimmee. There was no record of any accident victim with Danny's or Joan's names. David phoned the Osceola County Sheriff's Department, where Kissimmee is situated, and spoke with a Lt. Watco. Lt. Watco checked the O'Brien neighborhood and called back. No one had seen Danny all week.

Finally on April 13th, we went before Judge Roger Dykes and explained that Joan had not returned Danny, that there was implied force in his pick up. Judge Dykes signed three documents: Motion of Contempt, Writ of Attachment and Return of Minor Child, an Order Imposing Criminal Sanctions, and an Order Terminating Visitation.

A couple of days passed before these documents were typed and signed. Once this was accomplished, the documents were delivered to State Attorney Abbott Herring's office in Titusville, Florida, so that a warrant for Joan's arrest could be issued.

David asked that I talk to the Federal Bureau of Investigation to see if they could help us. We considered Danny's case a form of kidnapping. The FBI told me that it did not fit into the guidelines of kidnapping, but any request that we made to them for help would have to come through State Attorney Abbott Herring in writing.

I phoned the State Attorney's office. John Barnett of that office informed me he would not talk to us, except through David's attorney. More expense.

David had to ask Joe Caruso to go to the State Attorney's office to ask them to request the assistance of the FBI. The State Attorney's office then called the FBI. The FBI and Federal Attorney Wherry in Orlando, Florida, told the State Attorney's office that the FBI must have a written request before they could act. Meanwhile, the Federal Attorney told me to call the State Attorney's office and have them take care of the matter, but the State's Attorney John Barnett had refused to talk to us, except through Joe Caruso, David's attorney. Here was a maze beyond compare, with nothing being accomplished.

In the process of trying to get someone to help us, we called the Brevard County Sheriff's Department and spoke to Sheriff Leigh Wilson. Sheriff Wilson would not even file a missing person's report, so we made an appointment to see him. When we entered his office, Sheriff Wilson's opening remark to us, "If this child is with a relative, now mind you, I did not say *mother*, I can't help you," whereupon he left the room without further ado. We spoke with Sheriff Wilson's secretary; she couldn't help us either.

On the phone, I made an appeal to our State Senator Lori Wilson in Cocoa Beach. State Senator Wilson advised us, "Contact the Sheriff's Department." We were back where we began again on all fronts. In fact, it seemed nobody wanted to talk to any member of the Strickland family, regardless of the situation.

David made an appeal to the Governor of Florida, Reubin Askew. Askew replied, "Depend on your local law enforcement agency."

What a joke! But we pressed on.

Now David thought of Frank Demsky. Frank, a former football player with the Miami Dolphins, is handsome and intelligent with a master's degree in criminal justice. A State Marine Patrol officer and a licensed private investigator, Frank had attended Standard Police School with David.

Like the very good friend he is, Frank was willing to assist us in any way he could. Since money was going out faster than it came in on legal fees and expenses -- already Dewey and I had sold a lot we planned to build on in the Florida Keys and our savings account was destined for oblivion -- we reached an agreement with Frank that would serve all parties well without money changing hands.

I would keep Frank's two boys during the summer at no cost to him, while his wife attended nursing school, and Frank would see what he could learn about Joan's activities without fee. Frank was a light burning in the window on a very dark night. He went right to work, capable and interested.

While Frank did his checking, we concluded the next step in our search for Danny should be the newspapers. We hoped someone might read about Danny and contact us. I set forth with my friend Jackie Gunderson.

First we journeyed to the *TODAY* office in Cocoa, Florida. I told our story to reporter David Polhemus. From there we went on to the Cocoa office of the Orlando, Florida, *SENTINEL STAR* and talked to Jim Ball.

In both cases the reporters listened politely, studied the legal documents and pictures, and copied everything. They understood that Danny's life had been threatened by Willie Ng, according to Joan, that Judge Roger Dykes' court order had made it possible for Joan to abduct Danny, that Danny was taken with implied force and was, without question, missing.

By any newspaper's criterion here was a front page story. We anticipated eagerly. Not a word was printed

Frank, though, could not be denied. He had made several visits to Kissimmee. He learned that Joan had filed for divorce from Willie Ng. In the divorce proceedings, several statements were food for serious thought: Joan's statements that she was physically unable to work to provide income for maintenance for herself; Willie Ng was possessed of a violent and ungovernable temper; Willie Ng had assaulted her physically; she was in fear that Willie Ng would assault her again.

The divorce was recorded on February 23, 1976. Willie was ordered to pay alimony. Frank learned where Willie Ng was employed in Orlando and contacted him.

Since I was the only one in the family with any free time, I was sent off to interview Willie.

I asked my friend Grace Beck to accompany me to Willie's place of employment. Willie was out to lunch. Grace and I sat in the car and bided our time. From Danny's description of Willie, "Willie's a Chinese cowboy that rides a motorcycle," I was positive I would recognize Willie the instant I saw him.

Then, riding toward us on a Honda motorcycle, we saw a small man wearing cowboy boots. That had to be Willie!

We got out of the car and greeted Willie. To our surprise, Willie was very nice to us and very concerned about Danny. He said, "Joan wanted me to be a party to taking Danny earlier, but I refused. She's crazy. I don't want any part of her."

So that was that.

Frank talked with Mrs. Karen Deitemeyer, who lived in the trailer park that Joan and Willie had occupied. Joan, it seemed, had been helping as a volunteer for the Girl Scouts. Mrs. Deitemeyer told Frank that Joan, because of her conduct in relation to Scout work, had been asked to resign by the administrators of the organization. Furthermore, Joan explained her departure from the trailer park with the words, "I've got to leave and go to New York." According to Joan, she knew a female judge in New York who was going to assist her in getting custody of Danny. Mrs. Deitemeyer also said that Eileen O'Brien had telephoned her between the 9th and 11th of April and told her Joan was suffering from physical and mental problems and was tied up with plans for traveling to New York to solve her child custody problems.

Frank pursued the Scouting aspect in Joan's life. He talked with Sara Bowling, a Girl Scout leader. She confirmed the information Mrs. Deitemeyer had given him, relating a shocking incident involving Joan. Then, Mrs. Bowling recalled a conversation with Joan, wherein Joan had said she had to go to New York to solve custody of Danny; later Eileen O'Brien had telephoned to say Joan had gone to New York.

Now Frank went on to speak to Eula Morris, Joan's close friend. Mrs. Morris remembered a shopping trip with Joan. Joan had bought clothing for Danny and a blonde wig for herself -- for the trip to New York. Mrs. Morris said she had seen legal papers from New York on Danny's custody. Joan's explanation to Mrs. Morris for the New York trip: "I have to go, because I must have Danny in the physical jurisdiction of the court handling custody." Mrs. Morris said she had been convinced by Joan that the Stricklands were mistreating Danny and the only solution was to take Danny to New York with her. Mrs. Morris added that she had been questioned about Joan by the Drug Enforcement Administration. Later on, Eileen O'Brien had cautioned Mrs. Morris, concerning Joan's whereabouts with the words, "Keep quiet, if you know what's good for you!"

We began to think about New York in serious terms. But where in New York? Frank advised us to simmer down. He thought all of this talk of New York might be for our ears and our ears alone. Frank, as it turned out, is a very smart fellow.

During these sad and difficult days, when we discovered there were no books, no laws, no guidelines, governing child-snatching,

Frank was as comforting as Grandma's quilt on a cold winter night. Without Frank, David's dynamic attorney Joe Caruso -- we called Joe our 'Knight in White,' since he wore a white suit often, -- and Joe's personable secretary, Ruth Bowers, who cheered us on by pleading, "Yell at me; I won't blame you, if you do," I don't believe we could have made it. They were marvelous. We owed them so much, more than words or money. And, in fact, we did owe Joe thousands of dollars. But if worse came to worse, which it did in the end, we could sell SEA-TREK. For now, though, we concentrated on today. And today was more promising than New York.

The most revealing aspect of the interview with Mrs. Morris, Mrs. Bowling and Mrs. Deitemeyer was the name, David, which kept cropping up in their accounts of Joan's activities. Not David Strickland, but David, a fireman for the Killarney Fire Department in Orlando, Florida.

This David had been with Joan on April 2nd at a Scout picnic, and Mrs. Morris said this David was with Joan on April 5th. Joan and David had come to Mrs. Morris' house prior to leaving Florida, and had called her from Georgia that evening to report, "We got out of Florida okay."

To add to the now obvious conclusion that Joan had planned 'the snatching of Danny,' Mr. Charles Bowman, a neighbor of Joan's in Kissimmee, had watched Joan, Eileen and a man pack a car, a 1972 or 1973 white Ford Torino equipped with two antennas, with clothing, a television and other paraphernalia.

The Ford Torino stuck out like a sore thumb. The description fitted the car driven by the man who pointed the gun at me on the day Joan took Danny away.

While this was taking place, David, Dewey and I were *trying* to get the paper work through State Attorney Abbot Herring's office, making trips to the Courthouse in Kissimmee, Titusville, and running down leads that might give us some new information on Danny and Joan. Joe Caruso was busy getting depositions from Dan and Eileen O'Brien.

In Dan's deposition he said he hired two men to 'protect Joan,' both temporary circus workers, for the pick up of Danny, and they moved on. One of the hired men was identified as Tom Donoho. At this point, Eileen O'Brien handed over some postcards supposedly written by Joan with Miami, Florida, postmarks.

So far as we were concerned, the postcards were 'iffy.' In years gone by, Joan had told us that she had friends mail postcards to her mother, when she ran away, so her parents wouldn't discover where she was. We didn't trust the postcards, just as we had begun to distrust all the talk about New York.

In passing, though, Dan O'Brien did say to Frank and Dewey, when his deposition was being taken, "Money will buy anything. Just you wait and see." If this was the game we were playing, we were in deep trouble.

On May 5th and 6th, at the request of the O'Briens, Judge Roger Dykes held a hearing. The O'Briens wanted to quash criminal sanctions of Joan. Judge Dykes said, "No, not until the child and mother are in front of me."

Hooray for small favors!

Then Judge Dykes directed his remarks to the Strickland family: "If you go to the news media again, I will drop all criminal charges."

We didn't know how Judge Dykes knew I had been to the newspapers. Certainly no one else knew of my visit to the newspapers. The newspapers had seen to that by refusing to print a word on Danny's behalf. But now, Judge Dykes told us reporters had been hanging around his office, asking questions, and he wouldn't have it. We were under a gag order!

For the hearing we had subpoenaed Mrs. Morris, Mrs. Bowling and Mrs. Deitemeyer. They had spent two hours with Joe Caruso in the presence of Grace Beck and me. They repeated the stories they had told to Frank. Judge Dykes would not allow them to testify at the hearing.

Certainly these three women had pertinent, valid and perhaps important information to give the court. Judge Dykes didn't want to hear it. Why? We don't know and probably never will.

Over and above the name of David, the one positive fact from all of this was the name of Tom Donoho, circus worker. Frank, Dewey and David set out to find Tom Donoho, as if it might be the last thing they ever did.

They traveled from circus to circus throughout Florida. At one of the circuses, Dewey was tired and remained in the car to rest. When he saw David come out, David was handing a circus worker money. Dewey jumped to the conclusion that David had unearthed valuable information. When Frank and David got into the car, Dewey said anxiously, "What did you find out?"

David grinned and said, "The guy's boa constrictor is starving. I gave him a buck to buy a chicken."

Dewey laughed a badly needed laugh.

Since nothing came of the circus search, Dewey and I took time to drive to Orlando and visit the Killarney Fire Department. We wanted to check on the man named David, mentioned by Mrs. Morris, Mrs. Bowling and Mrs. Deitemeyer. We found a David, all

216

right.

This David told us he knew Joan through Dan O'Brien, but he didn't know Joan well. He claimed never to have been to our house on Merritt Island. If he was not telling the truth, he was a convincing liar.

As for my personal identification, there was no way I could identify him. I had been so busy looking at the car and the gun, the face of the man was a blur in my mind. So we took David, the fireman, at face value and went back to State Attorney Abbott Herring.

Abbott Herring could not seem to get the proper papers together for the FBI to act. We asked for help at the state capitol level in Tallahassee. They were comforting. But still the wrong paperwork came out of State Attorney Abbott Herring's office, time after time after relentless time.

In June, many people who knew of our plight wrote appeals to Governor Reubin Askew, asking him to assist us with the myriad problems we faced. I carried copies of some of these letters to State Senator Lori Wilson's office. Sorry, no results.

When July rolled around, State Attorney Abbott Herring pulled himself together and wrote a letter to David, suggesting David contact his congressmen and see if his congressmen could assist Abbott Herring in acquiring an Unlawful Flight to Avoid Prosecution warrant on Joan.

David acted on Mr. Herring's advice, though it was a bunch of foolishness, since the warrant could only be issued if Abbott Herring could get the paperwork done correctly.

During these months, I was at home, enjoying the company of Frank's boys, Eddie and Frankie. They delighted me with their laughter and games. I taught them to row a boat, and we made plenty of peanut butter and fluffy marshmallow sandwiches. As anybody knows, this kind of diet and exercise is good for the soul.

It was then that I decided to write a book about what was happening to us. I had been marking my calendar all along, and once Danny was snatched, I added to my calendar with copious notes. In the evenings, I worked to clarify facts and feelings. David and Dewey were not so fortunate; they had no time to spare.

Both of them were being called upon by the courts or attorneys to appear in two different places at once. It was a hectic schedule, when one considered they had to make a living and try to pay bills.

Along about here, Frank came up with the idea that perhaps Joan had married again. We wrote letters to several states where we felt Joan might have remarried. But no Joan O'Brien Ng showed up in

217

any files of vital statistics.

Now we received an anonymous phone call. The caller told us there had been a big drug bust in Columbia, South Carolina. We knew Joan's sister, Diane Lee, lived in Columbia. On a hunch, our friend Ralph Johns insisted that Frank and Dewey fly with him in his plane to Columbia, South Carolina to check on the drug bust. It was a wild idea, but we were grasping frantically at any and all straws.

When the threesome arrived in Columbia and showed Joan's photograph to a police detective, he said, "Yes, she was one of them." Three other policemen in the office agreed with this positive identification. The Columbia police searched the apartment in question. The apartment was empty. Frank, Dewey and Ralph gave up and flew home.

The same month I received a newspaper clipping in the mail from an anonymous source. The clipping was about a father and son being killed. Underlined in red on the note were the words: *"Is this what you want?"* Frightening! Was it meant for David and Danny or Dewey and David? I couldn't guess. But that clipping and note contributed to many wide awake nights.

A second anonymous note arrived in August with one typed line, "David, have you forgotten?" Along with the note was a picture of David and Joan on their wedding day. The photograph was an original Polaroid picture taken by Dan and Eileen, when David and Joan were married. I remembered it well. But I didn't know how anyone would possibly imagine that David could forget with Danny missing.

Now we considered ourselves and the future. We were gaining little ground in our search for Danny. By anyone's sense of perspective, we should have given up then and there. We didn't. The Strickland family pulled themselves up by the bootstraps, took a deep breath and trudged onward. We began a letter writing campaign.

We contacted all of our congressmen, House of Representatives and Senators, both in Florida and in Washington. We explained the situation and asked for legislation that would make snatching and concealing a child a crime. In our pursuit of the written word, we wrote the Justice Department, Washington, D.C., and, low and behold, they agreed to do a missing persons run-down on Joan!

That was something. Now what about State Attorney Abbott Herring? It seemed State Attorney Abbott Herring wasn't doing anything, though he claimed to be doing everything possible.

Summer was coming to an end. Soon Frankie and Eddie, Frank's boys would be off to school, and I would miss them. They had been a great comfort to me during this impossible summer; many days, I suspected, they were a factor in keeping us on an even keel.

In September, our illustrious State Attorney Abbott Herring began his campaign for re-election. Kathryn and Bill Case -- Bill and Dewey worked together at Kennedy Space Center -- joined Dewey and me on a jaunt to Merritt Square Mall where Abbott Herring was appearing in person to meet and greet voters.

With irony and malice aforethought, we thanked Mr. Herring for advising us to go through our congressmen to learn if his office had managed to get the correct papers together, so that the FBI could act on Danny's case.

Smoothly, blandly, the bespectacled, self-assured Mr. Herring made the monumental statement, "Everything is okay."

Incredible. We were still trying to get the Unlawful Flight to Avoid Prosecution warrant on Joan out of Mr. Herring's office for the FBI!

Each time the paperwork came down from Abbott Herring's office, it was wrong in some detail, and every paper, wrong as it was, took over a week to process. We were near the end of our rope with that man.

But we persisted. If Danny were dead, we had to know. If Danny were alive, he must be found and allowed to lead a normal, stable life. We could not understand Abbott Herring's indifference to the life of a child. We shall never understand Abbott Herring.

Now we appealed to President Gerald Ford in Washington. This was a kind of last ditch stand. Because it seemed nobody, except us, our attorney, our friends, Danny's friends -- that is, anyone in a position of authority -- really cared enough about Danny to give us constructive help. Words, words, words, useless words. Except for the encouragement of Children's Rights, Incorporated, a non-profit clearing house of child-snatching information, established by Arnold Miller, Washington D.C. -- Miller himself was the father of a snatched child -- we were utterly alone with our own resources. Then, glory halleluiah, President Ford came through for us in a back-handed fashion.

A representative of the Justice Department was sent to do a background investigation. As a result of this investigation, the FBI spent several days assisting Abbott Herring in surmounting the simplistic problem of getting the paperwork out correctly, so that the FBI could act.

While we sat back and wished the FBI good luck with Mr. Herring and his staff -- the FBI was going to need all the help it could get -- we contemplated David.

David had a girl friend, Sue Pace. Their relationship was becoming serious. Dewey and I were pleased David had found someone to love. Sue, a pretty, slender blonde with a level, sensible head on her shoulders, was a refreshing change in our lives. David and Sue became engaged, but they made the decision not to marry until Danny was found. They wanted Danny to get to know Sue and be a part of the ceremony when they wed.

Sue's birthday fell on November 4th. I made a big cake and invited her dad, Bob, and her brother, Robbie, over for ice cream and cake. It was a double celebration.

The FBI exceeded all expectations with Abbott Herring. We had at long last been assured by Abbott Herring's staff that the correct papers had been issued. In fact, as it turned out, all Abbott Herring had to do was file 'Information,' stating what statute had been violated and that he, Abbott Herring, had reason to believe Joan O'Brien Strickland Ng had left the State of Florida. So simple. But so very difficult for Mr. Herring. A mere seven screaming months had come and gone since we had called upon Abbott Herring to help.

Now we were anxious to see if the FBI would indeed issue the Unlawful Flight to Avoid Prosection warrant on Joan, so that a nationwide search could be initiated. November 11, 1976 was the stellar day. The warrant was issued!

We discovered the FBI does not work as fast in real life as it does on television. But they did go to work and almost immediately. After providing the FBI with all pertinent information, we relaxed a bit and let them shoulder some of the burdens.

To further improve our state of mind, State Attorney Abbott Herring went down to defeat at the hands of the electorate who seemed to know him as well as we knew him. Since Mr. Herring was packing his bags, getting ready to move on, I talked to Charles Wilson, an investigator in the State Attorney's office. Mr. Wilson said they were doing nothing now on the matter. Any effort they made would duplicate the FBI's efforts, and the FBI was much better equipped to find Danny and Joan. Truly, we looked to the FBI and the New Year with real anticipation and hope.

1977

David and I wrote letters to Charles Bowman, the O'Brien

neighbor who watched Joan and a man pack the Ford Torino, asking Mr. Bowman to please contact the FBI with any information he might have. Mr. Bowman obliged. Then, on a far out hunch, I wrote a letter to Tom Donoho, the circus worker whose name cropped up in Dan O'Brien's deposition, in care of Vision Enterprises, Dan O'Brien's employer, and requested a signed, return receipt.

Surprise!

I received a return receipt three weeks later. But the letter had done a lot of traveling, having been forwarded many times. We could not read the signature on the return receipt card. But the card had been stamped in Sarasota, Florida.

I called the post office, but they would not check the certified number through for us. So -- I sat down and wrote another letter with return receipt, specifying the address to which it was delivered.

The receipt came home on March 17th with the address: 3900 Roxanne, 10B, Sarasota, Florida.

Since David had to work the next day, Dewey and I drove to Sarasota. We found the apartment house and a Mrs. Ethel Freeman.

Mrs. Freeman, an old circus hand, had been a bareback rider for 40 years. We told her about Danny and not so incidentally asked about Tom Donoho.

Mrs. Freeman said she was a relative of Tom Donoho's in-laws and looked after their mail. "Tom's with Circus Vargas now," she said and promised to try to locate Tom on the circus itinerary.

After we departed for home, Mrs. Freeman made good on her word. Through a cousin, she acquired the route of Circus Vargas and called Tom Donoho in New Mexico on her own, asking him to please call us. When we arrived on Merritt Island, our daughter Kathy, who was baby-sitting the phone for us in our absence, told us of the call and said, "I told him to call back collect tomorrow at eleven o'clock."

He did!

Tom Donoho was helpful beyond wildest expectations. He said, "I was the man driving Mr. O'Brien's car. Benny Williams was the man in the car with me." Now we had the name of Muscles, as we referred to him.

Tom Donoho went on to explain how Dan O'Brien had hired the two of them. Tom Donoho had been told that Joan had allowed Danny to visit us. Everytime she let Danny come to see David for a few days, when she arrived to get Danny, we ganged up on her and beat her up.

The second car, according to Donoho, was a Ford; Donoho had been under the impression that the Ford was a county-owned vehicle, because of its red light and radio equipment. The driver's name was

David, a medic and a friend of the O'Briens!

Tom Donoho was a ray of sunshine. He went on to tell me that he would not have come to our house had he known the truth. He had suspected near the end of the venture that all was not well. "Joan just didn't act right with Danny," he said. Then, Donoho suggested we get in touch with Benny Williams' mother, Mrs. Buckles Woodcock of Circus World near Orlando. And wonder of wonders, he revealed that Danny and Joan had switched to the armed car behind the Pancake House in Cocoa, Florida.

Now we knew where they were when Grace, Dewey and I had been trying to catch up with them. Tom Donoho added, "Afterwards, I took Dan O'Brien's car back to a bowling alley in Kissimmee, the same place where I met the O'Briens to get the car," an entirely different tale from what the O'Briens had told about the car in their depositions. Tom Donoho promised to call the FBI agent in charge of the case the next day.

Mr. Donoho kept his promise. An appointment was set up for him in New Mexico, so that he might be interviewed by an FBI agent there.

Suddenly the worm had turned. We were thinking hopeful, really hopeful. We had three names to go with three faces. Our next move: call Circus World and speak to Benny Williams' mother, Mrs. Buckles Woodcock. Mrs. Woodcock invited us to come calling. We did.

The Woodcocks lived on the circus grounds. Mrs. Woodcock was a beautiful person in every sense of the word. She had hurt her back recently, but graciously invited us into her trailer for coffee.

Over the coffee cups, Mrs. Woodcock told us, "Benny's in Brazil, working with a circus." But Benny had told his mother the same story that Tom Donoho had told us. Benny had been concerned, though, about the gun, which he knew David, the man in charge of the operation, carried. Benny had said to his mother, "There was something wrong going on there." Mrs. Woodcock showed us a large picture poster of Benny, catching a leopard as it jumped off an elephant, and there he was, muscles and all.

Now we began to imagine success and reach. We would have Grace Beck hypnotized to see if she could come up with the remaining numbers on the car which the armed man, David, had driven the day Danny was abducted. We set up an appointment with Doctor Richard O'Halloran. This proved to be an interesting and expensive experiment only. It produced no new information. Well, what next?

We wrote down all the pertinent information we had gathered on the driver of the armed car. His name was David, he was a medic in the Orlando area; he drove a white Ford, and we had a partial license tag number.

David, Dewey and I began to check every ambulance service in the area. We had our facts; we had pictures of Danny and Joan.

First we tried the Kissimmee area. Nothing. Then, on April 6th, we hit the jackpot at the Holden Heights Fire Department in Orlando. It went something like this.

Firemen were standing around outside the station. Dewey showed them the photograph of Joan, asking, "Do you know her?"

A lieutenant said, "I've seen her around."

Suddenly I felt the hair on the nape of my neck begin to crawl. It was as if someone might be creeping up behind me, as if someone might be about to do me bodily harm. Instinctively, I swung around. What a shock! There stood the fireman we had talked to a year ago at the Killarney Fire Department. His name was *David Hall.*

David Hall denied ever coming to our house. But it fitted; it fitted. He was wearing an emergency medical technician's patch on his uniform. He had a white Ford Torino. I said, "What's the license number on your car?"

He filled in the missing numbers on the partial numbers Grace Beck remembered. But he continued to deny anything and everything. Nevertheless, we were confident we had unearthed the third man.

We turned the information over to the FBI. May 9th, the FBI agent in charge talked with me. David Hall was the third man and he was cooperating with the FBI!

I telephoned Joe Caruso. He thought he should get a deposition from David Hall. Joe subpoenaed David Hall for a deposition on May 16th in Orlando. That very morning the FBI called and said Hall could not be questioned. Hall did talk with Joe, though, without benefit of deposition. Hall claimed the last he had heard from Joan, she was in California. She had called him for money to return to Florida. Hall had sent the money, but Joan did not come home.

We were stymied again, but we had to go on living, especially David and Sue.

Finding Danny had proved to be such a long and complicated road, David and Sue were beginning to wonder if they would live long enough to see Danny's return. They decided to be married. Better for them to see this through together than separately.

Several times David and Sue set a wedding date. Then, some little something about Danny would crop up and they would change the date. Finally they settled on June 4th with a prayer that Danny would be home by then. It didn't happen.

Consolation was the sweet and simple ceremony that took place on our dock that morning at sunrise, when David and Sue became man and wife. Afterwards, our families and close friends came to the house for eggs, coffee and wedding cake.

The following day Sue received a wedding present in the mail. It was a finger with a gold wedding band on it, wrapped in blood-soaked rags and accompanied by a sympathy card. David and Dewey were at work. Sue came to the house frightened and crying, carrying the gruesome specimen.

I phoned the FBI. "Take it to the post office," they said.

I phoned the post office. "Don't bring it here!" they told me.

Nobody wanted anything to do with this horror. I didn't blame them. At last, in despair, I called our friend and private investigator, Frank Demsky.

Frank dropped everything and hurried to our home. He removed the finger from the box and unwrapped it. The finger was rubber! But the bloody rag was real. None of us could imagine who would play such a heartless and cruel joke on Sue. Sick is the only word that describes it.

Forgetting was hard. But we tried. We went on with our search. Now there was one more to help: Sue.

We wrote letters to all the state superintendents of schools in the United States, giving vital statistics on Danny including a picture of Danny and Joan. Some states allowed the information to filter down through their school systems. In spite of this tremendous effort, nothing came of it. Meanwhile, Dan and Eileen O'Brien were maintaining stoutly to the FBI that they knew nothing and had seen or heard nothing from Joan. Then, along came July 26th.

The FBI called and said Joan Ng had been located in California. Joan was using the last name of Martin. She was staying in contact with her family. She lived near a sister in Sacramento. She was drawing fraudulent Aid for Dependent Children, while David was perfectly capable of supporting Danny. And, yes, Danny was with her and alive!

What a day! What rejoicing! What tears of relief!

Certain it would be just a matter of days, perhaps hours, before Danny was returned, we waited; we sweated it out. We called the FBI. Keep calm. They were not neglecting the case.

Then, on August 12th, the FBI told us that they had made a positive identification of a man that was in Joan's company. His name was Dale Fremo. There was no record of marriage. But Fremo, Joan and Danny were together and on the run, heading east.

Supposedly, according to a report the FBI had, Joan was about four months pregnant.

Our spirits sank. Danny had been so close. Now he was lost again.

About the only encouraging word was on the home front. Florida adopted the Uniform Custody Act. Those states which have adopted the act will honor one another's custody proceedings, a tremendous assistance in curbing child-snatching, definitely a step in the right direction.

Another month passed with no news on Danny. In October, a new FBI agent was assigned to the case. He came to the house to review the file.

Dewey and I, as well as our very good friend, Kathryn Case, who happened to be there, listened carefully.

Joan and Fremo had been traced to Kansas City. The agent passed around a picture of Fremo along with his vital statistics. He was a shaggy-haired, bearded derelict. I remember Kathryn saying, "He's so thin." And he was. About the skinniest person I had ever seen. Fremo, a Mendicino County, California fugitive from justice, had applied for a job in Kansas City, Missouri. But he had fled the scene when a prospective employer began checking references.

The FBI agent remarked, "Fremo's mother lives in Colorado Springs."

Here I said, "Kathryn's going to Colorado Springs for the birth of a new grandchild after the first of the year." Inspiration struck. "Perhaps I could send some legal papers, a plea for help to Fremo's mother by Kathryn. Would you give us her full name and address?"

The FBI agent was sorry, but he didn't think he could do that. He did say, "Call me after Mrs. Case goes to Colorado Springs for the birth of her grandchild. Perhaps, by then, I can give you the full name and address.

Now we wrote letters to the California Welfare Department, asking for information on Danny. We hoped someone had seen him, talked to him, when Joan applied for Aid to Dependent Children, and could give us information on Danny's well-being.

We received answers to our letters, but nothing definitive, only the county in which Joan had been living, and, of course, she had moved on with Fremo, a man who didn't inspire confidence.

In December, I lifted the ringing telephone to an anonymous call. A man gave me two license tag numbers. He said, "Check them out. These two cars are at the O'Brien house." The caller thought one of the cars belonged to Joan.

My heart did a flip-flop as I dialed the FBI agent in charge of the case and followed through with a call to Joe Caruso. The FBI checked: one of the cars belonged to Joan's sister, Diane Lee, and the other belonged to Joan's brother-in-law, Patrick Bourquin. Joan was not at the house. So much for that!

We tried to look forward to Christmas. I was both glad and sad when Dewey took some pictures of Danny, framed and resined a large collage for my kitchen wall. At least, we knew Danny was alive. But how was he faring in an on-the-run world? We didn't know. Couldn't guess. It was better not to think too much.

1978

We began January, 1978 with renewed resolve. We mailed letters and petitions with thousands of signatures, collected mainly by Gary Hobbs at his drug store on Merritt Island, to U.S. Senator Richard Stone and President Jimmy Carter, urging intensification of the search for Danny. We could not understand why Danny could not be located, now that so many particulars in his case were known.

On an off chance that the FBI would give us the full name and address of Dale Fremo's mother in Colorado Springs, I prepared a packet of legal documents, a WANTED poster with pictures of Joan and Danny, and a cover letter directed to Fremo's mother. Already Kathryn Case was packing her bags, standing by, waiting for the call that would take her to Colorado Springs for her new grandchild's birth.

Kathryn wasn't too keen about the idea of carrying the packet to Fremo's mother, should the FBI part with the information necessary to deliver it. "I'm not accustomed to doing things like that," Kathryn protested. "What would I say?"

I said, "You'll think of something --"

Kathryn laughed and threw up her hands. "I couldn't refuse you, Margaret, and you know it!"

Since Kathryn and Bill Case had moved to Merritt Island from Denver, Colorado, we had become near and dear friends. Though Kathryn and Bill had never seen Joan or Danny, in fact, had not known us or any member of our family, until three months after Danny was abducted by Joan, they listened to our troubles, shared our burdens and cheered us up when we were down.

As for Kathryn herself, well, there's just no comparison. A

gregarious, fun-loving, blue-eyed blonde, she's as pretty on the inside as she is on the outside. Kathryn and I talked about the packet of legal papers for Fremo's mother off and on during the month of January and into February. She was ready, willing and able. Her bags were packed and so was the envelope of legal documents along with the plea to Fremo's mother.

While we waited for Kathryn's new grandchild to make its appearance, we kept busy. Dewey was president of the Canaveral Martin-Marietta Management Club, on the advisory board of Brevard Community College and active in the Coast Guard Auxiliary, where he taught several classes each month. David and Sue were getting their home in order. Sue worked at a local pet shop; David continued working 24-hour shifts at the Cocoa Fire Department. I stayed at home near the phone, awaiting developments. I learned all sorts of new and interesting things, while baby-sitting that telephone. I can refinish floors, 'fake' brick a house, do carpentry, furniture stripping, you name it, and I can do it, if it has to do with staying home. But I had reached the point of no return. There was nothing left to do around the house. Everything was ship-shape.

So that time would not lie heavy on my hands, the ever-thoughtful Dewey said, "I'm going to buy you a pile of rock."

We had been wanting to rid ourselves of the grass in our front yard and replace it with a contour rock design. "You're all heart," I told him.

During early February, I spread heavy plastic over the lawn. My load of rocks arrived. It was a huge mountain, hiding the front of the house. Dewey, generous to the core, promised to help me spread rock on Saturday, February 18th.

On Friday night, Kathryn and Bill Case came over to the house for the evening. They were elated by the prospect of becoming grandparents -- any minute now. Jackie and Kent Gunderson joined us. They were remodeling a house. And Dewey and I had my rock pile!

We sat, laughing and talking. Naturally, as in all our conversations, in time we came to the subject of Danny.

Kathryn said, "I've got the packet for Fremo's mother in my luggage. Don't forget to call me in Colorado Springs if you get the name and address."

I promised not to forget.

We talked a bit longer about Danny.

Then Kathryn, with her usual optimism, said, "Oh, don't worry. I'll just fly out to Colorado Springs, find Danny in a parking lot, scoop him up and bring him home!"

Now that was a pretty picture. We complimented her on her imagination. The evening ended on this nonsensical note of good will.

Saturday, Dewey and I rose early. We wanted to get started on my rock pile. The phone rang. It was Kathryn. "My son, Dave, telephoned, and he's taking Tina to the hospital. She's in labor."

"Oh, fine," I said. "Then, I guess you're on your way --"

"First plane out of Orlando --"

"Have you got the packet on Danny and Joan in your luggage?"

"I've got it --"

"I'll call the FBI on Monday and see what they say --"

"I'll be in touch --"

"Good luck!"

And Kathryn was away.

Dewey and I trudged out to my rock pile and got to work. Later on, the phone rang again. Grateful for a respite from slave labor, Dewey and I went inside the house. It was Bill Case.

Bill had received a long distance call from son Dave soon after he'd returned from seeing Kathryn off on the plane. "It's a boy!" he said. Kathryn was somewhere in the air, winging toward Colorado. Bill had called to share the glad news with us.

We went back to the rock pile, working until nightfall, when we crawled into the house, utterly, totally exhausted. After we had showers, Dewey stretched out on one end of the couch and I sprawled on the other end of the couch. We read the newspaper and watched television. Very late that night, the phone rang. For the first time since Danny's abduction, neither of us wanted to answer the phone. Both of us claimed we were beyond help. Too tired.

I said, "I can't move, Dewey."

But the phone continued to ring insistently. Dewey sighed wearily, got off the couch and made for the phone.

I heard Dewey say, "How's that new baby?"

It must be Kathryn, I thought, calling long distance.

Then, the tone of Dewey's voice changed abruptly, dramatically, drastically. "Where? At the airport? Where?" Then, "I can't think. Here's Margaret."

I yanked myself from the couch and ran to the phone.

It was Kathryn, saying, "I don't know how to tell you this, but to say it. I just saw Joan and Fremo, and I've talked to Danny!"

I knew Kathryn didn't drink. Certainly she wasn't crazy. "*What?*"

No, it was true. She was positive.

That night we made and received many phone calls. David decided that Dewey should be the one to go to Colorado Springs,

228

since Dewey had promised Danny the day Danny was taken away that we would come and get him if Joan didn't bring him home. Dewey aimed to keep his promise.

David and Bill Case drove Dewey to the airport in Orlando, Dewey carrying with him legal documents which stated that he could act in David's behalf, if Kathryn was right in her identification.

David, Sue and I drank coffee and prowled the house, while we waited the outcome of this unlikely turn of events. We could not quite believe ...

Kathryn had never seen Joan or Danny, let alone Fremo. Could it possibly be true? We couldn't quite convince ourselves. But we wanted to believe, had to believe that Kathryn had seen Fremo and Joan in the Colorado Springs Hospital, where her new grandchild had been born, and she had talked with Danny in the maternity waiting room. Incredible. Improbable.

We made a long distance call to the hospital. There was no baby in the hospital nursery by the name of Fremo or Martin, names we knew Joan had been using. More doubts. We made another pot of coffee.

Never did we imagine or suspect that while Dewey and I struggled with my rock pile, a remarkable and amazing series of circumstances had caught up with Kathryn Case in Colorado Springs, Colorado.

Here in her own words is Kathryn's story.

No matter what Abbott Herring says in court, I was not hired by the Stricklands to go to Colorado Springs and get Danny. I went to Colorado Springs for the birth of my grandchild, and in the doing, I found Danny Strickland.

It all sounds so simple. It wasn't.

Prior to my departure, I had packed two bags. Into one bag went the envelope for Fremo's mother. For some mysterious reason, before departure, I opened the bag with the envelope in it and shifted the envelope to the other piece of luggage. When I stepped off the plane in Colorado Springs, I discovered the airline had lost one of my bags.

"Never mind," I told the airline clerk, "Here's my son's address. Send the bag along when you find it," and hurried off with Dave and my first-born grandchild, two and a half year old Kimberly, to Memorial Hospital, where the new baby and mother Tina were waiting.

At the hospital, Kim and I sat in the visitor's lounge on the maternity floor. While we waited to view the new baby, Kim crawled into my lap. She entertained me with a song: SANTA CLAUS IS COMING TO TOWN.

Christmas was ten months off. So what! This was a celebration of birth. I urged Kim to sing the song again, lavishing hugs and kisses along the way.

We were interrupted by a small boy with a winning smile, large brown eyes and thick black hair. "How old do you think I am?" he asked soberly.

I try to please. "Eight?" I guessed.

"Six!"

"My, but you're big for your age," I told him.

"I go to school and draw pictures," the boy confided.

"That's nice. I'll bet you're good at it."

Satisfied, the boy wandered away. My eyes followed him.

He stood near the door to the room, a solitary figure, dressed in plaid shirt, faded blue jeans and scuffed cowboy boots. Obviously restless, alone and lonely, the boy returned to my side. "I have a new baby brother," he announced.

Kim bragged, "I have a new baby brother, too!"

Then, Dave and Tina, along with our other son, Coe, and his wife, Sharon, down from college in Denver, came in to see the new baby and visit with me.

Everyone laughed and talked at once as we looked at baby Kevin, now on display through the viewing window. The baby was perfect. Red-headed, too. Just like Kim. As I turned to exclaim my appreciation of Kevin, I noticed the little boy with whom I had spoken earlier, standing by a man and woman at the viewing window, looking at a tiny baby with the last name of Lehman on its bassinett. The woman was young, but she appeared old and worn. She was dressed in a frayed, quilted robe and leaned on a cane. What's more: she was disheveled, unkempt even, a fact that I couldn't comprehend in this immaculate environment. I suppose that's why I looked at them so long and hard. I shook off the thought and joined the family.

We settled into a cluster of chairs and continued our reunion. Then, the little boy appeared and tugged at my sleeve. "Did you see me crawl?" he asked too anxiously.

The boy seemed desperate for attention, "No," I said. "I'm sorry."

"Wait," the boy said. He stretched out on the floor and began to wiggle forward.

I applauded. "That's the best combat crawl I've ever seen!"

Pleased with praise for an accomplishment well done, the boy disappeared.

The family went back to talking, until I felt a small body entwine itself around my feet. Oh, my little friend, I thought. I reached beneath my chair, grabbed the boy by his boots and pulled him free. As I placed him on his feet, he said, "Hey, did you see my baby sister?"

"I thought you had a baby brother --"

"Naw, I have a baby sister."

Dave leaned forward and teased, "You have a baby brother!"

The boy placed his hands on his hips. "I said I had a baby sister."

"Okay, okay," Dave said with mock apology. "I saw you see your baby sister!"

The boy threw back his head and laughed with delight. "I fooled you. I had a baby brother all the time!"

We all laughed and told the boy how clever he was. Then, we returned to visiting, until a tug came on my sleeve again. "Hey, what's your name?" the boy asked.

"Mrs. Case." Pointing to my daughters-in-law and sons in turn, I said, "That's Mrs. Case and Mrs. Case and Mr. Case and Mr. Case;" and finally to Kim, "Meet Miss Case."

"Wow!" The boy grinned at me. "That's a whole bunch of Cases."

"It sure is," I agreed. "Now, what's your name?"

The boy threw up both hands, framing his small face, grinning, the large brown eyes sparkling, "Danny!"

It was as if the floor had dropped from beneath me and I was suspended on some ethereal plateau, where a composite of every picture I had seen of the kidnapped Danny Strickland etched itself upon a screen within my mind; and this Danny looked remarkably like the image my mind was seeing.

Danny leaned against my arm, touching ... But I couldn't look at him. I was misplaced in time, trying to cope with emotions entirely foreign to me. Perhaps, I thought, I've taken leave of my senses. No. This was too real, too right. Something deep within me said it was so, a persuasion too great to ignore.

From far away I heard Tina demanding, "Mom? Mom? What's wrong?"

I shook my head. Inexplicably my entire body was racked by pain. Finally I took a deep breath, got control of myself and focused my eyes squarely on the boy's face. "Danny," I said. "What's your last name?"

The beautiful brown eyes, so alive with laughter a few minutes before, went totally blank. The boy shrugged a dismal shoulder.

At six years old, I told myself, a boy as bright and alert as Danny should know his last name. Then, suddenly intuition was supported

231

by identifiable facts under rigid scrutiny.

Before Danny and Joan's trail diminished into thin air, the FBI reported to the Stricklands that Joan had lived with about a dozen different men and changed last names no less than twelve times. It would have been a difficult proposition for a boy Danny's age to keep track of a constantly shifting homelife, not to mention a name! Then, there was Dale Fremo's mother. She had told the FBI Dale and Joan visited her, borrowing $500, saying Joan was pregnant! And where am I now? I demanded of myself. Colorado Springs! At a hospital! On the maternity floor!

I considered the man and woman Danny had stood by at the nursery viewing window. They were seated in the corner of the room. On many occasions Dewey and Margaret had mentioned that Joan wore dark glasses constantly. This woman was wearing dark glasses! But the man beside her ... I had seen photos of Fremo; Fremo wore a beard and long hair ... This man was clean shaven with short hair. Yet, he was thin, so very thin, a physical factor upon which I had commented, when I'd first seen Fremo's picture. Still; I had to deal with the name of Lehman attached to the bassinett. But that made sense too. The changing names; after all, Fremo was wanted by the police in California.

Now the woman hiding behind the dark glasses called to the boy. "It's time to leave, Danny. Daddy's got to go."

Danny smiled, waved to me and departed reluctantly.

"That," I said to my family with conviction, "was Danny Strickland."

Both Coe and Dave knew the story of Danny's kidnapping.

Dave cocked an eyebrow at me and said, "Aw, Mom, why should you of all people, in a world of millions, think that you would come to Colorado Springs and find Danny?"

Good question. I had no ability to read the future. But I knew what I knew.

Even Coe, who had gone hunting with David Strickland, while visiting in Florida, didn't take heed. "Mom," he said, "you've gone and flipped your lid!"

Maybe so. But I went on believing, never doubting for a minute.

Hospital visiting hours ended. Tina returned to her room. We voted to dine at a restaurant before going to Dave's home for the night. As we rode in Dave's car, I was deeply disturbed and shaken. I could not escape the notion that I had seen Danny and Joan. Then, it dawned on me. "I have photos of Danny and Joan in my luggage. When we get to the restaurant..." I remembered the lost luggage. I ended lamely, "It's in one of my bags. Maybe I've got the right one."

At the restaurant parking lot, Dave humored me by lifting the trunk lid of the car and saying, "Okay, Mom. Have at it."

I unlocked the lone bag and reached inside. The envelope? It was there!

Around the restaurant dining table, I opened the envelope. The photographs of Danny and Joan were studied by my family. Nobody said anything, until Dave settled the issue. "Well, Mom, what are you going to do about it? I'm not saying it's them, but the pictures look like them. You could be right. I think a check should be made."

I did not want to encourage where they was no actual proof, except the unreality of my sixth sense. The Stricklands had suffered too much already, not knowing from one day to the next if Danny was alive. But Coe and Sharon agreed with Dave. Though the pictures were over two years old, they bore a striking resemblance to the woman and boy we had seen.

What to do?

Well, I had to telephone, that's all. Since David was often hard to reach, because of his professional responsibilities, I settled on a long distance call to Dewey and Margaret.

Once they heard me out, they said, "We'll call the FBI." Then, they called back. An immediate investigation was to be made. An FBI agent would get in touch with me. Meantime, Dewey would fly into Colorado Springs the next morning at 9:30.

That very night the local FBI telephoned me at Dave's house and asked me to relate my story. When the FBI learned I had pictures and copies of legal documents in my possession, the agent said, "I'll be right out."

Upon his arrival, he examined Margaret's letter to Fremo's mother, a letter from the Department of Justice, explaining the Unlawful Flight to Avoid Prosecution warrant on Joan, a letter from the Director of the FBI Clarence Kelley, a copy of Joan's divorce from her second husband, Willie Ng, the custody papers from Brevard County, Florida, a copy of the warrant for Joan's arrest on kidnapping, and a WANTED poster with pictures of Joan and Danny.

The FBI agent said, "Mrs. Case, I'd like your help. Meet Mr. Strickland at the airport and bring him here. Don't let him go near that hospital!"

Dewey arrived on schedule. I drove him from the airport directly to Dave's house.

Dewey sank into a chair and said, "Frankly, Kathryn, I'm afraid to hope." He sighed and picked up a magazine from the coffee table.

Time passed. Nothing happened. Then, at 2:00 p.m. the doorbell *rang.*

Dewey opened the door to two men. One of them was carrying the boy in his arms. Dewey said softly, "Hello there, Danny. Do you remember me?"

Bewildered, Danny shook his head.

Dewey gathered his grandson into his comforting arms. Tears streamed down his face.

Now Danny began to talk, faltering at first, then, faster and faster, recalling bits and pieces of the past.

I heaved a big sigh. I had not been wrong.

These days it is hard for me to believe all of this really did happen. I think of my joking remark about scooping Danny up in a parking lot and bringing him home. I think about the precise timing, the proper place, the envelope shifted from one piece of luggage to the other without rhyme or reason, this very important piece of luggage with the oh-so-necessary packet of information that went unlost. I think about these things, and I am awed.

Only God could have produced and arranged such a logical sequence of events, such happiness.

At 4:30 p.m. Sunday, the phone rang. It was Dewey. "Margaret.."

I said, "Dewey ..."

Then, Kathryn said, "Hi!"

"Was it really Danny?"

Tears in her voice, she said, "Yes, but I can't talk about it. Bye."

I hung up the phone and ran outside the house to tell David and Sue. We fell into one another's arms and cried, exhausted and happy.

After a while, Kathryn called back. "Dewey's on the way home with Danny. He's due in Orlando at 11:32 tonight."

"Tonight?" Very hard to believe.

"Yes. And I don't think a crowd should be at the airport to meet Danny."

I was glad Kathryn was thinking, because David, Sue and I were so ecstatic with happiness, we were beyond thought.

Finally, though, we got ourselves together and telephoned Frank Demsky for advice. After some discussion, it was decided that the best course of action was for David and Frank to meet Danny and Dewey at the airport. We had no idea how it might go. We were aware that Dan O'Brien had hired men to come and get Danny in the first place. It could happen again.

Frank explained the picture to Airport Security in Orlando. They allowed Frank and David to drive around to the back of the airport, so that Danny would not be exposed to the public at large in the lobby.

Danny's first words to David were awe struck. "Daddy -- are you a ghost? I though you were dead!"

At home I was counting the seconds. Sue, our daughter Kathy, her husband Cary and Bill Case were with me. We were sitting around the kitchen table, drinking coffee, when a car entered the driveway. Now I heard Danny talking a blue streak. I started to get up from the kitchen table. My legs wouldn't work. I sat down on the kitchen floor. Danny came running in and sat on my lap.

We did hug and kiss. I couldn't talk. Danny made up for my momentary conversational disability. He told me about his flight in the airplane; he had saved some peanuts and colored a picture for me. "Grandma," he said, "I used to dream of this house and you, after I went to bed. It was real and I thought it was a dream."

What a night to remember!

During the next few days, many friends came by the house. Nancy and Jerry Brown came bearing gifts. Jerry had graduated from high school with David. The Christmas before Danny's recovery, Nancy and Jerry had brought us a card and a check for $100 to be used for Danny, when he was found. Such a nice gesture; and they were saving for a house and baby of their own. But Nancy and Jerry were typical of the kind of people that saw us through those desperate twenty-two months. We shed many tears of gratitude. But we did laugh. How we laughed!

A few months earlier, I had applied for and received a Visa charge card. Since Dewey and I are great ones for paying our way in this world with cash -- or we don't get it -- we had never had a charge card. So we had tried to think of everything that would lighten our search for Danny. We had joked and said, "Now's the time for that charge card." We figured when Danny was found it would be a Saturday night and we wouldn't have thirty cents between us; and it *was* a Saturday night.

That Visa charge card had done its best work. It paid for the airplane tickets necessary for Dewey to go out to Colorado Springs and return with Danny. Everything had come out just right; and all at once!

We spent days catching up with Danny. He remembered most things. He became very animated at his old toys, the swing, the fish pond. Three days passed. "Where are my trees that Daddy and I used to play army in?" he asked.

We had removed a row of six large pine trees on order from the county, so that a storm drain might be installed!

Danny recalled many of the good times we had enjoyed on our dock. But he didn't remember other people too well. He did remember his best playmate Jeramy Moore, the grandson from next door.

Jeramy came over, just like before. Danny stood looking at him for what must've been a full minute. Then, he said, "You're my best friend, Jeramy!" and wiped away the missing years.

Joan called from her hospital bed in Colorado Springs. The only aspect of that conversation which I remember, "I don't want Danny to forget that Dale Fremo is his daddy."

My reply, "David is his daddy."

We had our telephone number changed and unlisted.

After everyone had settled in comfortably, the first order of business was a physical check-up for Danny. The doctor unearthed no problems, except an eye infection. Medication cleared that up. Next we took him back to the Baptist Church School, which he had been attending prior to his abduction. He would have to enter the four year old class, exactly where he was when he'd been taken. Danny was too old for four year olds. David and Sue registered him in kindergarten at Mila Elementary School near their home.

Danny stayed with Dewey and me. David and Sue spent their nights in the spare bedroom. But each day David took Danny to his own home for a while. He wanted Danny to adjust gradually to new places and new faces.

Sue was ready to assume her new role and she did an excellent job. In no time at all, Danny was ready to move in with his father and Sue. Many of his weekends were spent with Dewey and me, though. Danny so loved the dock and fishing.

Now the news media got on our case. We had never been released from the original gag order handed down by Judge Roger Dykes. The very newspapers which would not print an item against Judge Dykes' wishes in 1976, knowing full well we could not respond, went to work on us and did a fine job of libel.

It did not interest the news media that David had stayed within the framework of the legal system and against great odds had been successful in finding his son. We came to regard THE SENTINEL STAR and THE COLORADO GAZETTE as one might regard the plague. The untruths they printed about the Strickland family were staggering. If they had removed the inaccuracies from their newspaper articles, nothing would have remained.

We realize motherhood is a sacred word in the English language. But motherhood should never be used to excuse someone who has planned and carried out the abduction of a child and concealed that child contrary to court order.

Likewise, the television news coverage imitated the newspapers; they could not resist Joan's persuasive personality. Everytime Joan opened her mouth, there was someone there to record it. Nobody once bothered to check the validity of what she said, tried to ascertain the facts and report accordingly.

While our character was being assassinated, Joan knew full well that we could not respond without being held in contempt of court. So there we sat, reading and listening to the same lies, day after endless day. It was humiliating.

Just a few of the more blatant untruths: the Strickland home had been checked by the Health Department and was an unfit home in which to raise Danny; Dewey Strickland was a wealthy construction man; the Strickland family had wealth and political influence.

If anyone had bothered to check the record, they could have seen readily that our political influence was nil, that we were fast going broke, that our home was a fit place in which any child lucky enough to live would be happy.

No newspaper ever bothered to print that Joan had given birth to an illegitimate child and was not married to Dale Fremo when the FBI took Danny from Fremo; that Dale Fremo had an outstanding warrant for his arrest in California for jumping probation parole, stemming from an original charge of felony kidnapping; that Joan's second husband was Willie Ng, not Fremo -- Joan married Fremo over the telephone, after Danny's pick up by the FBI; that a threat had been made on Danny's life when he was taken; that Dan O'Brien hired three men, who used implied force when Joan took Danny and disappeared with him; that Joan drew fraudulent welfare under the name of Joan Martin in California. None of these facts saw the light of day. None of them.

We had never lived in the public eye. We did not like it. We did not know how to counteract the lies; and even if we had, we could not do so, because of the court order.

Thus, Colorado, unaware of the true facts in the case, refused to allow Joan's extradition to Florida. It wasn't that David wanted Joan punished. Far from it. He simply wanted some legal assurance that Danny could not be taken again, and if that terrible day should occur, the legal system would work in Danny's behalf. For surely Danny was the loser. Not David. Not Joan. Not Dewey. Not me. It was Danny; and it was Danny still about whom we worried.

Soon David had additional worries on that score. Our former State Attorney Abbott Herring became Joan's attorney and biggest defender.

Oh, dear ... Here was the man who had filed the original charges against Joan, the man who had taken seven long months to make out the correct papers for the FBI to enter the case, and he was once again working against us. He was trying his case seemingly on every street corner and in every newspaper, getting the cart before the horse, so to speak, while giving the truth a good shellacking.

Said Abbott Herring, "David Strickland never came to see me while I was State Attorney." But that was only the beginning. Abbott Herring was shocked -- personally, I gathered -- by the fact that the Federal Bureau of Investigation had entered the case. With Mr. Herring as State Attorney, who needed the FBI! The truth, according to Abbott Herring, was highly elusive, particularly since Danny would never have been found without our efforts and the efforts of the FBI, not to mention the perceptive Kathryn Case.

As if all this wasn't enough to choke a horse, when the case came up for trial, we discovered legal papers in conjunction with the original filing missing from the current State Attorney's files. A very strange code of ethics. But nothing phased the intrepid Abbott Herring.

Mr. Herring was adding fuel to our fire by saying that during his term in office evidence had turned up which made him feel justice would not be served by pursuing prosecution of Joan. We would appreciate knowing what that evidence is, since he did not feel called upon to reveal it in his own defense.

Many people who knew the facts of the matter and read the newspapers rushed to the telephone to call us and to complain to the newspapers. But we were entering a new era in our fight for Danny's life. Better not to look back.

In May, we had to make several trips to Titusville to talk to State Attorney Douglas Cheshire's office. Danny had to miss school and attend some of these meetings. Consequently he heard the whole story from beginning to end with nothing remaining for his imagination. He was questioned by the State Attorney without the presence of any of the family. During these interviews, State Attorney Cheshire used a 'Tennessee truth stick.' It was a harmless bit of wood, I gathered. But these tactics did not improve Danny's state of mind. Danny returned from these sessions highly agitated, as if he might be losing his grip on reality. A confused six-year-old child should never be subjected to such tactics.

I told State Attorney Cheshire that Danny had told me about a bank robbery involving Joan, a man named Paul, and a bald-headed man named Jack. Danny said, "We lived with Paul and Joan wrecked Paul's car." He spoke of Paul frequently. State Attorney Cheshire wasn't interested. We turned the information over to the FBI.

One day Kathryn Case and I took Danny out for lunch. Two men entered the restaurant and sat in an adjacent booth. Danny took one look at them, began to shake, and crawled under the table. When we managed to retrieve him, calm him down, he said, "I thought one of them was my daddy Paul."

Kathryn took charge of Danny. I rose and went over to the gentlemen's table. I introduced myself and asked their names. I'm sure they thought I was crazy. But I had to know. Neither of them was named Paul, but our lunch was ruined.

Indicative of Danny's two years on the run was a visit to the fire house with David to meet David's fellow employees and friends. At the sight of badges and uniforms, Danny flew into a frenzy. He had been taught that police were bad.

Occasionally Danny would look at us all with a dazed expression in those big brown eyes, as if he didn't believe we were real. But, of course, that was understandable; he had been told incessantly, when he talked about us to Joan, that we were all dead.

David and Sue made an appointment with the Mental Health Clinic for Danny. After several visits to Mental Health, the recommendation was made that Danny not be exposed to any pressure situation whatsoever. But this was a nearly impossible recommendation to follow. The legal system was pulling in the opposite direction with their 'Tennessee truth sticks.'

We decided to depend on our best judgment, weigh and balance everything we said and did. We knew, though, that Danny had to be told the truth when he asked questions. We wanted him to understand the value of truthfulness in the years ahead.

Then, in June, much to our amazement, Joan returned to Florida to stand trial. Judge William Woodson presided.

When we entered the courtroom, there sat Joan, cuddling the new baby, Charlie, in one hand and clutching a Bible in the other hand. We sensed we were about to go down the tube again. How right can one be!

In spite of David Hall's crucial testimony that he took Joan from our house to the airport and purchased one-way tickets to South Carolina, an out-of-state destination, for Danny and Joan under fictitious names, Judge Woodson refused to allow the trial to go to the jury.

Judge Woodson directed a verdict of acquittal. He ruled the state had not proved criminal intent!

Once again, let me make David's position perfectly clear: he did not want to see Joan in jail; she was Danny's mother. But he felt the least Judge Woodson could have done was to have given Joan a stern lecture and given him some legal assurances that the law would be more cooperative should Danny be taken again. Then, I picked up the newspaper TODAY and read that Joan's attorney, Abbott Herring, and Judge William Woodson had been football teammates at the University of Miami in 1946 and remained bosom buddies to this day!

We were not alone with our feelings of helplessness in the face of the judicial system. Many friends and total strangers felt strongly about the trial. They wrote letters to the newspapers, charging that Judge Woodson had let Joan use her baby as a prop in court and saying that the trial should have gone to the jury, where impartial, freeminded people could have made a decision with proper recommendations.

We agreed. We had talked to the newspapers, both SENTINEL STAR reporter Blanton McBride and TODAY's managing editor Ron Thornburg. But nobody was listening. Odd. Now that we were free to speak the truth, only deaf ears greeted us. We were told by the newspapers that legal aspects of the case alone would be printed from here on in.

Oh, well . . . With this behind us, Danny improved both mentally and physically. David and Sue enrolled him in summer camp. He loved it. But he was not allowed to complete camp, or enjoy it like the other little boys, since he was at the beck and call of court-related matters.

There were better times, though. One day I was in a department store shopping. Over the loudspeaker came a message, "Will Danny Strickland's grandmother please meet him in the toy department?"

A bit bewildered, I made my way to the toy department. There stood Danny. I laughed and said, "How did you know I was in the store?"

Danny's brown eyes filled with love. "I saw your car in the parking lot."

David was in the nearby sporting goods department. But Danny had asked a clerk to page me.

I bought Danny a book. Little things like that had come to mean so much to our family.

I remember one Sunday morning after church, when David, Sue and Danny stopped by the house. Danny ran to his bedroom, the one in which he sleeps when he visits us. In a few minutes he called, "Grandma, come here!"

I went to see what he wanted. The door to his room was closed. I opened it. On the floor he had laid out his best clothes. From the bedroom closet came Danny's voice, saying, "This is Danny's holy spirit, and I love you."

Danny listened, really listened to The Reverend Tom Alston at the Central Brevard Christian Church. Danny wanted to be able to take communion. David and Sue explained that he must be baptized first.

Danny argued, "I've already been baptized twice!"

When we got to the bottom of this remark, we learned Joan had had Danny baptized to change his name, so that she could collect welfare.

Although we felt we were doing well with Danny, there were too many moments when Danny seemed bewildered and out of touch. David made an appointment with psychiatrist Doctor Burton Podnos.

For Doctor Podnos, David listed Danny's background problems in detail: Danny was afraid of the police -- he would hit the floor of the car and his heart pounded wildly, if he so much as saw a police car; Danny insisted he knew bank robbers; Danny had been raised on welfare; Danny knew how to get groceries without paying for them; Danny became extremely agitated and hid himself away when he heard Joan's name; Danny had lots of fake 'dads,' which confused him greatly; Danny had been told we were all dead; Danny had no idea what his last name was when Kathryn Case found him; Danny never mentioned Joan's name, except when he asked me to go get his new halfbrother, Charlie.

Doctor Podnos proceeded with his tests. Joan was to be present in Doctor Podnos' office. This was the first time Joan had been with Danny since February. We were not permitted to prepare Danny in advance for this encounter with his mother. Though I believe Danny loves Joan, nothing very good came of this surprise meeting, including the bill Doctor Podnos sent to David for Joan's personal request for counseling.

After seeing Joan at Doctor Podnos' office, Danny came home to cry and repeat, "Don't let them take me away again." He was like a broken record. Calming him down, getting him into bed that night was no easy feat.

Now the newspapers took after us again. SENTINEL STAR reporter, Blanton McBride, telephoned and asked, "Have you been making threatening phone calls to the O'Briens?"

"Of course we haven't. Ridiculous." I hung up.

I had more urgent matters on my mind. The custody case had

been assigned to Judge Dominick Salfi. Abbott Herring, feeling stronger by the minute and knowing David's attorney Joe Caruso was out of town, filed motions to restore Joan's visitation rights and to modify custody. Since Judge Salfi was hearing another case, the emergency hearing would be held before Judge Tom Waddell on June 22nd, and Judge Waddell would advise Judge Salfi on what to do!

David telephoned Judge Waddell's office and explained that Joe Caruso was out of town. That was no excuse. The hearing would be held. Well, I could imagine why. I understood from other people that Judge Waddell was Abbott Herring's close friend.

David telephoned Joe Caruso. Joe came to the rescue, flying home during the night, leaving the bedside of his very ill and hospitalized son. Once Joe was on deck, the hearing was called off.

In Joan's petition for modification of custody, she asked for custody of Danny, and for David to pay child support and Abbott Herring's attorney fees. Beyond belief. David couldn't understand why he should pay Herring's fees when he would not have been involved in a custody case hearing if Joan had not kidnapped Danny in the first place. David felt Joan should pay Caruso, if anything.

Along came July. A hearing was to be held before Judge Dominick Salfi. He said he would hear two items and two items only: visitation and security. The terms and conditions he set forth: Joan must provide a cash bond of $7,000 surety bond or security and comply with court orders, return Danny after visitation on time, and not remove Danny from the State of Florida without consent of the court. The visitation schedule was a ragged, crazy-quilt, designed as if by a madman. It was one day here, five days there, ten days over yonder with a clock work that only an Einstein could have deciphered.

At the end of this impossible schedule, if Joan and David could not agree on visitation, the court would set another schedule.

Joan failed to secure bond, so the visitation schedule was not used. Now Judge Salfi ordered an investigation by the Health Department and appointed an attorney, Joanne Butt, to represent Danny. Also, Judge Salfi joined Dewey and Margaret Strickland and Dan and Eileen O'Brien as parties to the cause. He ordered all parties involved to encourage love and affection for the other parties in their conversation and relationship with Danny.

Next Judge Salfi decided that Joan could begin visitation with Danny at the Health Department. David didn't mind, especially since Judge Salfi had ordered *direct* supervision in the presence of authorized personnel.

David explained this very carefully to Danny. He wanted Danny to have a good visit without fear or fright, since Danny was concerned so greatly about being taken away.

During the first visit, David and Sue had an appointment with other Health Department personnel. Their appointment would last longer than Danny's visit with Joan, so Kathryn Case and I drove over to get Danny. Joan had brought him a blow-up toy and a picture. Danny was pleased. Danny laid his head on my shoulder and said, "Grandma, I lied."

"What do you mean?"

"Nobody stayed with me like Daddy promised. And I lied. I was afraid."

Then, Danny rambled on about a tape recorder -- how Joan would ask him questions, and he would answer them. She had asked him, "Do you want to go back to Colorado?" and he had answered, "Yes," because he was afraid to say, "No."

I told Kathryn to turn around and go back to the Health Department, where I spoke to Billy Rollings. I explained to him what had happened and how fearful Danny had been. Mr. Rollings didn't know anything about anything. I departed, and Kathryn and I took Danny to the park to play. But Danny couldn't calm down. Finally we gave up and drove to Joe Caruso's office. Joe wasn't in. We sat and talked with Joe's secretary, Ruth. Danny repeated the story he had told Kathryn and me. He had to tell everyone and anyone who would listen. In times of crisis, Ruth was a super sounding board.

The following Monday was the first day of school. On Wednesday, Danny was to visit his mother again. He was reluctant. He felt David had lied to him. He had been alone with Joan and he was afraid. David tried to convince Danny to visit Joan on the promise that either he or Sue would stay with him. Danny wouldn't commit himself.

Sue and Mr. Rollings had several telephone conversations. Sue understood Mr. Rollings to say the meeting room had a two-way mirror. Mr. Rollings said they would watch what went on during Joan and Danny's meeting, through the mirror.

On this premise and with much explanation to Danny, Sue and David managed to arrive at the Health Department with Danny in fairly good form. But there was no mirror. Danny refused to cooperate. The visit was terminated by the Health Department.

In the process of all this needless suffering for Danny, Sue learned Mr. Rollings' memory was mighty short. He did not remember why I had returned to his office after the first visit, but he remembered every detail concerning Joan's problems with her car that day.

Now David received a report Abbott Herring had sent to the Health Department. This piece of paper contained a list of witnesses -- among them a man arrested with Dale Fremo in California -- who would testify that Danny had never once mentioned David or the Strickland family name during the twenty-two months Danny was away from home. Since Joan had convinced Danny we were dead, we felt this was not a pertinent point. We were amazed that a man who had been arrested for felony kidnapping should be a character witness in a parental kidnapping!

Along with this report was a psychological evaluation on Joan from Colorado Springs. Joan is very good at saying what she suspects people want to hear, if it's to her advantage. This report was no exception. She passed with flying colors. But it was the cover page that irritated David most.

Here Joan stated that she and Fremo had no significant indebtedness, and the expense for the custody conflict would be covered by a trust fund created by friends. A social worker had placed a statement in this report, noting that it was indeed 'noteworthy' that the Fremos were able to organize and obtain public exposure in behalf of their cause. We thought it was pretty 'noteworthy' ourselves. David was flat broke and Dewey and I were heavily in debt with SEA-TREK up for sale. But for Danny's sake, we had to stay within the legal framework of the law, regardless of the cost.

A copy of Joan's deposition arrived next. It was the most interesting and remarkable reading I've done in a long while. Joan admitted to using eight different names. She had never used her legal name of Joan Ng throughout those twenty-two missing months. But, then, she had been very busy.

Joan had moved seventeen times. For her telephone marriage in the hospital, she had used the O'Brien name. In California, she acquired a driver's license under the name of Joan Martin and used this name, plus her birth certificate with the name O'Brien on it, explaining to the welfare people in California that she used the name Martin because she was living with someone by that name and had used it for years.

In her deposition, she went on to state that Danny was allowed to choose his own name when she had him baptized. Danny Martin was a nice name, she felt. As for the several baptisms, she said, "It doesn't hurt." With these baptismal records, she was able to obtain welfare.

Twice Joan had risen to great heights of responsibility by entering Danny in school, once in Lincoln, Nebraska, and once in Colorado

Springs.

In California, she had purchased a sports car and traded that in on a Volkswagen van. She had traveled much, camping out with the van. She was not employed, because she was occupied "sewing, baby sitting and what not."

Joan claimed she considered Dale Fremo her husband from the beginning of their relationship. She said she and Dale had made up some vows, said a prayer, and started living together. She said Fremo returned to court in California for trial. The case was laughed out of court, according to Joan, and Fremo was put on self probation. Fact: Fremo had plea bargained the original kidnapping charge which involved physical damage, money, drugs and holding or detaining an individual to commit extortion with a threat to kill; he pleaded guilty to battery, which is unlawful use of force upon another person, and was placed on probation, which he ignored promptly by removing himself from the State of California. At this writing, the warrant on Fremo is outstanding.

Joan stated her parents left town the day before she came to pick up Danny at the beginning of the twenty-two month disappearing act. Dan and Eileen were at cross purposes with Joan on this score. In their deposition, they had left town after breakfast the same day. David Hall in his deposition said the O'Briens met Joan and her three companions at the bowling alley, and Dan O'Brien had given the circus workers the keys to his car and said, "Take it and go."

In Joan's deposition, she went on to say that she traveled to the airport from our house with David Hall, having drawn a map for the circus workers, so they could return the car to her parents' home. Joan had written a letter to her parents, saying the car was at the airport. Eileen said in her deposition that the car was at home. Dan said the car was at home, that he had talked to Tom Donoho and that Joan had driven Tom back to Tom's car in Kissimmee, and Joan had brought the car home. Tom, the man driving the O'Brien car, said he took the car back to the bowling alley, the same place the O'Briens had given it to him, left it, and drove off in his truck. David Hall's deposition said that he took Joan straight to the airport from our house.

How did the O'Brien car get to the O'Brien house? Confusing? To say the least.

Mr. O'Brien's deposition said he hired two circus men to come to our home with Joan. He did not know the third man. David Hall said he went to the O'Brien's home the night before to discuss the matter with Joan's parents. David Hall was the third man!

Now for the postcards. In Joan's deposition, she said she

departed Florida on April 4th, 1976. David Hall said he took Joan to the airport and bought one-way tickets to South Carolina for Danny and Joan under fictitious names. All through April of that year, Eileen and Dan had presented postcards stamped in Miami as proof that Joan had not left the State of Florida.

Who sent the postcards? Your guess is as good as any.

Back to Joan's deposition. Joan said she had asked several attorneys what would happen to her if she took Danny. She claimed each of the attorneys had told her, "Nothing. It's not a crime."

Well, everyone of those attorneys was right, because nothing was happening.

Joan claimed Dewey pushed her around outside our house on that fateful Sunday morning, until he saw David Hall and the circus roustabouts. Dewey was across the road at the end of our 250 foot long dock. Two sets of neighbors and Grace Beck, all reputable people, knew the truth. But did anyone else?

Not if Joan had her way, for the deposition dribbled down into the absolute and positive pointless. Joan accused me of teaching Danny that to nurse her baby was to be a pig. But this item was not so pointless to the newspapers.

Oh, how the newspapers reveled in writing about Grandma Margaret Strickland and her lack of sensitivity. Of course, that's putting it sweetly.

Once we had studied the entire deposition, we looked at one another and agreed: it was good to have Danny home!

With the deposition behind us, and following the Health Department's cancellation of visitation rights for Joan, Abbott Herring asked Judge Salfi to impose sanctions of contempt on the Stricklands. Mr. Herring said we had ignored the order which encouraged love and affection for the other party. Nonsense! Danny knew what was going on. He had heard the full story at the State Attorney's office. He had been assured a third party would be present at visitation. We didn't blame him. It had been a hard row for a little boy to hoe, especially a little boy who was confused about his identity for far too many months.

Along with the motion for contempt, Mr. Herring requested that Danny visit Joan under the supervision and responsibility of Eileen O'Brien. David refused. Understandable.

This was the household where Danny's kidnapping had been planned in front of him, while Dan O'Brien had promised responsibility for Danny. Danny understood that Dan O'Brien had hired the men who came for him; and he understood muscles and guns.

Now Joan wanted Danny placed in a foster home. Judge Salfi

had said more than once that this was a third alternative. Joan had evidently decided, if she couldn't have Danny, David couldn't have Danny. Truly beyond reason.

Danny had had enough insecurity. He needed a home base with a loving family. He had it. If Danny did not trust Joan, one had only to look at the record. We wished it were different. But Danny knew too much. He loved Joan, true, and even said as much. But he did not trust her. He had every reason not to trust her.

Finally, in a positive move in the right direction, Danny's court appointed attorney, Joanne Butt, requested counseling for Danny. Zack Price of Family Services became Danny's counselor. He and Danny hit it off from the word go.

We had no idea what they did or discussed. It didn't matter. We knew only that the most important event in Danny's week was his visit with Zack Price. Zack Price will be Danny's friend forever. Report or no report. The improvement in Danny was dramatic.

On November 20th, we went to court to hear Joan's motions to impose sanctions on the Stricklands. Since Judge Salfi couldn't find time to hear everything, he put all parties under an order which prohibited them from discussing any matters concerning the other parent with Danny or discussing the other parent in Danny's presence with another person, regardless of whether the comment was favorable or not. Suddenly we thought we were losing our minds.

We were under two orders that conflicted directly. We were to encourage love and affection for the other party on one hand, and we could not discuss anything, not even the good, concerning the other party!

Danny's court appointed attorney, Ms. Butt, married and moved away. She was replaced by Joan Bickerstaff. Danny fell in love with Ms. Bickerstaff; he kept her card by the phone. He could call her anytime he liked; and he did often. We didn't blame him. She was young and attractive, full of get up and go.

And go we all did, back to court on December 29th to finish the hearing of November 20th. Judge Salfi found David, Dewey and me guilty of *not* encouraging love and affection. He felt we should not have answered any of Danny's questions. None. This was the result of a harmless little scene.

Danny had received a jacket from Joan on his birthday. He liked the jacket. But he said, "Joan lied to me."

I said, "She did?" and hoped it would end there.

Danny said, "She told me this jacket was like my daddy Dale's." Then, he looked up at me with those soulful brown eyes and said,

"Grandma, is Dale Fremo my real dad?"

"No, he isn't!" I answered firmly.

I wish Judge Salfi had been in my shoes.

Little things like that didn't bother Judge Salfi, though. He seemed above human emotions. But since we weren't, he handed down a new order: all parties to the joint conflict would receive counseling.

Dewey and I refused. Judge Salfi had played fast and loose with us once too often. We felt we were his personal social experiment, since he refused to consider the true facts in the case. David agreed to counseling. Anything. He went that second and third and fourth and fifth mile.

John B. Curtis was the conflict counselor. He phoned and asked Dewey, "Is there any chance of David and Joan getting back together?"

Dewey said dryly, "I doubt it. David's happily married to Sue, and Joan has been married twice, so far as we know, since she married David."

David liked Mr. Curtis well enough. But he considered the counseling money down a rat hole, primarily because Mr. Curtis suggested that David hold Joan's hand and listen to her talk. David had no desire to hold Joan's hand and listen to her fiction. The whole business was useless.

As anyone can see, after Danny's return, we were on a legal merry-go-round that never stopped. Seldom did Danny go two consecutive days without court ordered activities. Keeping track of the whole mess was close to impossible.

There was visitation, counseling, appointments with the Health Department, personal lawyers, the State Attorney, judges and psychiatrist. The minimum number of Danny's appointments and activities were three a week and the maximum three a day on a school day. This went on month after month after month.

Sue was under a court order that she could not take Danny to some of his appointments, since it seemed to upset Joan if Sue was anywhere around. So I delivered Danny to many of his things-to-do when David was at work. Besides Danny's busy schedule, we had our own obligations which had to be fulfilled; hearings, trials, conflict counseling, home checks, interviews, psychiatrist, State Attorney, *ad infinitum*.

Fortunately, we learned to take one day at a time. We knew Danny had to stay in school as much as the court would allow -- he was a year behind in school as the result of his abduction already. But, Danny had precious little peace of mind. He was kept in a constant daily turmoil. We complained often and bitterly, but there was no stopping it. The victimized parent and the abducted child had no rights. Sad, but true.

Nevertheless, it was much better having Danny home, though the circumstances were not perfect, than having him lost, not knowing if he were alive. Yes, Danny was home. That's what counted. But for how long? Too often we had our doubts.

1979

On February 6th, Joan returned to the bosom of Dale Fremo in Colorado Springs. Don't get your hopes up; it didn't mean a thing. Abbott Herring was there pitching. He asked for a trial date to be set on the issue of Danny's custody.

While we waited for the date to be scheduled on the court calendar, as a gesture of consideration, Joe Caruso wrote a letter to Abbott Herring, telling him that it would be all right for Eileen O'Brien to visit Danny with security.

Eileen hadn't requested a visit with Danny. But with Joan gone, David considered this a reasonable move in the right direction. As for the security, David would not waive it. For Eileen had maintained she did not know Danny's whereabouts, when, in fact, she had been in Colorado with Danny, Joan and Fremo while the FBI searched for Danny.

Finally the custody trial date was set for April 24th, Judge Joe Cowart presiding. A lot of prayers had been said for Judge Cowart. We knew we had stayed within the framework of the legal system; we had not lied to Danny or anyone else. We were prepared.

Joe Caruso went to the courthouse at 9:a.m. He would call us when the case was to be heard. About 11:30 a.m., Ruth, Joe's secretary, called and said, "Ready?" I phoned Dewey at his office, so that he could meet us at the court house. David, Sue and I stopped by to pick up Ruth, and we were on our way. Danny's Sunday School teacher, Martha Franco, met us at the courthouse door to supply support and testimony if needed.

We did not expect what Joe Caruso told us. Joe said that Judge Cowart had studied the case and the various reports, and had made his decision. David would retain custody of Danny, and Joan would be allowed a forty-five day visit each summer, providing she posted a $5,000 security with the court to insure Danny's return.

We heaved a collective sigh of relief. David and Sue would provide a stable home for Danny, love and heritage. Joan and Dale would stay in contact with Danny and enjoy him. Of course, we did not dismiss our remaining concern: Joan might choose to take Danny and hide him again. But we made up our minds to be optimistic and hope, and give Danny a new lease on life.

As summer approached, Joan posted bond for Danny to visit her in Colorado Springs, where she was living with Fremo. As the time to depart came closer, Danny became apprehensive. Danny refused to go. Danny's court appointed counselor and court appointed attorney knew Danny well. They went before the court and asked for a delay in Danny's visit with Joan. It was their opinion that Danny was responding well at this time and to delay the visit would be best for Danny's mental welfare. The court decided that the mother had rights. Danny must go *now*.

Suddenly we were in the same legal position we had been in when Joan kidnapped Danny in 1976. The only change in the situation: Danny was older.

This time Danny did return home, though. Joan set up a press conference with the SENTINEL STAR for Danny upon his return to Florida. It was hard to believe that a mother would do this to a seven-year-old child; it is even harder to believe that a responsible newspaper would take such an unfair advantage of a seven-year-old child. Did Danny count for nothing?

To those who were a party to this farce -- well, I think not. Eileen O'Brien was quoted as saying, "I'm not taking any chances on bringing Danny home late and losing the bond money." This seemed to be the paramount issue, not Danny.

As we continued to read the newspaper article, we understood we faced the same old problems all over again, only worse. Danny was quoted as saying he did not like himself and would like to kill himself. Danny's counselor and attorney had been right in their requests to delay visitation.

Like so many other child-snatched victims, Danny has paid a horrible price, through no fault of his own. The scars will be with him forever, and his future remains uncertain. But for the first time, we are beginning to see the light of day . Little did we imagine that Danny's case would become a precedent in the years to come in another appalling child-snatching.

SECTION XIII

THE AFTERMATH

Scott and Alice Adams reside in a lovely home on a quiet street in Cocoa Beach, Florida. Their lush, green backyard slopes to a canal, beneath well-placed shade trees, suitable for fishing and boating. It's the perfect place for the children to grow alongside their pet fish Oscar, Jean and George, the parakeets, and a dog named Bones.

Behind this serene facade, though, lies a parental kidnapping which I have come to think of as 'the aftermath' of the Danny Strickland case. But first, let's go back in time, before Scott married Alice, to the day when Scott met a girl named Sally at Scott's mother's condominium in Miami, Florida.

Sally was pregnant and unmarried. Scott felt sorry for her, and he assisted her by insisting she have the proper foods so that a normal child would be born into the world. When the baby was born, Sally gave the child up for adoption, and Scott and Sally went their separate ways.

After a while they met again and decided to take up where they left off. Though they would not marry, they agreed that any children they had were to be shared.

Two boys were born to them, one in 1971 and the other in 1973. But Sally grew restless, and she left, taking the boys with her, moving from place to place around the United States.

Occasionally Scott would catch up with Sally, and the boys would be his for a few weeks; then they were gone again. At one point, Sally took the boys from the United States to Israel for nine months. In desperation, Scott journeyed to Israel to see the children. When he returned to Florida, he purchased a new home and sent Sally tickets for her and the boys to return. He was making every effort to reconcile his family.

In 1976, Scott gained temporary custody of the two boys. But Sally didn't return to Florida with the boys. Finally, in 1979, the children were located in North Carolina through school records.

Since both North Carolina and Florida had passed the Uniform Child Custody Jurisdiction Act, North Carolina recognized Florida jurisdiction under the U.C.C.J.A. The children were returned to Florida. Scott retained custody. But on the first unsupervised visitation by Sally, she fled with the boys. Again, they were missing for nine months.

Once more Scott began to search for his missing sons. This time he found them in Illinois. When discovered, the boys were using different names, they were dressed in rags, and they would not come near Scott because their mother had so prejudiced them against him.

During the hearing in Illinois, the judge placed the children in a shelter home for a week. Upon the advice of his attorney, Joe Caruso, the excellent lawyer who had seen us through our legal problems when our grandson Danny was snatched, Scott hired an Illinois attorney.

In the hearing which followed, the Illinois judge honored Florida custody, and the children came back to Florida with Scott. Now they attend school, making good grades. One of the boys began taking violin lessons and the other boy learned the organ.

Since it is a felony to remove children from the State of Florida contrary to a court order, Sally was charged with a felony. Sally was returned to Florida and the felony charges were dropped, although she did go to court on a civil contempt violation. The verdict or court order: (1) 45 days in jail; (2) a fine; (3) deferred visitation.

What a different story from the Danny Strickland case. The new laws worked. And what's even more interesting, Scott's attorney, Joe Caruso, based his plea upon an aspect of the Danny Strickland case!

Meanwhile, during this period of searching for his children, Scott met Alice, a charming girl from North Carolina, and they married, creating a family environment for the boys. The only fly in the ointment was Sally.

Sally suggested to the boys, in lieu of paying the $23,000 court fine, that Scott hire her to live with them and be a nanny. Imagine the position in which this placed Scott in the eyes of his sons, since he refused to hire their mother. But one senses Scott had every right to refuse. Sally felt the art of learning how to roll cigarettes gave children dexterity to their fingers and their minds!

Of course, both boys would be happiest if their parents were there. But one of them told me, "Everybody's dream sometimes doesn't work." At least in this case, justice had a hand in righting a terrible wrong.

In discussing the case with Scott, I mentioned a newspaper article which concluded that Sally had received a very stiff sentence. I will never forget his answer:

"I would have gladly spent 45 days in jail and spent $23,607.09 instead of the hell I went through for months, the loss of about $100,000 in legal and search fees, and the upheaval it brought into the children's life."

Then, our conversation took on a lighter tone, as if we were trying to put it all behind us temporarily. For years I had referred to our mutual attorney, Joe Caruso, as our 'Knight in White,' since he is addicted to white suits.

We decided to buy Joe and his capable secretary, Ruth, a gift. But what? At length, we concluded Joe should have a white hat to go with his white suit. As for Ruth, we felt she deserved a white hat, too!

SECTION XIV

"AFTERMATH" VERDICT

"AFTERMATH" VERDICT

IN THE CIRCUIT COURT IN AND
FOR BREVARD COUNTY, FLORIDA

CIVIL ACTION NO. XX-XXXX-XX-X/X/X

In the Interest of:
STEVEN and SHANE ADAMS*
SCOTT B. ADAMS,
     Petitioner
vs
SALLY RUTH JOHNSON, f/k/a
SALLY RUTH GREEN
     Respondent

AMENDED

ORDER SENTENCING SALLY RUTH
JOHNSON TO FORTY—FIVE (45)
DAYS' INCARCERATION AND DEFER-
RING RULING ON THE RESPON-
DENT'S MOTION FOR VISITATION
AND PETITIONER'S MOTION TO IM-
POSE SANCTIONS INCLUDING AN
AWARD OF ATTORNEY'S FEES AND
COSTS.

THIS CAUSE coming on to be heard the 20th day of
December, 1982 upon the outstanding order of this Court dated
September 2, 1981, and the Respondent's Motion for Visitation and
Petitioner's Motion to Impose Sanctions Including an Award of
Attorney's Fees and Costs, and the Petitioner, SCOTT B. ADAMS,
being present and represented by Joe Teague Caruso, Esquire, and
the Respondent, SALLY RUTH GREEN, being present and
represented by John Allen Doe*, Esquire, and the Court finding that

an Order of Contempt and Imposing Sanctions and Writ of Attachment was previously entered on September 2, 1981 and immediately preceding this hearing, the Respondent, SALLY RUTH GREEN, surrendered herself to the custody of the Brevard County Sheriff and the Court having heard argument of counsel and being otherwise fully advised in the premises, it is

ORDERED as FOLLOWS:

1. That the Respondent, SALLY RUTH JOHNSON, f/k/a SALLY RUTH GREEN be, and the same is hereby sentenced to forty-five (45) days' incarceration in the Brevard County Jail.

2. That the Sheriff of Brevard County shall incarcerate the said SALLY RUTH JOHNSON, f/k/a/ SALLY RUTH GREEN, for a period of forty-five (45) days in the Brevard County Jail beginning December 20, 1982.

3. That the Court reserves ruling on the Respondent's Motion for Visitation and the Petitioner's Motion to Impose Sanctions Including Attorney's Fees.

DONE AND ORDERED in Chambers, Titusville, Brevard County, Florida, this 21st day of December, 1982, nunc pro tunc, December 20, 1982.

Circuit Judge

Copies furnished to:
Joe Teague Caruso, Esquire
John Allen Doe, Esquire

*This court order is based on an actual case which has been detailed in the 'Aftermath' chapter of this book. Real names of the parties involved have been changed to protect their privacy.

IN THE CIRCUIT COURT IN AND
FOR BREVARD COUNTY, FLORIDA

CIVIL ACTION NO. XX-XXXX-XX-X/X/X

IN RE: In the Interest of
STEVEN ADAMS and SHANE ADAMS*
SCOTT B. ADAMS,*
        Petitioner

and

SALLY RUTH JOHNSON,* f/k/a/
SALLY RUTH GREEN*
        Respondent

COST JUDGEMENT

THIS CAUSE coming on to be heard the 4th day of
February, 1983, upon the Petitioner's, SCOTT B. ADAMS, Motion
to Impose Sanctions Including An Award of Attorney's Fees and
Costs, and the Petitioner being represented by Joe Teague Caruso,
Esquire, the Respondent, SALLY RUTH JOHNSON, f/k/a/
SALLY RUTH GREEN, being represented by John Allen Doe*,
and the Court having received the sworn testimony of the parties and
having considered the Motion and Affidavit filed by the Petitioner
and further finding that the sum of $23,607.08 was in fact actually
expended as attorney's fees and costs by the Petitioner over a period
of nine (9) months and in several states to obtain the return of the
children and the Court further finding that the Order of this Court
dated September 2, 1981 holding the Respondent in contempt and
imposing sanctions provided in Paragraph 3:

"3. That the Respondent, SALLY RUTH JOHNSON, f/k/a/ SALLY RUTH GREEN shall be responsible for all attorney's fees and costs incurred by the Petitioner in obtaining the return of the children which sum shall be determined and awarded by the Court at a subsequent proceeding.",

and the Court being otherwise fully advised in the premises, it is
ORDERED as follows:

1. That the Petitioner's, SCOTT B. ADAMS, Motion to Impose Sanctions Including An Award of Attorney's Fees and Costs be, and the same is hereby granted.

2. That a Cost Judgment be, and the same is hereby entered in favor of the Petitioner, SCOTT B. ADAMS and against the Respondent, SALLY RUTH JOHNSON, f/k/a/ SALLY RUTH GREEN, in the amount of $23,607.08.

3. That the Petitioner, SCOTT B. ADAMS, shall have and recover from the Respondent, SALLY RUTH JOHNSON, f/k/a/ SALLY RUTH GREEN, the sum of $23,607.08, for which let execution issue.

DONE AND ORDERED in Chambers, Titusville, Brevard County, Florida, this 23rd day of February, 1983, nunc pro tunc, February 4, 1983.

                                        Circuit Judge

Copies furnished to:
Joe Teague Caruso, Esquire
John Allen Doe, Esquire

IN THE CIRCUIT COURT IN AND
FOR BREVARD COUNTY, FLORIDA

CIVIL ACTION NO. XX-XXXX-XX-X/X/X

IN RE: In the Interest of
STEVEN ADAMS and SHANE ADAMS*
SCOTT B. ADAMS*
          Petitioner
and
SALLY RUTH JOHNSON,* f/k/a/
SALLY RUTH GREEN
          Respondent

ORDER DENYING RESPONDENT'S
MOTION FOR VISITATION AND DE-
FERRING FURTHER CONSIDERA-
TION OF VISITATION UNTIL AFTER
THE FIRST DAY OF APRIL, 1983.

     THIS CAUSE coming on to be heard the 4th day of
February, 1983, upon the Respondent's, SALLY RUTH JOHN-
SON, f/k/a/ SALLY RUTH GREEN, Motion for Visitation and
the Petitioner, SCOTT B. ADAMS being represented by Joe Teague
Caruso, Esquire, and the Respondent being represented by John
Allen Doe*, Esquire, and it appearing that this Court terminated the
Respondent's rights of visitation in its Order of September 2, 1981
when the Respondent failed to return the children following a period
of weekend visitation and proceeded to remove the children from the
State of Florida and secrete the children in violation of this Court's

Order. The Respondent continued this course of conduct for a period of approximately eight or nine months which required the Petitioner to expend a sum in excess of $20,000 in an attempt to locate and obtain the return of the children. The Court further finds that the willful and contemptuous conduct of the Respondent which resulted in the termination of her rights of visitation interrupted the permanance and stability which the Court attempted to establish for the minor children in awarding custody of the children to the Petitioner, SCOTT B. ADAMS. The Court further finds that at the present time the Respondent is unfit for purposes of visitation due to the past and reoccuring acts on her part of disrupting the permanance and stability of the children's environment all of which are contrary to the best interest and welfare of the children. The Court further finds that it is necessary to protect the best interest and welfare of the children and in so doing defers further consideration of the question of visitation until after April 1, 1983 but upon such future application finds that any visitation would be conditioned upon the posting of a bond by the Respondent in the amount of $7,500.00, and the Court having heard argument of counsel and being otherwise fully advised in the premises, it is

ORDERED as follows:

1. That the Respondent's, SALLY RUTH JOHNSON, f/k/a/ SALLY RUTH GREEN, Motion for Visitation be, and the same is hereby denied.

2. That the Court defers further consideration of the question of visitation until after April 1, 1983 and further determines that any future visitation shall be conditioned upon the Respondent, SALLY RUTH JOHNSON, f/k/a/ SALLY RUTH GREEN, posting a bond with the Clerk of the Circuit Court, Brevard County, Florida, in the amount of $7,500.00, the terms and conditions of which will be set forth in any subsequent Order relating to visitation.

3. That the Respondent, SALLY RUTH JOHNSON, f/k/a/ SALLY RUTH GREEN shall be allowed to communicate with the children by letter or other written communication and the Petitioner, SCOTT B. ADAMS, shall be responsible for maintaining such open line of communication between the Respondent and the children. The Respondent shall further be entitled to speak with the children telephonically once each week as shall be mutually arranged between the parties so as not to interfere with the children's schedule. In the event the parties cannot agree the telephonic call shall be arranged through agreement between the attorneys of the parties and in the event they cannot agree, application may be made to the Court

to set the definite time for telephonic communication.

DONE AND ORDERED in Chambers, Titusville, Brevard County, Florida, this 23rd day of February, 1983, nunc pro tunc, February 4, 1983.

Circuit Judge

Copies furnished to:
Joe Teague Caruso, Esquire
John Allen Doe, Esquire